Cultural Frames, Framing Culture

Robert Newman, Editor

I'm No Angel

The Blonde in

Fiction and Film

Ellen Tremper

UNIVERSITY OF VIRGINIA PRESS *Charlottesville and London*

University of Virginia Press

© 2006 by the Rector and Visitors of the University
of Virginia

Printed in the United States of America
on acid-free paper

First published 2006

9 8 7 6 5 4 3 2 1

Library of Congress Cataloging-in-Publication Data

Tremper, Ellen, 1942–
 I'm no angel : the blonde in fiction and film /
Ellen Tremper.
  p.   cm. — (Cultural frames, framing culture)
  Includes bibliographical references and index.
  Includes filmography (p.).
  ISBN 0-8139-2521-5 (cloth : acid-free paper) —
ISBN 0-8139-2520-7 (pbk. : acid-free paper)
  1. English fiction—19th century—History and
criticism. 2. Blondes in literature. 3. Thackeray,
William Makepeace, 1811–1863—Characters—
Blondes. 4. Blondes in motion pictures. I. Title.
II. Series.
PR868.B56T74 2006
823'.8093522—dc22   2005017751

Contents

Illustrations

Preface

I count being read to as one of the great and necessary pleasures of childhood. It satisfies our need to be comforted by hearing stories that help us make sense of the often mysterious and confusing world. The British child psychiatrist D. W. Winnicott described it as one of a group of "transitional phenomena . . . that wide area that is indeterminate between living in the external world and dreaming." These are crucial to our growing up.

I remember with great fondness (and have read to my own children) *The Pokey Little Puppy* and, my all-time favorite, *The House at Pooh Corner*, about adventurous and curious and—conspicuously—male characters. But there also were stories of another kind. When I was four, my father brought home for me a yellow and forest-green boxed volume of the Grimms' fairy tales. The box itself was a mystery—dark inside, as I peered into it. In the anthropomorphic way of children, I told myself (and I'm not making any of this up) it was a home for the book and those strange stories—so different from my own experience—that became real as my mother read them. The initial capital letter of each tale was illuminated, a complicated calligraphic scroll, which I examined with great interest as she read. And then the delight of the story! But "delight" probably misrepresents my feeling, for it suggests a quickened sensitivity, a liveliness, whereas what I felt was a drowse of consciousness, a delicious, still lapsing into a space that was not the one I occupied in my fully wakened state. The pleasure was the transport of "Once upon a time" into, paradoxically, a timeless and bodiless world.

The stillness of being read to by my mother, especially about beautiful young girls, must have carried a message learned unconsciously by my small child's body. Rachel Brownstein writes in *Becoming a Heroine* that a teenage girl comes of age through her reading of novels; she is "doing mysterious solitary researches into her own importance by becoming, as she reads fiction, a heroine." But personality is probably formed by the age of three or four—just when I was hearing about blond princesses. My notions of femininity—fashioned as later I, too, read novels, watched movies and television, and breathed in the air shared by my girlfriends and the boys telling dirty jokes in the schoolyard—could cover over but never entirely erase my early encounters with the stories of these girls.

I am not insinuating a conscious conspiracy on the part of mothers. Yet the stillness of sitting, leaning against my mother's side with her arm around me, was, indeed, a prize that, ironically, re-created the fate of all the heroines in these cautionary tales I was hearing. They got their reward, and it was always the same one—the prince—by not moving. Unwittingly, I was learning the lesson that for girls it was important at least to be quiet and patient, if not also long-suffering.

For those of us who grew up listening to these stories, the blond and beautiful girl who obediently did what she was told, who could spin straw (or her hair?) into priceless gold, seemed part of the natural order of things. Of course Sleeping Beauty, Rapunzel, and Cinderella had golden locks. Thank goodness for Snow White, I've thought, for those of us not so genetically endowed. She was the great exception, saving me and probably many others from complete ego-deflation. But otherwise blondes seemed always to be the heroines. They were always beautiful. And, unlike me, they were always as good as the gold on their heads. How could I succeed? My failures—not least, my failure to be a blonde—were already very apparent to me. Mirrors don't lie, as the queen in "Snow White" found out.

As an adult I've come to realize a few things that escaped me as I sat rapt by these fairy tales. For one, these girls, even Snow White, were all victims. They were locked up—in towers, like Sleeping Beauty and Rapunzel, in cottages, like Cinderella, or in the occasional glass box, like Snow White. And although there are Bluebeards and ogres in other stories (fortunately, these were not the ones my mother read), the girls in mine were imprisoned by jealous and vengeful older women. Then—what had seemed, in childhood, quite reasonable—each owed her freedom to a prince. All she needed to do was bear the pain and period of her confinement. And of course she succeeded handily because her *heroinism* was not like the heroism of active, questing boys. Patience and passivity were her great virtues.

My early experience played its part in *I'm No Angel*. Blondes were not on my mind when, about eight years ago, I was reading Mary Elizabeth Braddon's *Lady Audley's Secret*. But then I came to the place in which Lady Audley pushes her husband down a well, and I had one of those shocks of recognition or, really, the opposite. "This woman is angry!" I said to myself. "But . . . she's a blonde!" I was suddenly transported back to my introduction to the girls in the fairy tales who looked like Lady Audley—those uniformly beautiful but, unlike her, also eternally sweet and amiable beings.

But then more recent reading experiences flooded in. I remembered Rosamond Vincy's "quiet steady disobedience" in George Eliot's *Middlemarch* and Becky Sharp, who coquettes the men with her "famous frontal development" in *Vanity Fair*, and realized that Lady Audley wasn't unique in her transgressive blondness. I believed I might have stumbled across something worth pursuing. And it didn't hurt that everyone to whom I mentioned this possible project suddenly became animated. It seemed that it wasn't only gentlemen who preferred or were interested in these unsettling blondes.

That stumble was a fortunate fall. Like Alice's tumble down the rabbit hole, the trip into hitherto unknown (to me) territories has been an exciting adventure from which I've learned much about subjects as various as early travel narratives, landscape gardens, costume and cosmetics, lighting technology, and music—to name just a very few of the domains that have come into relation as I've worked. Some of them that seemed important at one stage became mere sidebars to my story of women's transformation into active, natural, and entitled beings. But even as entire chapters fell to my cutting room floor (well, delete key), there was pleasure and profit in my getting to know so many very helpful, generous, and knowledgeable people. I've also visited places I would never have known about had it not been for an obsessive interest in all things blond these past eight years.

Graduate school forced me to find a century, more narrowly, a genre and a writer, about whom I was expected to become an expert. Years of teaching did nothing to restore any generalist inclinations. But blondes gave me what few other subjects could have done. They allowed me to roam freely in fiction, poetry, and drama, from the Renaissance to the present—even to dip into another medium. Perhaps one of Shirley Polykoff's great ad campaigns for Clairol—redacted, of course—sums up what I've felt about researching and writing *I'm No Angel*. Having only one life to live, I've very much enjoyed living it through these blondes.

Acknowledgments

Acknowledgments are a pleasure but also a worry. So many people, over the past eight years, have helped me as I've worked on *I'm No Angel* that I'm fearful I will have forgotten some. If I have, it's owing to midterm memory loss rather than the importance of their contributions. Of those in mind, I begin with my colleagues past and present at Brooklyn College and the Graduate Center of CUNY who have supported me in various ways—through their friendship and productive conversations, by reading portions of the manuscript, and with their suggestions for films and books. Roni Natov, Herbert Perluck, Julie Agoos, Wendy Fairy, Geri DeLuca, Barbara Gerber, Robert Viscusi, David Corey, Carey Harrison, Patricia Laurence, Rachel Brownstein, Patricia Hopkins, Lindley Hanlon, Liz Weis, Anne Humpherys, Nancy Hoch, Linda Hamell, and Emma Wunsch have enriched my life and my thoughts. I also thank John Belton, Geoffrey G. O'Brien, and Teddy Wayne for their recommendations. I owe a special debt to my colleague Lillian Schlissel, my co-digger for gold in the mines of American popular culture, who suffered through more drafts than anyone else as well as my bursts of enthusiasm for discoveries and ideas, communicated in 8 a.m. phone calls. I want also to thank Nancy Pardo for her generosity and office skills and Florence Bello for her cheerful assistance. I am grateful to the librarians of Brooklyn College—Sally Bowdoin, William Gargan, and Martha Corpus—who went beyond the request to retrieve valuable information and books for me. I wish to thank, as well, all those who listened to early versions of chapters: members of the Women and Society Seminar of the Columbia University Seminars and of the Brooklyn College English Department Works-in-Progress Seminar. I thank my friend Toni Clark, dean of women and, in 1999, chair of Women's Studies at Pomona College, for inviting me to talk at the Women's Union. Thanks, too, to Norris Pope for sharing with me his interest in and knowledge of glamour photography of the 1930s and '40s.

The staff of the Humanities Rare Book Room of the British Library and of the Fawcett Library of London Guildhall University, now the Women's Research Library of London Metropolitan University, were all courteous and helpful. To David Doughan, reference librarian of the Fawcett, now retired, I owe a great debt. I thank him for the breadth and depth of his knowledge of women's history, which informed this project, and, particularly, for his informal tutorial in nineteenth-century women's magazines, which he offered me in October 1998. I thank Margaret Beetham of the Department of English and Women's Studies of Manchester Metropolitan University for her gracious hospitality and the present of her invaluable book *A Magazine of Their Own?* To Anthea Jarvis, principal curator of costume, and Miles Lambert, curator of costume, at the Gallery of Costume of the Manchester City Galleries, I owe much information, an enjoyable day of research, and a tip on a terrific book.

The Museum of Modern Art's Film Study Center was closed during the time I was writing *I'm No Angel*. Without Piermont Pictures, "the best video store on the East Coast," according to *Premiere Magazine*—and the rating seems entirely justified—it would have been almost impossible to view the many hard-to-get films of the teens through the 1950s I've included in this study. Rick Pantale, owner of Piermont, and Mercedes Ross were helpful in my searches for videos and fabulously generous and forgiving, never charging me late fees for videos I kept for weeks at a time. The closing of MoMA's Film Stills Archive was also the occasion for my discovering Photofest, recommended on the Museum's Web site as the place to go for movie stills. Howard Mandelbaum, principal, and Tom Toth of Photofest were very helpful in arranging for me to see and select photographs from their large collection of stills and advertisements. Thanks also to David Rozenblyum of Brooklyn College for his rephotographing of some of the stills and transparencies.

I wish to thank the Rare Books Division, The New York Public Library, Astor, Lenox and Tilden Foundations, for permission to reproduce Thackeray's sketches from *Vanity Fair;* the British Library for permission to reproduce the cartoons from Florence Claxton's *The Adventures of a Woman in Search of Her Rights;* the Victoria & Albert Picture Library for permission to reproduce the poster for *A Sensation Novel in Three Volumes;* the Bridgeman Art Library for permission to reproduce Frederick Leighton's *Flaming June;* the Hearst Corporation for permission to reproduce the Varga Girl of September 1941, and *Photofest* for permission to reproduce the film stills and advertisement. I also wish to thank Farrar, Straus and Giroux for permission to quote from Robert Lowell's "For the Union Dead"; and A. P. Watt Ltd. on behalf of Michael B. Yeats for world rights in English, exclusive of the United States, to quote from W. B. Yeats's "For Anne Gregory." For rights in the United States, the citation from "For Anne Gregory" is reprinted with permission of Scribner, an imprint of Simon and Schuster Adult Publishing Group, from *The Collected Works of W. B. Yeats, Volume 1: The Poems, Revised,* edited by Richard J. Finneran. Copyright © 1933 by The Macmillan Company; copyright renewed © 1961 by Bertha Georgie Yeats.

I especially wish to thank Cathie Brettschneider, acquisitions editor of the University of Virginia Press, and Robert Newman, editor of the Cultural Frames, Framing Culture series, for their sensitive and intelligent advice. Thanks also to Mark Mones, project editor, for helping me over the hurdles of permission requests and formatting requirements, and to Susan Brady, for her meticulous copyediting. Unlike me, she's never met an unrestricted clause she didn't recognize!

Finally, I want to thank my husband, Peter Wayne, for his company all the way through this project. He kept hearth and home together when I went off to England to begin my research, read almost all of the novels I wrote about (and those I eliminated), and watched every movie with me. It was great fun and a terrific benefit to have his companionship while I was thinking and writing. Without his computer expertise, I would have struggled to prepare the text and notes for electronic submission in conformity with the specifications of the Press. I dedicate this book, with love, to him and to our children—Gregory, Teddy, Elizabeth, Geoffrey and Joanna.

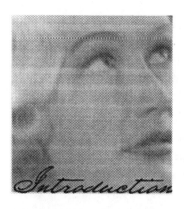

Introduction

"... love me for myself alone
And not my yellow hair."
—W. B. Yeats, "For Anne Gregory"

A brunette walks into the doctor's office and complains, "Doctor, I hurt all over." The doctor says, "That's impossible." "No, really! Just look. When I touch my arm, ouch! it hurts! When I touch my head, ouch! it hurts! When I touch my chest, ouch! it really hurts!" she wails. The doctor just shakes his head and says, "You're really a natural blonde, aren't you?" The woman smiles weakly. "Why, yes, I am. How did you know?" The doctor replies, "Because your finger is broken."

Why was the blonde upset when she got her driver's license? Because she got an "F" in sex.

Did you hear the one about the guy who was blond? . . . Neither did I!

Why did jokes like these—always about women—begin to circulate in the ether? What is it about the blonde that invites adjectives like brassy, sexy, hot, and dumb, or names like bimbo and bombshell? On the other hand, why did platinum, or honey, or golden, or ash, or any other number of blond shades become the requisite colors for women of influence in public life—for television anchors, for CEOs, and for a certain senator?

Blondes, of course, haven't always been the butt of jokes—always about a shortage of intelligence and surfeit of sex. But then, too, they haven't always been figures of power. Once upon a time, they were the most beautiful girls in the kingdom, with souls of perfect beauty to match. They were graceful and modest, their dispositions of the sunniest. They were always meek, mild, and gentle. Even in 1860, Wilkie Collins was thinking of that sort of blonde when he wrote in the preamble to *The Woman in White:* "This is the story of what a Woman's patience can endure, and what a Man's resolution can achieve."

Yet something happened to make Collins's words as silly as any "dumb blonde" joke. The history I'm about to recount explains the radical alterations in blond iconography, from the nineteenth century to the present, from fiction to film—the morphing, that is, of Ivanhoe's childhood love, the "flaxen Saxon" Rowena, into Marilyn Monroe. Stephen Jay Gould's neo-Darwinian model, "punctuated equilibrium," aptly characterizes the fitful nature of this social and aesthetic evolution. The long periods of stability that had marked the representation of the blonde in northern European culture were twice signally "broken by shorter spurts of evolutionary change":[1] during the twenty-five-year span from 1847 to 1872, when women novelists found their voice and gained a popular audience; and again in the 1930s, the first decade of the "talkies," when "voice," no longer merely metaphor, became technical reality in cinema. These novelists wrote, and blond movie stars acted, refreshingly against the grain and expectations. By subversively alienating blondness from its long-lived association with "feminine" character traits, they made the color do social work, which benefited all of us. George Meredith in his "Essay on Comedy and Uses of the Comic Spirit" argued that evolved civilization cannot prevail without equality between women and men. The story of the blonde, at its roots, and with its (sometimes) dark materials, kept pace with, but also participated in, the changes in real women's lives, essential to the evolution of modernity.

On or about January 1847, the blond character changed. The challenge to meanings associated with blondes in folk- and fairy tales—purity, patience, modesty, endurance, docility—indeed, the beginning of a blond insurgency, began in this watershed year in which William Makepeace Thackeray's *Vanity Fair* appeared. Dynamic and aggressive "sandy-haired" Becky Sharp, the most animated puppet to come out of the workshop of the "Manager of the Performance" (xxx), was followed in October by a cameo appearance of a more traditionally hued but very ill-tempered blonde, Georgiana Reed, in Charlotte Brontë's *Jane Eyre*. In December came Emily Brontë's fair, ringleted Catherine Linton in *Wuthering Heights,* with her "cool, regardless manner, exceedingly embarrassing and disagreeable" (18). Despite differences in their hair tints and characters, these three figures had something in common. They were *not* the flawless and always lovable, placid, pliant, good-as-gold blondes familiar to readers from fairy tales. But neither were they demons. They occupied the middle ground of ordinary life, being merely active or captious, but always desiring, women. They thwarted readerly expectations by perplexing, disobeying, or manipulating their fellow characters to achieve their ends. Often purposely straying outside the social fold, they were "bellewethers," leading the way toward an active and natural femininity that, by the 1930s, had unquestionably arrived in Hollywood.

The first recorded use of the word "blonde" as a noun, to mean a female with light hair, was in 1822: "*Edin. Rev.* 199 Brenda, the laughing blue-eyed blonde" (*OED* 1:233). In 1847, both Thackeray and Charlotte Brontë used it disparagingly to lessen public admiration for this iconic beauty. Marina Warner is thus off by a century when she writes, in *From the Beast to the Blonde:* "Only in the 1930s and 1940s, under the influence of Hollywood, did the word emerge as a noun, and acquire its hot, vampish overtones, based in the jaunty and ironical reversal of meaning cultivated by popular media this century" (363). The Brontës' new-fashioning of the blonde reflected their resistance to the social and cultural privileging of women of infantine and/or coquettish beauty—loved not for themselves alone but for their yellow hair—above those exhibiting (like the authors) intelligence, enterprise, integrity, and perseverance. Charlotte, especially, wrote stories in which women who are the captains of their souls become, as well, the masters of their fates. Like Thackeray, she scorned the fairy-tale blonde and her counterpart in Romantic novels from earlier in the century—admired primarily for their beauty. The dedication to the second edition of *Jane Eyre* suggests that Brontë believed this model of womanhood helped to keep young girls from the full exercise of their intelligence and talents—from a life of economic and social engagement. Her novels, with brunettes for heroines, also featured aggressive blondes, who—as much or more than the brunettes—disturbed the ages-old image of the passive and pliable young woman. Between that season in 1847 when readers encountered Becky Sharp impersonating a vengeful Clytemnestra, about to plunge a dagger into sleeping Agamemnon, or scowling Catherine Linton, surlily refusing tea to Mr. Lockwood, and the sunny moment in 1932 when moviegoers watched Clark Gable in *Red Dust* plunge the platinum-blond head of Jean Harlow into a rain barrel, the terrain of the playing field for women and men had been leveled considerably. The development of intellectual, social, sexual, and economic freedoms—in short, of modernity—is partly owing to the Victorians' first re-presentations of the blonde.

But why blond hair? First, because acquisitive and sentimental Victorians were obsessed by hair, in general. Its cultural and economic consequence is clear from this statistical analysis of the hair industry in "Honeycomb," a monthly feature in the midcentury magazine *The Ladies' Cabinet of Fashion.*

> The importance of the trade in hair in this country, and the attention paid to its culture and due order, may be estimated from a glance at the statistics of those engaged in it in the metropolis alone. Pigot's directory for 1840 contained the names of 950 hair-dressers in London, and about the same number in the provinces. According to the London directory of the present year (1853) there are the following persons devoted to the speciality of the human hair:—Three hair-merchants (large importers probably); seventeen hair-manufacturers; twenty-four artists; or workers in hair—hair-jewellers, or device-workers as they may be termed—who elaborate the hair of our deceased friends and relatives into such *memento mori* as rings, brooches, earrings, chains, and other fanciful ornaments; 650 hair-dressers, barbers, &c., and twenty-seven wig-makers. (6 [January 1855]: 54)

And so on and so on. Then think of Krook in Dickens's *Bleak House,* on first seeing blond Ada: "Hi! Here's lovely hair! I have got three sacks of ladies' hair below, but none so beautiful and fine as this. What colour, and what texture!" (39).

The Victorians were especially enchanted by blond hair because, beyond its associations with wealth, fertility, and ideal femininity, it provided material evidence of a Saxon political and cultural (that is, "racial") heritage. After the Napoleonic Wars, the long-standing antagonism to the French was supported by historians eager to erase Norman cultural contributions by tracing "Englishness" in an unswerving line back to Saxon institutions. The effort even trickled down to popular women's magazines, in which one could read, for example, that the Saxons' "laws betray a spirit of natural equity," their institutions "founded on notions of freedom and justice." "How many advantages we enjoy," wrote M.S.R. in the *Englishwoman's Domestic Magazine,* "that are traceable to their influence and institutions! and probably we are not very far wrong when we say that this nation owes more to the Anglo-Saxons than to any of its other rulers and governors; for it was through their influence that the foundation was laid of nearly all that is great and honourable in the English character" (2nd ser., vol. 1, no. 1 [1860]: 20).

Racial proof of English moral superiority could always be manufactured when needed. Although her maternal ancestor is Italian (and profligate), the heroine of "Blanche D'Aubigné," a novella by Sarah Symonds that also appeared in the *Englishwoman's Domestic Magazine*, "was as perfectly the opposite of her mother, as if not one drop of the same blood flowed in their veins. . . . Her complexion was beautifully fair, and that, and her light, flowing ringlets, were certainly derived from her English grandmother, who had been of one of our most ancient Saxon families" (1, no. 7 [1852]: 203). Stories like this one united revision of British history and the color legend for the map of behaviors—gentleness, consideration, stoicism, and patience—recommended to marriageable girls.[2]

But an ambitious group of women began to express other notions of feminine excellence in journalism and fiction. Having escaped the common lot, a growing number left home, traveled, even established a publishing enterprise. In articles supporting women's rights or in novels in which their heroines' superiority denied beauty as the only criterion of merit, these writers visibly disputed commonly held values and assumptions by making the blonde a "sight" of cultural contestation. But they did something else, as well. In their journalism, they promoted collective endeavor; in their novels, they downplayed competition between women—blond and dark—the feminine vertices of the old Romantic romantic triangle. Cooperation and deep feeling between their characters, however momentary, transformed the literary representation of heroines but also the landscape of possibilities for women's friendship and progress toward greater social and educational freedoms.

With the migration from Romantic fantasy to realist fiction, the exotic, dark, intelligent woman—Corinne in Germaine de Staël's *Corinne, or Italy* (1807) or the Jewess Rebecca in Scott's *Ivanhoe* (1819)—became the dark-haired, intelligent heroine: Jane Eyre or Esther Summerson or Dorothea Brooke. But the virtuous blonde, Cinderella, or her later avatar—Lucile in *Corinne* or Rowena in *Ivanhoe*—was fading away. While her patience and beauty were still revered by the middle-class incarnation of the handsome prince in the novels of Dickens and Collins, in those authored by English, and soon after by American, women, her golden gleam had begun to fade into the ordinary light of day.

Her imperfections were becoming obvious. She might be bad-tempered, acquisitive, or even sexually curious. These novelists resisted the assumption that beauty is matched by virtue and, moreover, that virtue is a strictly "feminine" attribute.

Of course, transformations in the representation of character depend on the intersection of many social, economic, and cultural influences. But such changes, always in dynamic relationship with the forces that have brought them into being, also provide a "social register" of the very influences that have created them in the first place. Such is certainly the case in the fictional representation of women who were, by the mid-nineteenth century, moving in the real world, at an accelerating pace, from being merely *desirable* objects to *desiring* subjects. The new-style blonde between the covers of a book was proof of the social corrections now challenging masculine power—power that had kept the vast majority of women in their homes and in their place.

That such representations of British blondness should emerge in Victorian culture—undergirded by a robust nationalist ideology dating back, as I've suggested, at least to the Napoleonic Wars and stoked by its current vigorous imperialist policies—might seem a paradox. For in a society eager to capitalize on the differences between its members and the dark peoples of its subject dominions, there was reason to discriminate degrees of whiteness, with the blonde the whitest of whites, and her security and continued privilege a powerful raison d'être advanced for and by the economic and military agenda.

Surely the blonde, the embodiment of idealized femininity in this Anglo-Saxon society determined to remind itself and the world of its members' superior genetic stock ("Their energy, their talents, their integrity,—so far beyond those of the native population, and, we may add without vanity, usually so far beyond those of other foreign visitants")[3] ought not to be a figure of subversion and rebellion. And yet the women novelists were representing her as just that. Perhaps the "rewards and privileges" bestowed by whiteness (Dyer, *White* 20), they reasoned—that is, playing-by-the-rules whiteness—were not as powerful an incentive as men believed them to be. These women could conceive of an even more fundamental desire—freedom to control one's fate—especially now that women's fate was becoming less mysterious. Through studies by such groups as the British Association for the Advancement of Science, which formed a statistical section in 1833, the Statistical Society of London (1838), and the later National Association for the Promotion of Social Sciences (1857–84), questions about women's lives in the aggregate—the miserable rates at which they married and were educated, or their poor wages—could now be accurately answered.

Feminists in the United States had acknowledged that the exclusion of women from the 1840 World Anti-Slavery Convention in London was the decisive event in their organization of the first Woman's Rights Convention in Seneca Falls, New York, in 1848. Women in England, trained from childhood to put others first, had characteristically joined altruistic movements like the antislavery cause rather than fight to win rights for themselves (Anderson and Zinsser 2:358). But now they were deeply moved by their American sisters' actions. The women of Seneca Falls, they wrote, "lighted a flame which has warmed . . . [those of us who had] thought *not* of our bondage."[4] The creative writers took another route to feminine selfhood. In their novels, they showed that the blonde's independence is inversely proportional to her Saxon inheritance. Her fortunate fall from grace and immobility—which left her free only to "suffer and be still"[5]—was then and has been ever since a boon to all women. Happily, the blonde has been getting "darker"—through impersonation, disguise, and "adulterating" cosmetics (all of which stratagems we will see in these pages), but also, since 1847, through her unruly behavior and reputation.

It's true that the fictive representation of blond rebellion was at first mild—only the turbulence created by the flutter of a butterfly's wing. It might mean a "corrugated" forehead (*Wuthering Heights*) or, more consequential, an attempted elopement (*Jane Eyre*). But from such local disturbances storms may brew. And by 1847 they were in formation. These literary embodiments and events were some of the many agitations in a more general intellectual, moral, and political climate change.

Women activists-turned-feminists, those who had come to think of "our bondage," were beginning to organize on many fronts: for better education and public hygiene; shortening of the work week; improvement of governesses' pay; alteration of the regressive laws regulating prostitution; for property and divorce rights, and many other issues affecting women's lives. They were even starting their own journals, different in focus from the "women's" magazines devoted to housekeeping and fashion. *Eliza Cook's Journal* (1849), *The English-woman's Review* (1857), and *The English Woman's Journal*[6] (1858) were organs for the promotion of their political and social efforts. Equally important, these penetrations into a formerly exclusive male preserve, the political, gave them the opportunity to work outside the home in a communal endeavor, putting into practice the very values they espoused. The restive blondes of fiction had their counterparts in the real world.

Like Jane Austen, in whose stories no blonde appears, Charlotte and Emily Brontë, George Eliot, and Mary Elizabeth Braddon gave their heroines dark hair. Sympathetic, sometimes willful, and intelligent—these were the prototypes for the later "New Woman." The novelists challenged notions of moral virtue and behavior that had enchanted middle-class women into remaining compliant and cooperative homebodies. But the phenomenon of "blond insurgency" speaks louder about the ardent desire to stir the cultural and social pot. They dared more with their blondes, who were usually secondary characters in their books, ascribing to them emotions and behaviors unacceptable for their dark-haired heroines, whose virtue had to be acknowledged (through a happy marriage or, far less frequently, professional success) by story's end. They might, that is, explore the blond creature's transgressions with greater license. Yet, remarkably, they often did not punish her for her un-standard deviations. If Braddon sentenced her character Lady Audley, she "naturalized" her behavior, blaming society for creating the conditions that forced the blonde to do the "wicked" things she'd done.

A range of vexing desires and failings distinguished these blond characters from their counterparts in male-authored fiction of the period (Thackeray being the great exception). The contrast in treatment, I think, is owing primarily to male writers' importation of the conventions of Romance into their domestic fiction, long after the disappearance of the older genre.[7]

Romantic fiction is, in its formal attributes, the late eighteenth-, early nineteenth-century literary expression of the imperialist impulse, as in poetry, one might argue, the epic had been. The hero's voyage out into the world, his subduing or conquering of dark "Others" (whether Cyclopic or Saracenic), and his requisite temptation by the dark woman (from Calypso to Dido to Rebecca) ends with the actual creation of a new Rome or just back in his old home (Ithaca, Ivanhoe), with a faithful Penelope or Saxon blond Rowena. In this regard, its prototype was the travel narratives of the Renaissance, in which were recorded encounters with licentious dark others—of Africa, the "Orient," or the New World. For example, John Leo Africanus in *A Geographical Historie of Africa* wrote of the women of Tunis that they "lead an unchast life. . . . Most part of their substance and labour they bestow upon perfumes and other such vanities. They haue here a compound called Lhafis, whereof whosoeuer eateth but one ounce" "is by the said confection maruellously prouoked unto lust"

(249). Women like those of "Mount Merniza" he held responsible for the rout of male control and order in the household and community as they leave "their saide husbands and children . . . for any light iniurie offered by their husbands" and "will depart unto some other mountaine, and seeke them newe paramours fit for their humor" (192). Such depictions of dark peoples have prevailed in literature, more or less subtly, down through the centuries.[8]

Especially in the social and economic climate of imperialist enterprise at midcentury—its public expression crowned by the Great Exhibition in London of 1851 (the first World's Fair, organized to demonstrate the superiority of British industry and science) and the state's practical encouragement of Anglo civic and commercial participation in Her Majesty's Indian dominions—the presence in the domestic novel of leftover conventions of Romance and the denigration of dark colonial subjects are far from mysterious. But female novelists said no to a cold, perfectly behaved blonde, a mainstay of such fictions and, presumably, the antithesis of the licentious women believed to live in tropical climes, and gave us true nasties like Georgiana Reed, complex young women like Ginevra Fanshawe and Rosamond Vincy, and "manmade," not "natural-born," killers like Lady Audley. Unlike their counterparts in the male-authored Pre-Raphaelite poetry of the same period, these blondes from the realist novel weren't demonic. They were merely of the "fallen" commercial world, worldly.

By conventions of Romance, the dark-haired woman is the tempting, exotic, and forbidden object of the hero's outbound quest, while the blonde is the haven (as is his nation) to which he returns. On the other hand, the narrative focus of the domestic, realist tradition is "home" in its more limited sense of personal domicile. While the very developed domestic ideology of the Victorian period was the complement of, and basis for, successful imperialist ventures abroad, female writers would understandably be attracted to the genre that allowed them freedom to explore a woman's potential "subjectivity" in her "natural" environment—her home—from which, like Antaeus when he touched earth, she derived her power.

Nevertheless, these writers also recognized the limitations of hearth and home. The blonde's breaking out registers their novelistic challenges to a confining domestic space and ideology. Later, a genre with unusual culture ballast that was enthusiastically supported by women writers and readers alike, the "sensation novel" of the 1860s and '70s, featuring "the lovely fiend of fiction, / With the yellow, yellow hair," exposed other constraints on women's freedom. That it was satirized by W. S. Gilbert (in his comic operetta *A Sensation Novel in Three Volumes*, 1871) or gothically twisted by Bram Stoker (in *Dracula*, 1897) into an appeal for the darkened blonde to return to her light (domestic) roots is the cultural record of the disapproval and/or fear of women's growing sexual independence and, as many men believed, unsuitable arrogation of power in the public sphere, toward the close of the nineteenth century. Alexander Pope, who, almost two hundred years before, had offered similar advice to "a whole sex of queens" in his second epistle, "To a Lady"—"For foreign glory, foreign joy, they roam; / No thought of peace or happiness at home. / But wisdom's triumph is well-timed retreat, / As hard a science to the fair as great!" ("To a Lady," 2276)—would have sympathized.

"For better or worse," catching the man—whether to lure him into (frequently) marriage or (less often) mischief, as in the 1980 comedy *Nine to Five*, in which Jane Fonda, Lily Tomlin, and Dolly Parton teach their boss a lesson in gender relations—has usually driven the narrative of women-centered novels and films. But whereas charms of only the most unsexual of body parts (head, neck, arms, feet) and, far less frequently, intelligence are the means by which the husband is secured in the Victorian novel, the visual medium of film and new license in representation (at least in "pre-Code" Hollywood, 1930–34, before the Production Code Administration [the Hays Office] cracked down on "indecency"), together with the greater freedoms enjoyed by women in 1927—the first year of the "talkies"—permitted a far franker acknowledgment of women's sexuality and desire in movies.

A succession of types—the platinum vamp or "gold digger," her sensational hair color achieved through a process developed in 1909 by the French chemist Eugène Schuller;[9] the comedic bombshell and the romantic-comedy heroine of the '30s; the "fast-talking dame"[10] of the '30s and early '40s; the film noir victim/accomplice of the late '30s to early '50s; and the deceptively mindless (and underrated) "dumb blonde" of the 1950s—proved the blonde's shape-shifting abilities. Far more complicated than the ingenues played by Mary Pickford or Lillian Gish in the "silents," she was a "double" subject, her chemically acquired tresses and darker substrate suggesting the provocatively ambiguous behavior of which she was capable (think of the comedically sexy Jean Harlow, the sultry and ironic Mae West and Marlene Dietrich, the mysterious Kim Novak in *Vertigo*, and Marilyn Monroe, in both her noir and comic roles). At once more radical and subtle than blackface in minstrelsy, the bleached hair—which, in its outrageous unnaturalness demands attention—simultaneously points to the something beneath: the naturally dark hair that, without treatment, must reappear in a few weeks' time and, even further down and inside, the contradictory emotions issuing from the "gray matter." The blonde-who-is-not-a-blonde is variously a bombshell or comedienne, manipulating men with her newly acknowledged strengths—sexiness, witty words and humor, even physical aggressiveness—in her self-assertive star-turns. These versions of blondness were not merely "jaunty ironical reversals of meaning." They also were long-overdue representations of women's growing self-determination and (occasionally) old-fashioned anger.

The white's "natural" rhythmic awkwardness is part of the on-stage business in *Show Boat* (1927), based on Edna Ferber's novel of the same name (1926). Black Queenie and the mulatta Julie Laverne teach Magnolia, dark-haired daughter of Cap'n Andy, to sing and move to a "black" song, "Can't Help Lovin' that Man of Mine." This marvelous moment of women's connection translates the description of Magnolia's childhood in the novel: "The routine of her life . . . had been made up of doing those things that usually are strictly forbidden the average child. She swam muddy streams . . . read the lurid yellow-backed novels found in the cabins of the women in the company . . . roamed the streets of strange towns alone; learned to strut and shuffle and buck-and-wing from the Negroes whose black faces dotted the boards of the Southern wharves as thickly as grace notes sprinkle a bar of lively music" (19). Ferber follows the dark/blond distinction of Romance, describing Magnolia as "pale, dark-haired," and "distinguished-looking" (117). The licenses of Magnolia's unusual childhood, its risks, her freedom of movement, early (literary) initiation into sexuality, and "the moves" learned from blacks are consistent with stereotypical assumptions about dark-haired heroines. Today this transcription of her experience seems an all-too-evident reminder of the long and persistent history of whites' perceptions of Otherness, first and anxiously remarked in the records of the earliest cross-race encounters—the Renaissance discovery narratives.

But more surprising, dating from the same period, is the blonde's apparent familiarity with Magnolia's experience. In contrast to the product achieved through the tight control exercised by directors today, the cinematic representation of blondes of the 1930s was a matter not only of the writer's scripts and the director's "takes" but also of the "auteurship" of resistant and self-defining women (like Mae West), many of whom came to Hollywood with their own "backstories," well-publicized in the new venue of fan magazines.

Stanley Cavell wonders that "the word 'actor' keeps on being used in place of the more beautiful and more accurate 'star'" for such performers; "the stars," he says, "are only to gaze at, after the fact, and their actions divine our projects" (*World Viewed* 29). Cavell's "after the fact," implying that light from a star reaches us only long after it has been emitted, is not a mere playing with words. Star is "more accurate" than actor because it also suggests the psychological luminousness of past performances that followed these women into their subsequent movie roles; their personalities glowed recognizably from one to the next. And aptly, as with stars (I'd add), thousands of people could view them simultaneously as they sat in darkened theaters all across the country. John Bayley puts the same idea more concretely: "In the old days of the star system . . . their public simply and avidly wanted the stars to be themselves—to be the fabulous Greta Garbo or Rudolph Valentino. The fans were not so much interested in the way they performed, the role they were supposed to be playing. . . . The actor replaced, in the past, the character whom he was acting" (1).

The actresses of the pre-Code era who managed their performance and image sometimes exploited black idioms. Freedom to "play it as it lay," for Mae West, took her "uptown." If in the nineteenth century the blonde got darker through her increasingly unruly behavior, now that her hair dazzled, her relationship to black culture was often explicit and positive. The mainstream interest in the African American culture of 1920s Harlem—particularly in jazz and blues and in popular dances like the Charleston (1923) and the Black Bottom (1924) was obvious. Mae wanted her public to recognize "the black sources of her comedy and attitude" (Schlissel 9). She moved, talked, and sang like the blues singers she knew from Harlem's nightclubs. Flo Ziegfeld had his chorines coached by black dancers (Schlissel 8). Marlene Dietrich, who made a point of dressing in tuxes and trousers offscreen as well as on, was her own director, her own lighting designer, and costumer (Bach 6, 191, 197). But she was no Fay Wray, screaming with fear in the clutches of King Kong as he clings to the spire of the Empire State Building. In *Blonde Venus* (1932), her worldly character is nonchalantly at ease in an even closer bestial grip. Singing in a New York cabaret, she is *inside* the black gorilla, or, more accurately, gorilla suit, chained to a conga line of spear-toting, shield-bearing "Africans"—black

American chorines. And even closer . . . she sways rhythmically on her very safe perch at the edge of the stage, singing "Hot voodoo, in my blood"—her confession that the "African" (sexual) beast is within *and* so compelling that her conspiring "conscience wants to take a vacation." The surprising apotheosis—demonstrating the blonde's complicated affinity with blackness—arrives as, slowly, with white hands now freed from their hairy mitts, she lifts the gorilla head-piece and substitutes for it a blond "afro" wig, all the while wooing her two "audiences," Cary Grant, at a table in the club, and the moviegoers seated in the darkened theater, with her song of erotic promise. This image of the blonde, the collaborative effort of Dietrich and director Josef von Sternberg, shaped by whites' newly admiring embrace of black culture but old, presumptuous flattening of black experience to sexual indulgence and license, may have been merely another turn in the complex history of race relations, but for women it was emancipating.

The vision of the blonde in the '30s was also complicated in another way. Rising stars like Jean Harlow, Carole Lombard, and Miriam Hopkins—younger than West and less exotic than Dietrich—redefined femininity through their animated bodies and mouths. "Sedate" was an adjective put up in mothballs as these women asserted their right to make choices, to move freely through the world, and, above all, to be funny. Whether the blonde was working-class or high-class, she was also defined by a characteristic courage, perseverance, and honesty—traits valued during the Great Depression, by way of representational mystification, as the ticket out of the economic slump.

But pre-Code and even later '30s moments of unprecedented freedom for women, both cinematically and culturally, were replaced by a negative representation of the blonde—the darkest version yet: her passionate, intemperate, socially alienated avatar in film noir at the end of the decade. With hindsight, it's clear that as the Great Depression dragged on, women would be linked misogynistically through cinematic representations of the blonde to the general social and economic malaise.

This noir blonde prevailed, beyond the hiatus of the war years and for new reasons, into the early '50s, when competition arrived in the form of more domesticated, sunnier versions like Marilyn Monroe's brilliantly comedic dizzy dame in *How to Marry a Millionaire* (a later variation on the girl-catches-man theme of early '30s "screwball"), with Doris Day's virginal career-girl blondes in romantic fantasies like *Pillow Talk*, and (reaching new lows both in IQ and entertainment value) with the new breed of teenage stars (like Sandra Dee) in the first celebrations of teen culture of the late '50s and early '60s. These blondes (almost half a century in the past but many of whose movies are still shown on late-night television or the cable channels) were embodiments of women's (and girls') roles in a society that, after World War II, was supersaturated with oxymoronic domestic desire. Like the cyclical "cage crinoline" that made its one-hundred-year return in the 1950s (the 1850s being the years of fullest skirts for the entire nineteenth century, as were the 1750s for the eighteenth),[11] a reinvigorated, confining "blond" domestic ideology reigned in new suburban settings and in cinematically scripted versions of real life. The plot was simple but thick: sooner rather than later, the blonde's dominant gene—producing the twinned desires for home and husband—would be expressed. With the exception of Monroe's contradictory images on- and offscreen, these blondes were, unfortunately, a far less interesting phenomenon than that of their audacious predecessors of the early '30s—incredibly a mere twenty years earlier—a number of whom distinguished themselves by refusing to accept marriage as "their pleasantest preservative from want" (*Pride and Prejudice* 93). Such domesticating figures and scripts, denying women's abilities and independence, required and still require rewrites to represent other possibilities and to erase color-coded, retrograde distinctions.

In 1694, Charles Perrault, the creator of Mother Goose, revised a traditional French fairy tale, "Peau d'âne," or "Donkey Skin," to support a group of extraordinary women of the court of Louis XIV. They desired relationships of equality with men without the burden of unwanted pregnancies or arranged marriage. The heroine, golden-haired Donkey Skin, escapes her king-father's incestuous overtures by wearing the filthy skin of his prized donkey and fleeing to a neighboring land, where the prince falls in love with her. In 1970, almost three hundred years after Perrault wrote his story because *les précieuses* refused to accept the ordinary lot of women, Jacques Demy, director of the more famous *The Umbrellas of Cherbourg* (1964), wrote and directed a film version, *Peau d'âne*, starring Catherine Deneuve as the beautiful blond princess Donkey Skin, and Delphine Seyrig, another beautiful blonde, as Lilac Fairy, Donkey Skin's charmingly subversive fairy godmother. Demy, riding the second wave of feminism, also did his part to help women in their struggle for independence and power. Closely following the plot of Perrault's story, he altered it just enough—and comically—to make it a parable for our times.

As with Perrault's story, Demy's mise-en-scène is the always timeless yet always medieval world of northern European fairy tales. The first departure is that Lilac Fairy isn't an old crone but a blonde of considerable beauty and charm herself. She's impish but wise, humorous but serious. Donkey Skin is disturbed by the king's marriage proposal yet—unlike the girl of the original tale—really wants to marry her father. She loves him very much, she tells her godmother. But no, she is mixing up two kinds of love, says Lilac Fairy. Of course young girls desire to marry their fathers, as young boys do their mothers. This is a natural feeling, she continues, but it would be very bad for the offspring, who would be "tainted." Thus, Donkey Skin gets a lesson in both Freudian psychology and genetics.

The king, as he woos her, reads her poetry by Guillaume Apollinaire and Jean Cocteau—"poetry of the future," he explains, given to him by Lilac Fairy. With references to "Calliope phoning in a scoop" and "Urania turning on the gas lights," it's no wonder that, as he says, Lilac Fairy's "knowledge of the future amazes me." Moreover, muses are now a*mus*ing!

When Lilac's ruses to prevent the king from marrying Donkey Skin have all failed, she cryptically laments that her spells are weakening—"like a battery." She advises her to run away. It will be an ordeal: "Life is not so easy as you think—even for the daughter of a king." This is an important lesson for Donkey Skin, who might be a little too fond of gazing at her beautiful reflection in the mirror. But as in the original tale, a handsome prince from a neighboring land falls in love with her.

With the marriage about to take place, a helicopter carrying Lilac Fairy and the king alights on the lawn. Lilac kisses Donkey Skin, whispering in her ear: "Oh, darling! I'm going to marry your father. Try to look pleased." She and the king, who had once "behaved badly [to her] in an affair," have clearly reconciled.

Because of the king's revelation about his future wife's "knowledge of the future," we assume that it was she who arranged for the convenient mode of transport. Obviously, Lilac's a forward-looking woman, knowledgeable about poetry, both symbolist and modernist, and technology, as well. She's also the mover and shaker behind the action in this story—its ideological locus, even if Donkey Skin is more often the camera's focus. And she's far more interesting than the beautiful girl who, with respect for authority—except in the case of choosing her husband—does exactly as she's told. Lilac Fairy, golden godmother, is our great maternal role model!

Back to Perrault, forward to Demy, this history extends over a very comprehensive time-space continuum, from 1694 to the present, over two continents, and from fiction to film. Although the "bookends" I name here are men, women writers and actors, like imaginative Lilac Fairy, have been the main players in altering representations of the traditional blonde and, thus, advancing the liberty of women and men, too.[12] The plasticity of their collective story—the ways in which their representations have altered to meet new historical challenges—is as interesting as any of their individual contributions. Like "Peau d'âne," the story of these stories offers much instruction.

Thackeray's Blondes

Rebecca and Rowena

> "Revenge may be wicked, but it's natural,"
> answered Miss Rebecca. "I'm no angel." And, to say
> the truth, she certainly was not.
> —William Makepeace Thackeray, *Vanity Fair*

The two-year period 1847 to 1849 was critical in the re-representation of women—both in print and in the public sphere. And 1847, alone, was a banner year for nascent feminism and the new blonde, with Becky Sharp leading the way in January, and Jane Eyre, Georgiana Reed, and Catherine Linton following in October and December. The next year, against the background of ferment and revolution in Europe, American women held the Seneca Falls Convention. Then, in 1849, the year in which William Makepeace Thackeray published his send-up of Scott's *Ivanhoe*, *Rebecca and Rowena: A Romance Upon Romance*, Eliza Cook published her magazine, *Eliza Cook's Journal*, the first of a new breed of periodicals produced by women and mixing articles on serious social issues with poetry and fiction. Although women were not yet at the barricades, they were moving to change their lot as never before. Representation played an important role in their advance.

Like Bessie Rayner Parkes, Barbara Leigh Smith Bodichon (both originally Unitarians), and Matilda ("Max") Mary Hays (who would publish the *English Woman's Journal* in 1858), Cook came from a family of intellectuals and religious nonconformists. She was interested in an array of progressive, not radical, social issues: female education; governesses' poor pay; the benefits of gainful employment for "ladies" in the business world; improved education for middle-class clerks; temperance. All of these issues, directly or indirectly, affected the quality of women's lives. Indeed, that women were able to start magazines, enter into the nation's political debates, win legislative battles (like the Divorce Act of 1857), and fight for better sanitation and education was an index of the movement of middle-class women out of the home and into the wider world. However, the metaphorical language through which Eliza Cook describes the aims of her new publishing venture suggests just how vexed by restraining conventions and self-restraint their journey was. The sanctity of home and housekeeping dominates her self-conscious, precious rhetoric.

She draws on a range of figures that would have kept her readers in the comfortably familiar worlds of mainstream literature and their own experience. In setting out the editorial policy in "A Word to My Readers" in the first number of the *Journal* (5 May 1849), she declares that she is no "mental Joan of Arc" in the war against "Ignorance and Wrong," but, rather, calling herself a homemaker (and perhaps playing on her name), she deploys culinary metaphors, proposing to prepare "a plain feast" of "viands" of her choosing that are "wholesome and relishing." Borrowing the Romantic poets' "corresponding breeze" to suggest the similarity between nature and the human spirit, she punningly confesses that she has listened to the "active breath of nature," which "awoke wild but earnest melodies, which I dotted down in simple notes." Yet these "airs" haven't been heard, as one might expect, out-of-doors. Rather, they are "strains hummed about the sacred altars of domestic firesides." Her tune is scored entirely in D (for domestic) major.

It's only when she describes her new venture more particularly that she delicately distances herself from this traditional woman's space. Punning all the way, she travels beyond the limits of home, transforming her magazine into an emporium or "market-place," its "house-wares" into "goods," and her readers into customers (but customers still buying for home-use), expressing confidence that her "friends," if "I offer them a combination of utility and amusement," "will freely take the wares I bring, and not think the worse of me for mixing with them in the market-place of Activity and Labour." Then expressing hope that they will accept the exchange of the privacy of the hearth for the public sphere of the marketplace—that is, welcome the inclusion of articles on public policy in addition to poetry and fiction in her magazine—she trades in Romantic for commercial metaphors to move her readers from the home into a broader, and broadening, intellectual sphere and, truly, into the world of actual commerce, where her ideas will be especially relevant and serviceable.

Yet while the articles and stories in her magazine address new interests and concerns of her primarily female readers, she doesn't challenge their position as matriarchs and housekeepers. A woman was defined by her relations to the other members of her home and the actual place in which she lived; she was wife, mother, sister, or daughter, to which many of the articles in women's political magazines would attest.[1] To question this social/biological meaning of the word "woman" was beyond the limits of Cook's worldview, even though, unmarried and employed herself, she was proof that a woman could think and act independently. The late-blooming sensitivity of the Lady Augusta, originally the most undomestic and callous of women, in "The Three Hyacinths before Heaven" by "Silverpen" (Elizabeth Meteyard)—the lead story in the first number of the *Journal*—reveals Cook's reluctance to challenge the home and charitable work outside it as the primary feminine spheres. Domesticity was too powerful a cultural force to fight openly.

But Cook got stronger as she wrote and edited longer. She condemned the infantilization of women that marked and (as she believed) diminished the intercourse of polite society. She complained in the number for September 25, 1852:

But even in the most intelligent European circles, woman is still regarded too much in the light of an ornamental object. If we pay her a compliment, it is generally at the expense of her intellect. It is her beauty, or her grace, or her accomplishments,—rarely her good sense, judgment, or her womanly qualities, that are praised. In genteel society she is often treated as a creature incapable of a serious thought. When the "ladies" enter a room where conversation is going forward, it is immediately changed to some puerile and frivolous subject. Compliments begin. . . . And the young ladies are trotted out, one after another, to show their paces and be admired. Pretty flatteries are bandied about—gilt lies—sweet nothings—rising into an agony of small talk; and worship of weakness seems to become the order of the day. (no. 178: 337–39)

She was not alone. Progressive mainstream periodicals like the *Pall Mall Ga-zette* also tolled the bell for these "gilt lies" and "sweet nothings."

Thackeray, too, was an ally. Troubled by the constraints imposed on women, he restored motive, activity, intelligence, and sexuality to his blonde. Unlike Dickens, fettered by his commitment to middle-class domesticity as the indispensable solution to social woes, Thackeray cared not at all about good housekeeping. But he did mind very much about the materialistic values of his world, to which women were not immune, and which were responsible for their "indentured" position. And he knew that his "darker purpose," his social critique, must begin with the iconic figure of the blonde.

By midcentury, the adventures of Romance had been replaced by the "domes-tic" reinterpretation of the genre: stories that either centered on, or made incidental reference to, the colonial venture going forward in the British Raj. Racism and anti-Semitism were surreptitiously coded in the popular middlebrow literature of women's magazines, with their abundance of fair and flaxen-haired heroines, through characters' names and passing comments on skin and hair color. Many of the plots of serialized stories turned on the extended absence of an acquaintance or lover on colonial business. Geographic and climatic differences provided an opportunity for pejorative comparison of women elsewhere in the world—in India, but also in the southern European countries the voyager had to travel through to get there—with the pale-complected "daughters of Albion" admired on his return. In Sarah Symonds's story "Destiny: A Tale," in the *Englishwoman's Domestic Magazine* beginning in February 1853, complexion is an index of racial purity or impurity, either the result of being born on English soil or of living south of the thirty-eighth parallel. The heroine's dancing partner, a sallow-faced guest from the colonies, remarks in an interval: "Nothing strikes me more on a return to England after some years of absence . . . than the fresh complexions and transparent skins of our fair countrywomen; it is so singular a contrast to the colourless and often sallow skins of the daughters of more glowing climes. In Asia this is almost universal, and even in the Southern countries of Europe the same absence of all beauty of complexion prevails" (1, no. 12 [1853]: 363). Sunburn, yellow fever, parasites, liver complaints—causing "sallow skins" in southern "climes"—were perceived as signs of racial inferiority, while fairness was tantamount to moral excellence.

"Light and Dark," a poem in the May 1858 *English Woman's Journal* commemorating those who died in the Indian Mutiny the previous year, celebrated the sanctity of the blond Saxon woman, for whom (it was understood) the dangerous occupation of a hostile land was undertaken. The moral contrast between the dark-skinned predators and their victims—the "white-limbed" English mothers with their "fair Saxon hair," "soft pale breasts," and infants of "rosy beauty"—is made in racial terms.

> And golden mosque and minaret
> With severed mangled limbs are set;
> Fair Saxon hair all dimmed with gore,
> And babes whom English mothers bore,
> Are brought out day by day to die;
> Sweet stars quench'd 'neath that cruel sky,
> Prey to each hungry morn.
>
> (1, no. 3 [1858]: 164)

Highlighting the genetic and moral purity of the Anglo-Indians and deploring the loss of their innocent lives,[2] the poem is a call to patriotism and duty, a tribute to their "buoyant spirits of conscious and indefeasible superiority,"[3] covertly arguing the morality of remaining in India to fulfill the colonial mission of civilizing the barbaric and primitive indigenous population. An exception in the pages of this generally progressive magazine, "Light and Dark" suggests how widespread the assumption of Saxon superiority was in Victorian culture. Even if covered in gore, the poet proclaims, pure Saxon women—golden and pale—remain unsullied by contact with the dark races.

The connection between women and imperialism/colonialism, although not as maudlinly portrayed as in "Light and Dark," is never much below the surface in Thackeray's fiction. However, Thackeray, an incomparably greater writer than any appearing in the pages of the middlebrow magazines, exploited the relationship to point out *home* truths about the "home" country. Imperialism is found at home—in the intemperate treatment of women—not only abroad in intemperate climes. He depended on representation to iron out the very wrinkled social fabric.

His attack was two-pronged. It began in 1839, when, at twenty-eight, he wrote *Rebecca and Rowena: A Romance Upon Romance*—although this satire on the Romance form wasn't published until ten years later. His avowed purpose in writing it was to administer retributive justice, giving the dark-haired

Jewess Rebecca her desserts and showing up the beautiful Saxon Rowena for the materialistic, chilly creature she really is. Alfred Hitchcock's ice-blondes weren't originals.

Refashioning Scott's Romance about the beginnings of the English empire into a domestic romance about a blonde and brunette, he wrote: "Rowena, that vapid, flaxen-headed creature . . . is, in my humble opinion, unworthy of Ivanhoe, and unworthy of her place as heroine. Had both of them got their rights, it ever seemed to me that Rebecca would have had the husband, and Rowena would have gone off to a convent and shut herself up, where I, for one, would never have taken the trouble of inquiring for her" (14). He ridiculed Rowena, the boring, unexceptional beauty, like many in his own world, correcting Scott's errors, of which the biggest is the conclusion: marriage for the blonde and virginity and exile for the dark, exotic girl.

Because his romance is "upon" Scott's Romance, it's a double negative—which, as we know, makes a positive. Thackeray set things to rights in the "realist" mode, overcoming Scott's objection to a Rebecca-Ivanhoe union by having his heroine convert to Christianity (highly improbable, and he knows it, but we grant him the license). And so, toward the close of his amended version, he writes that he is "quite affected," "now her head is laid upon Ivanhoe's heart." He has been thinking of this scene of reunion of Ivanhoe and Rebecca "ever since, as a boy at school, I commenced the noble study of novels—ever since the day when, lying on sunny slopes, of half-holidays . . . I grew to love Rebecca, that sweetest creature of the poet's fancy, and longed to see her righted" (101).

The "noble study of novels" . . . Thackeray meant to name this activity so grandly, for he felt, as a boy, and more fully as the adult writer, the power of novels to mold the reader's perceptions of reality. He was inspired to show his contemporaries (for their own good) the world as (he believed) it truly was. That meant substituting the realist for the Romantic mode of representation. He articulated his criticisms of his culture with the publication of his early and farcical "romance upon romance," but two years before, he had done it seriously in *Vanity Fair*, the novel he considered until the end of his life his best work. In naming his satire of Scott's story after its female characters and choosing the title *Vanity Fair* for his novel of 1847, he was the first Victorian to expose the immemorial relationship between imperial aggression, women, and the debasement of values in his fallen, commercial world.

Through details even more miraculous and exaggerated than Scott's, he explodes the fantastic elements of *Ivanhoe*. Instead of giving the reader the story as Scott *should* have told it, he coyly respected the parameters of the original plot: "But after all," he wrote, "she [Rowena] married Ivanhoe. What is to be done? . . . There it is in black and white at the end of the third volume of Sir Walter Scott's chronicle, that the couple were joined together in matrimony" (14). He has only one choice: to extend the story beyond the day of their nuptials. But the decision to begin his tale after the wedding is more than a clever evasion of narrative constraint. It's a cornerstone of his literary realism. "Thus Sir Wilfrid of Ivanhoe, having attained the height of his wishes, was, like many a man when he has reached that dangerous elevation, disappointed. . . . Life is such, ah, well-a-day! It is only hope which is real, and reality is a bitterness and a deceit" (19). Poor Ivanhoe will take the true and uncomfortable measure of his exquisite blonde only after he's tied the knot. Then (like Thackeray, who always knew better) he'll wish he'd married Rebecca instead. His silent hankering after her (in both Romances) was mirrored by Scott's readers' preference. In his introduction to the 1830 edition of the novel, Scott felt called on to defend Ivanhoe's choice.

The Romance is a natural target for Thackeray's critique of the treatment of women because the hero invariably chooses the woman of his own "race"—no matter the qualities of the Other. Frederic Jameson in *The Political Unconscious* argues that "from the earliest times, the stranger from another tribe, the 'barbarian' who speaks an incomprehensible language and follows 'outlandish' customs, but also the woman, whose biological difference stimulates fantasies of castration and devoration . . . are some of the archetypal figures of the Other, about whom the essential point to be made is not so much that he is feared because he is evil; rather he is evil *because* he is Other, alien, strange, unclean, and unfamiliar" (115). The exotic, dark-haired woman is doubly the Other, by virtue of her ethnic or racial difference and her sex, a figure of fascination but also one who must be rejected in order to safeguard the "purity" of the "tribe" or the enlarged tribe, the nation. Rebecca is equally beautiful and skilled in the healing arts; she's also an unbelievable polyglot, outdistancing Ivanhoe in language acquisition, speaking fluent Saxon (253), French (253), and Latin (273), reading (425) and writing (420) Hebrew, and reading Arabic when Bois-Guilbert passes a "slip of parchment" to her on which she reads "in the Arabian character, '*Demand a Champion!*'" (414). Rowena, ignorant even of French, remains silent when addressed by the Normans, while her guardian, Cedric the Saxon, must answer for her: "The Lady Rowena . . . possesses not the language in which to reply to your courtesy, or to sustain her part in your festival" (118). But whom does Ivanhoe choose? Well, who wants a leech or a babbler at home?

Thackeray was a realist who believed his society needed stronger medicine than the simple solutions of Romance for its moral recovery. Like Peter Cook and Dudley Moore, he knew that "reality bites." His mordant satire on the vanities of his world required a hard, realistic look at its injustices. But he also knew that the fiction writer isn't effective merely because he supplies a "history of the real world." Rather, as he wrote some years after the publication of *Vanity Fair:* "The Art of Novels *is* . . . to convey as strongly as possible the sentiment of reality—in a tragedy or a poem or a lofty drama you aim at producing different emotions; the figures moving and the words sounding, heroically" (quoted in Iser 39–40). I understand Thackeray to mean that reading a novel does not actually reproduce the "real" world but pleasantly burdens us by making us *feel* the weight of those emotions we recognize as also existing in the rest of our lives. The effective novel, in other words, is *affective,* moving us as we read. Thackeray's description of the reader's emotions in response to the language of the novel might be better expressed as "the reality of sentiment." We respond to the novel and remember it for the strong feelings we had as we were reading, as even late in his life he recalled Rebecca in *The Roundabout Papers:* "Rebecca, daughter of Isaac of York, I have loved thee faithfully for forty years! Thou wert twenty years old (say) and I but twelve, when I knew thee. At sixty odd, love, most of the ladies of thy Orient race have lost the bloom of youth, and bulged beyond the line of beauty; but to me thou art ever young and fair, and I will do battle with any felon Templar who assails thy fair name" (quoted in Monsarrat 21). In his Keatsian evocation of womanly perfection, Thackeray indirectly invoked not only that from which it was forever inseparable—his youth—but also the immense pleasures of reading and the exercise of the imagination, the readerly counterparts of "the poet's fancy."

For Thackeray, as he read *Ivanhoe* at the age of twelve or thirteen, his "love" for Rebecca made the experience real and memorable. Irony bears witness that admiration for her was matched by an equally strong aversion to Rowena, that "vapid, flaxen-headed creature": "Those who have marked her conduct during her maidenhood, her distinguished politeness, her spotless modesty of demeanor, her unalterable coolness under all circumstances, and her lofty and gentlewomanlike bearing, must be sure that her married conduct would equal her spinster behavior, and that Rowena the wife would be a pattern of correctness for all the matrons of England" (15). Thackeray, the sentimental man who distrusted anyone who didn't show her feelings, disdains Rowena's invariable ice-maidenly coolness and frozen correctness of behavior. He writes a humorous send-up of these qualities (too frequently found in the world beyond the novel), describing Rowena's "grief" over Ivanhoe's putative death through her rapid translation of "immaterial" sentiment into the material: "That she truly deplored the death of her lord cannot be questioned, for she ordered the deepest mourning which any milliner in York could supply, and erected a monument to his memory as big as a minster. But she was a lady of such fine principles that she did not allow her grief to overmaster her" (51). Rowena's the kind of girl who cares more about a fancy new wimple to cover her blond curls than the man who would have paid for it. But then all Romance is a "fabrication": "*Entre nous,* I . . . sometimes doubt whether there is a single syllable of truth in this whole story" (56).

But if there is any syllable of truth, it's that there is *truth in reading* it or in the reality of sentiment—the memory of which remains for the reader long after the plot details are forgotten. It's also the only "unconditional truth" that we may confidently believe in when reading *Vanity Fair,* for the Stage Manager–narrator, despite his name (which suggests both his control and full knowledge), is like the lying Cretin, giving directions at the crossroads, who may or may not be telling the truth. Yet here there is no "right" question to help us out. The Stage Manager is not intentionally malevolent or duplicitous. Rather, our dilemma results from the enticing corruptions of the Fair itself. His point of view must be unreliable because, as he admits, his judgments are tainted by the same egotism and striving he sees all around him. He recognizes his own weaknesses for the "vanities" of society as when he offers us an archly distancing homily on its attractions. He's like the "honest newspaper-fellow who sits in the hall and takes down the names of the great ones who are admitted to the feasts." Like him, he is "scorched" by "the glare of fashion": "It is all vanity to be sure: but who will not own to liking a little of it? I should like to know what well-constituted mind, merely because it is transitory, dislikes roast-beef? That is a vanity; but may every man who reads this, have a wholesome portion of it through life, I beg" (518–19).

A good foothold is difficult to maintain in this morally slippery terrain. Offering a commentary on the others at this feast, the Stage Manager implicates himself as well; like the guests, he desires the attractive pleasures afforded by irreducible and delicious life. The truth of Thackeray's, as well as his Stage

Manager's, susceptibility to the blandishments of this world is well-documented in his many letters on the subject. Thus, because he implicates himself, he suggests that he is hardly one to pass judgment on his complex and flexible puppet, Becky Sharp, whom he also needs to observe the various booths from another vantage point and so, through triangulation, take an accurate reading of his culture. She represents a critical retreat from the corruptions of Vanity Fair even as she lives in and epitomizes it. But she is not, as some readers have maintained, the quintessence of corruption in the fallen world. Although she says, "I'm no angel," and the narrator adds, "And, to say the truth, she certainly was not" (9), Thackeray never asserts that she's an angel's contrary—a demon. Seconding Becky's sentiment, Mae West chose this self-evaluative comment for the title of her 1933 film. Film critic Molly Haskell, in *From Reverence to Rape*, argues persuasively that there are scenes in the movie in which West takes a moral position "against the prevailing wind" and shows an "honesty proceeding from intelligence" (20). I can say the same for Becky. And so, after disabling the flaxen blonde by outing Rowena's frigid rectitude, Thackeray, to make his point about the position of women, chose her opposite: a sexy, smart, ambitious dirty-blonde—just as, but no more guilty, than anyone else in Vanity Fair.

Thackeray was one of those men who don't feel, in the abstract, the rightness of a political or social question but translated his very personal, intense love or friendship for an individual into the representative case. He was a social inductionist; his modus operandi probably accounts for his being a novelist rather than a philosopher. His satires, generated by a particular instance, grow in relation to the metastasized cancer that threatens all of society but especially victimizes the people he cared most about: women and children. In *Vanity Fair*, he stage-managed his critique of the plight of women, using his dirty-blonde as a "sharp" instrument to dissect the figure that the poet Coventry Patmore would call the "angel in the house." But it was also necessary to raze that "house," in which she willingly or wilfully chose to live.

Yet as sentimental as he was about women, Thackeray recognized the complexity of their victimization, believing that they were not mere hapless pawns in a game played by men solely for their own benefit. In his novel of 1847, he created, as well as Becky, the very different character Amelia Sedley, the one very "lively on the wire" (xx) and the other tediously passive—whose adult lives provide the motive-force for his narrative: the scrutiny of the destructive social aspirations and relations that guide women and everyone else in Vanity

Fair, not excepting the Stage Manager and reader. "This, dear friends and companions," says the Stage Manager, "is my amiable object—to walk with you through the Fair, to examine the shops and the shows there; and that we should all come home after the flare, and the noise, and the gaiety, and be perfectly miserable in private" (185). He seconds Mephistopheles' confident judgment in *Doctor Faustus:* "Why this is hell, nor am I out of it" (1.3.76).

As he does in *Rebecca and Rowena,* Thackeray ridicules Lady Crawley, the "vapid, flaxen-haired creature" with which his society was in love: "She wore light clothes, as most blondes will, and appeared . . . in draggled sea-green, or slatternly sky-blue. . . . She had not character enough to take to drinking, and moaned about, slipshod and in curl-papers, all day. Oh, Vanity Fair!—Vanity Fair! This might have been, but for you, a cheery lass; Peter Butt and Rose, a happy man and wife . . . but a title and a coach and four are toys more precious than happiness in Vanity Fair" (80–81). He denigrates her only attractions, youth and Saxon fairness—color-code for superiority—as bad reasons for choosing a mate, especially when blondness is subversively linked to dullness, lack of character, and the materialism that dominates his world. But Lady Crawley, née Rose Dawson, the social-climbing iron monger's daughter, isn't different from any other girl in Vanity Fair "this season." She's Thackeray's portrait of the "*fade* and insipid"[4] icon of popular culture.

But while his "pen and pencil sketch"[5] hints at his disdain for the Saxon ideal, it doesn't allow him to explore more than superficially women's position in his culture. He needed a full-color portrait of another sort of blonde, "pale, sandy-haired," with "large, odd, and attractive" eyes (10), for this important work. Becky, although variously described as having "fair ringlets" (34) and "yellow hair" (423), is, like the alloy steel, stronger than pure iron alone. To the "true blonde," Thackeray added another element. His vector of social criticism would be a woman of true grit:[6] the sandy-haired Becky Sharp.

To be sure, the "malignant" or malevolent blonde existed in poetry and painting long before Thackeray conceived of Rebecca's "fair ringlets." Coleridge's "Life-in-Death" "nightmare" woman of *The Rime of the Ancient Mariner* (1798) is such a figure.

> *Her* lips were red, *her* looks were free,
> Her locks were yellow as gold;
> Her skin was as white as leprosy,

> The nightmare Life-in-Death was she
> Who thicks man's blood with cold.
>
> (183–84)

This "nightmare" is no transparent wraith, despite her "ribs through which the sun / Did peer," but a golden-haired, ruby-lipped Saxon. She's an incarnation of Robert Graves's archetypal "White Goddess," "mother, bride, and layer-out" of the warring "God of the Waxing Year" and "God of the Waning Year" (24–26).[7] Her Medusa-head, "with its numbing look," "freezes up the blood of man." Her threat to the men of the Mariner's ship is registered as sexual aggression: "*Her* looks were free." Percy Bysshe Shelley's closet-drama *The Cenci* of 1819 told the story of a parricide, the golden-haired Beatrice, who was a threat only to the man who had raped her—her father, the Count Cenci. His violent passion—"Might I not drag her by her golden hair? / Stamp on her?" (167)—is the occasion for Shelley's denouncing "domestic and political tyranny and imposture" (131). Yet while Shelley and Thackeray wrote about the disastrous consequences of the tyrannical treatment of women, Beatrice is very different from Becky. "The young maiden," Shelley wrote in his Preface, "urged to this tremendous deed by an impulse which overpowered its horror, was evidently a most gentle and amiable being, a creature formed to adorn and be admired, and thus violently thwarted from her nature by the necessity of circumstances and opinion" (447). Becky, however, is by no means only a victim. Thackeray deliberately fashions her as a character of ambiguous moral nature to universalize his claims about the spoiled social and sexual relations of women and men.

In 1852, five years after *Vanity Fair* appeared, an American admirer of Thackeray's, Herman Melville, described a portrait of Beatrice in *Pierre or the Ambiguities*. He called it the "most awful of all feminine heads—The Cenci of Guido" (489)—in words that newly confounded blondes with chaos and violence. Of a copy of the Guido painting, Melville wrote:

> The wonderfulness of which head consists chiefly, perhaps, in a striking, suggested contrast, half identical with, and half analogous to, that almost supernatural one—sometimes visible in the maidens of tropical nations—namely, soft and light blue eyes, with an extremely fair complexion, veiled by funereally jetty hair. But with blue eyes and fair complexion, the Cenci's hair is golden—physically, therefore, all is in strict, natural keeping; which, nevertheless, still the more intensifies the suggested fanciful anomaly of so

sweetly and seraphically *blonde* a being, being double-hooded, as it were, by the black crape of the two most horrible crimes (of one of which she is the object, and of the other the agent) possible to civilised humanity—incest and parricide. (489)

Despite his admission that Beatrice is the victim of a heinous crime, Melville conflates this golden-haired woman with a culturally recurring image of untrustworthy, aggressive, non-European females as in *Typee*, in which travel book he also described the beautiful island girl Fayaway as having "strange blue eyes" (104). The "natural keeping" of blondness with sweetness, meekness, and mildness—as in fairy tales, assumed attributes of the blonde in Victorian culture—has been distorted by venomous treachery, the fatal sting of the "double-hooded" cobra already cloaked in mourning ("black crape"), anticipating the crime the "Cenci" will commit. Melville's portrait recalls Coleridge's "Life-in-Death" and the misogynistic poetry and painting of the Pre-Raphaelite Brotherhood, formed in 1848, which obsessively focused on disastrous, powerfully tressed blondes and (less surprisingly) redheads. Dante Gabriel Rossetti, a founder and leader of the group, at the age of eighteen, in 1846, had written "The Blessed Damozel" about a "mild" woman, already dead, leaning out "From the gold bar of heaven" with "hair that lay along her back / . . . yellow like ripe corn [wheat]" (1461). She longs, patiently and unthreateningly, to be reunited with her earthly lover. In 1869, an older Rossetti wrote a fragment of a poem, "The Orchard-Pit," in which the woman's "hair / Crosses my lips and draws my burning breath; / Her song spreads golden wings upon the air, / Life's eyes are gleaming from her forehead fair, / And from her breasts the ravishing eyes of Death" (1472).[8] The last stanza—with its variation on the topos of *vagina dentata* or female cannibalism—is dominated by the poet's fear of the inseparable and unholy trinity: woman/sexuality/death:

> My love I call her, and she loves me well:
> > But I love her in the maelstrom's cup
> The whirled stone loves the leaf inseparable
> That clings to it round all the circling swell,
> > And that the same last eddy swallows up.
>
> > > > (1472)

The treacherous blondes of the Pre-Raphaelites represent the type-in-formation of the "Fatal Woman," a Romantic phenomenon that fully flowered only in the second half of the nineteenth century. She is always pale, intimating an inability to survive without the life-blood of her younger, less powerful lover, whom she sexually cannibalizes as does the female spider.[9] This figure, although appearing in a variety of genres in continental literatures, in England was primarily the fantastic creation of poets rather than novelists at midcentury and later.

Thackeray's demythologized "natural" blonde, Becky, should not be grouped with the fatal women of these poets, who were largely responsible for the revival of interest in figures like the man-eating Lady Lilith. In fact, neither Rebecca nor Shelley's Beatrice is the creation of misogynistic fantasy. The "famous little Becky Puppet," "uncommonly flexible in the joints" (xxx), bends all ways and simply cannot be typed. Following Shelley's purpose, Thackeray was the first to create a blonde in a novel who would expose the treatment, position, and behavior of *all* women through his narrator's intentionally ambiguous representation. If vital Becky, the first realistically "difficult" blonde in the English novel, is a "fallen woman," it's only because she inhabits the already "fallen world," suggested by the Miltonic motif of expulsion from the First Garden: "The great gates were closed. . . . The world is before the two young ladies" (7).

Thackeray's criticism of Scott in *Rebecca and Rowena* is an explicit indictment of the Romance formula that makes too simple a contrast of heroines. The variant hue of Becky's hair—sandy, not flaxen—suggests the ambiguity that defines this indeterminate character. When he began *Vanity Fair* in 1847, there was no clearly defined "fatal woman" type, and, in any case, Becky is both too comic and brainy (perhaps these characteristics are twin-born) to be one of this sisterhood. His decision to make his ambiguous character blond rather than dark-haired *and* call her "our heroine" overturns cultural assumptions of the period about blond women as "most gentle and amiable being[s]." Indeed, Thackeray did what no writer before him had done. He married the image of blond innocence with "knowledge" of the fallen world to liberate women from the very pressures that caused them to adopt guile as their stratagem for social success.

Guile, however, need not be not lethal. Instead, like his captivating, witty, and teasing friend Jane Brookfield (Monsarrat 194), Becky is of a metaphorical order of "man killers" who exist in his unheroic, debased, commercial society. Like the mythic Narcissus, she's autoerotic, seeing herself in the pools of her lovers' eyes and falling in love with her own reflection. But the comparison stops there because Narcissus tipped in and drowned, while Becky's a survivor, a coquette.

Coquettishness is of the fallen world—an exaggerated femininity women have been taught men "fall" for. It insists on innocence when its basis is sheer theater and artifice. Yet Thackeray doesn't blame Becky for her efforts. Rather he's in awe of this force, "man-made," in both senses, unleashed on the inhabitants of Vanity Fair, who aren't as clever as she at the serious game of "getting on."

The coquette specializes in exaggerating the body language and behaviors culturally coded as feminine and, when successful in attracting men through her ploys, heartlessly holding them at arm's length.[10] Her narcissism prevents her from suffering the heartbreak of women who, like Amelia Sedley, allow themselves to love not wisely but too well. Thackeray's double vision of Becky, not best-natured yet a heroine, permits some sympathy for her as she successfully coquettes the men of Vanity Fair, while it cynically distances us from her exaggerated feminine behavior. Through these competing perspectives, Thackeray dissects the values of the upper- and middle-class milieus by which, almost universally, women voluntarily lived.

Any assumptions about the personality traits of blond fairy-tale heroines are overturned by Becky, who is neither meek nor tractable. While they may be her crowning glory, her pretty blond curls are also the tip of a potentially dangerous iceberg, colored to shock. She's like the drag queen whose performance gives pleasure precisely by creating an unsettling cognitive dissonance for his audience. The coquette's parodic exhibition of femininity, which renders her invulnerable, resembles the queen's "camp" performance—his outrageous exaggeration of the feminine—which similarly announces his refusal to suffer for his sexuality. As we're enjoying it, we're simultaneously aware that his masquerade disrupts our faith in the immutability of sexuality. Our attraction to it is partly owing to the comedic exaggeration of feminine traits, but there's also pleasure in the subtle danger created by the audacious transgression of sexual boundaries. We watch with astonishment and wonder—altering the words of the song—"Why can a man be more like a woman?" Like the drag queen, Becky is a "female impersonator,"[11] comically exaggerating traits Victorian culture considered feminine, which Thackeray determined to expose because they enslaved women.

Becky gives many performances as a coquette, impersonating the behaviors of the Victorian ingenue but with a cunning that tweaks not only her victim but the role. When Jos gallantly says, "By Gad, Miss Rebecca, I wouldn't hurt you for the world!" the Stage Manager reports that Becky assured Jos she believed him, "and then she gave him ever so gentle a pressure with her little hand,

and then drew it back quite frightened, and looked first for one instant in his face, and then down at the carpet-rods" (25). We recognize a performance, but Jos is taken in by "the simple girl" (25) with her "sad and piteous look" (29), "blush[ing] as she bent her fair ringlets over the netting" (34). In her maiden days and even after, Becky appears "with eyes habitually cast down" (10).

However, the "charades" and song of chapter 51—"In which a Charade is acted which may or may not puzzle the Reader"—are Becky's chance, on the grand scale, for performing female impersonations at Lord Steyne's residence. They're also Thackeray's opportunity to use his aggressive blonde to indict his culture's treatment of women by showing it as only the latest manifestation of violations recounted in the foundational myths of Western culture: the story of the House of Atreus and of the imperialist Trojan War and regicide that followed. As entertainment or "art," the charades stand in relation to the narrative of which they are a part, as the novel does in relation to the real world from which it comes and in which we, "the reader[s]," live. Thackeray joins art to novel to world, implying that the meaning of the charades is applicable to his larger fictive world and to ours, as well. Our proof of his novelistic "home" truth is the "reality of sentiment" with which we'll be left when we shut up his "box" of "puppets."

The "rising action" of this chapter focuses on Becky's "performances" in the world of fashion and anticipates the meaning of the charades as it parses the aristocratic "booth" of Vanity Fair. The inhabitants of this acquisitive, spiritually bankrupt world have nothing better to do than to "talk . . . about each others' houses, and characters, and families: just as the Joneses do about the Smiths. . . . the poor woman herself was yawning in spirit. 'I wish I were out of it,' she said to herself" (521–22). Money, power, and sex make both the aristocratic and commercial worlds go round.

Becky's history in the fashionable quarters of London has parallels to actual theatrical performance. As must be true of an actor in a long-running Broadway hit, "Her success" in the world of *ton* "excited, elated, and then bored her" (521). The thrill of conquest soon turns into its opposite as she learns by sheer repetition the tedium of a society governed by Saxon sameness and "Britannia of the Market," John Ruskin's "Goddess of 'Getting-on.'"[12] Thackeray describes the perpetual, compulsory social activity of the Victorian upper class, "the fine dinner parties" followed by the "fine assemblies" (521) with the same dramatis personae. With the inexorability of classical fate, young men become portly, polite, and prosy elders; "the young ladies, blond, timid, and in pink" (521), age into "sumptuous," humorless matrons in diamonds. Thackeray's indignation at this predictable evolution was the inducement for making his Becky puppet blond *but* sexual, "inventive," and aggressive. Women were systematically deprived by the conventions of their class, indeed of an entire culture (and not least by their own complicitous desires), of an interesting and well-spent life. He had only to think of his friend Jane Brookfield for a reality check.

The "audience" at Gaunt House guesses the "answers" to the charades (which Thackeray thoughtfully supplies his readers): "Agamemnon" and "Nightingale." We think of the Greek myths and Homer's epics—of the destruction of ancient families and empires—but the meaning also reverberates through other stories down the centuries.

He has carefully prepared for and deepened the social meaning of the "answers" by previously introducing them in the novel. Their second "appearance" in the charades, acting their "polysemic" parts, as Becky multifariously acts hers, is then suggestively enriched by our previous knowledge of them. The reader's ability to recognize the similarities between the exotic locales and distant events of the tableaux (Turkey, the Egyptian desert, ancient Greece, England in the eighteenth century) and the contemporary aristocratic milieu constitutes the possible "puzzle" of the chapter heading. Thackeray challenges the reader to experience the "reality of sentiment"—unease over the familial and social injustices not only of the charades but also of the "offstage" actions of the rest of the novel. The bad "domestic relations" we read about are the contemporary and local equivalents of the "foreign" and exotic dramatized here.

In this sense, Thackeray is importantly different from earlier writers, who had emphasized the distinctions between the "primitive" "Oriental" and the "civilized" Western European or Briton. While, for example, Scott suggests an underlying similarity between the aspirations of Rebecca and the Christians—we have, all of us, one human heart—the narrative of *Ivanhoe* affirms the savagery and otherness of Brian de Bois-Guilbert and the East, from which he has returned with his ferocious-looking black slaves. But Thackeray, at midcentury, leads us back to his own culture through "foreign intrigue." The attractive blonde is his secret agent.

He prepares for the exotic locales with the information that Becky was invited to the Prince of Peterwaradin's residence, "Levant House" (519), among whose other guests were "'H. E. Papoosh Pasha, the Turkish Ambassador (attended by Kibob Bey, dragoman of the mission) . . . Hon. Sands Bedwin, Bobbachy Bahawder,' and an &c." (523). He buttresses the connection between the meaning of the charades and the Orient, describing "young Bedwin Sands," traveler to the East, by comparing him to the "felon Templar" of *Ivanhoe*. Sands traveled "with a black attendant of the most unprepossessing appearance," "just like another Brian de Bois Guilbert" (528). The similarity between the two broadly reinforces the Oriental connection but also specifically introduces the linked themes of sexual aggression and imperialism. In *Rebecca and Rowena*, Thackeray had written that he would fight any Templar who would assail Rebecca's fair name.

Becky doesn't participate in the tableaux meant to illustrate the syllables "Aga" and "memnon," which pair sexual exploitation of women and aggression. The "Aga," the petty tyrant of Turkish origin, acted by Bedwin Sands, receives the "wares"—the beautiful Zuleikah—from a slave merchant played (ironically) by his own black slave, Mesrour. This scene reinforces Thackeray's previous assertion: "We are Turks with the affections of our women; and have made them subscribe to our doctrines too. We let their bodies go abroad liberally enough, with smiles and ringlets and pink bonnets to disguise them instead of veils and yakmaks. But their souls must be seen by only one man, and they obey not unwillingly, and consent to remain at home as our slaves—ministering to us and doing drudgery for us" (172). Substitutions of other names, roles, places, or times, do not alter universal wrongs. *Plus ça change* . . .

In this dramatization, the woman's status as victim of barbaric patriarchal prerogative is underscored by the casually given information that Mesrour has "sewn up ever so many *odalisques* in sacks and tilted them into the Nile" (528). Sexual and overt physical violence against women, the heart of this little play, suggested already through the comparison to Bois-Guilbert, is the basis for the prurience of the audience's reaction: "A thrill of terror and delight runs through the assembly. The ladies whisper to one another" (528). Thackeray implies that not only the men in the audience but also the women are titillated by this display of male power and aggression. They are complicitous in their victimization.

The next tableau transports the "Turks" of the first scene to the desert: "An enormous Egyptian head figures in the scene" (529). Signifying the last two syllables, "mem" and "non," it asserts the power and wealth of the Egyptian Pharaoh Amenhotep III, through the pharaonic, "monumental" bid for immortality. Amenhotep had a huge statue of himself built at Thebes.[13] Thackeray derides such affirmations-in-stone of the pharaohs' material importance as, in another vein, Shelley did Ozymandias's, by undercutting the solemnity of the project: the head "sings a comic song, composed by Mr. Wagg" (529).

He assumes his readers will understand the metamorphosis of this Egyptian head, for the "comic song" it sings is succeeded by other "signifying" music—"The band plays the awful music of *Don Juan*, before the statue enters" (529)—just before Becky makes her own dramatic entrance. Thus the statue of Amenhotep is transformed, for the culturally astute reader, into that other statue, the "Commendatore," who appears just before sexually exploitative Don Giovanni is engulfed in hell's fire. Imperial power and sexual domination are again joined; the worlds of Amenhotep and Mozart are closer than we may have imagined.

"Agamemnon" evokes many associations: Clytemnestra's adultery and regicidal act, as played out in the final scene of this charade; Paris's "rape" of Menelaus's wife, Helen; Agamemnon's conflict with Achilles over the concubines Chryseis and Briseis (Bullfinch 216) with which Homer's *Iliad* begins. It also recalls the curse of the House of Atreus. Long before the adultery and regicide, Agamemnon's father, Atreus, killed his brother Thyestes' children and served them to him at a banquet. And it reminds us of another child's slaughter—Agamemnon's sacrifice of his virginal daughter Iphigenia on the altar of Diana, who, enraged over the killing of one of her sacred stags by Agamemnon, had prevented the Greek fleet from setting sail for Troy (Bullfinch 213–14). The interrelatedness of these stories offers more evidence of the connection of violence against women and children and imperialist aggression.

But women, too, play active parts. It had been Becky who "incited" (527) Lord Steyne to mount the tableaux performed at Gaunt House. Now, with her own husband as Agamemnon, she's ready for her grand role—Clytemnestra. Sandy-haired Becky is finally impersonating a type different from the innocent or coquette: the aggressively sexual woman, about to make her psychic mark on European literature. But Thackeray plays on the readers' assumptions about such women to invalidate them.

As the narrator sets the scene by mentioning that Cassandra is a prisoner and Iphigenia has been slain, Thackeray invites a "feminist" interpretation of the events of *The Agamemnon*. Rather than see the death of the king as does his daughter Electra in Aeschylus's play, we're encouraged to participate in, to experience the reality of another sentiment—Clytemnestra's grief and rage over her great loss. Why shouldn't she seek revenge against her husband, who has sacrificed her child to further the bellicose intentions of the Achaeans? The "fatal woman" has reason for being so, *if,* indeed, she is a fatal woman.

Clytemnestra glides swiftly into the room like an apparition—her arms are bare and white,—her tawny hair floats down her shoulders,—her face is deadly pale,—and her eyes are lighted up with a smile so ghastly, that people quake as they look at her.

A tremor ran through the room. "Good God!" somebody said, "it's Mrs. Rawdon Crawley." (529)

Except for her green eyes, she's Robert Graves's White Goddess. Mother, lover, sister, "layer-out," the White Goddess is all things to men, desirable and fearful: "A lovely slender woman with a hooked nose, deathly pale face, lips red as rowan-berries, startlingly blue eyes and long fair hair; she will suddenly transform herself into sow, mare, bitch, vixen, she-ass, weasel, serpent . . . mermaid or loathsome hag" (24). Becky, too, as her picaresque story shows, is past master of metamorphoses. Thackeray's sketch, "The Triumph of Clytemnestra" (figure 1), appearing on the page of the novel after the charade, shows her nose as long—not like Amelia's, "rather too short than otherwise" (4). But Becky only performs the role of the White Goddess. And there's further uncertainty, for Thackeray contrives the scene to make us wonder if she's really fatal. Although she "scornfully . . . snatches the dagger out of Aegisthus's hand, and advances to the bed" (529), and "you see it shining over her head in the glimmer of the lamp" (529), "the lamp goes out, with a groan, and all is dark" (529). The Stage Manager leaves us in the "dark," unlike Aeschylus, about whether this Clytemnestra murders her husband.

The White Goddess is a male's, or, more accurately, many males', invention. With his feminine, unmythic point of view, Thackeray sabotages the fiction through the ambiguity of the charade as he will later when Becky makes her "second appearance in the character of Clytemnestra" (727), accused but then acquitted of murdering Jos for his insurance policy (729). What she is and what she may or may not have done will never be known with certainty. The homage she receives after she plays her part "with such ghastly truth" (530) is sensational, especially from Lord Steyne, who "said between his teeth," "By—, she'd do it too" and, aloud, as a clever remark, "Mrs. Rawdon Crawley was quite killing in the part" (530).

But despite suggestions, serious or punning, about playing the fatal woman "to the hilt," Becky quickly resumes the role of the less lethal coquette, looking "gay and saucy" and sweeping "the prettiest little curtsy ever seen" (530). She

The Triumph of Clytemnestra

Fig. 1. Becky coquettes after playing Clytemnestra. (By permission of the Rare Books Division, The New York Public Library, Astor, Lenox and Tilden Foundations)

ends the evening with the same ingenue-coquette impersonation. Her song, "The Rose upon the Balcony," follows the second set of charades representing the word "nightingale." The band plays "a nautical medley" (533), including "Rule Britannia." The themes of sexual exploitation and imperial aggression are again joined as Thackeray brings his meaning closer to "home." Although perhaps harder to see in one's own culture, these violations are still committed.

The lighthearted character of these charades is denied by the meaning of its one-word answer, "nightingale." A brutal prototype of sexual and physical violation shadows the jocular "music hall" action on the stage. By translating the word "nightingale" into its Greek equivalent, "Philomèle, Thackeray deftly accomplishes more than a linguistic metamorphosis. Following the pantomime, Lord Southdown, fast becoming Becky's rival in female impersonation, is, this time, an "old woman" who "gurgles" from behind "a sweet pasteboard cottage covered with roses and trellis work" (534). Then Becky appears.

Maria DiBattista has pointed out the significance of the myth of Philomel, the story of King Tereus's rape of his sister-in-law (92). Thackeray symbolically suggests the darker meaning of the nightingale's song—her violation followed by the violent ripping out of her tongue (which in the Ovidian myth is mutely expressed by Philomel through the tapestry she weaves)—by reminding the audience of the Greek name for the bird. In the unheroic fallen world of his contemporary culture, the Victorian woman was less violently treated but praised for her silent suffering. Thackeray purposely undermines the convention of the nightingale as the bird of love in western lyric poetry by reminding us of the potentially dark side of sexual relations in the midst of political and cultural decadence. In the myth, the queen, Philomel's sister, kills her son Itys, cooking and serving him to her husband in reprisal for his defilement of her sister. The story of the two women, Procne and Philomel, freed through their metamorphosis into a swallow and nightingale, ends as Agamemnon's story begins, with the atrocity of filial cannibalism.

The darkness of sexual and familial violation are missing from Becky's song about a nightingale. Everything about it is false or a cover-up, beginning with the "pasteboard" cottage. Thackeray implies that this is the way Victorians prefer their reality, including sex. Rape in the Ovidian myth has been replaced by the merely prurient—the sexual unsavoriness of the cross-dressing Lord Southdown, who impersonates the whiskered "mamma" of "Philomèle." The girl "comes in laughing, humming, and frisks about the stage with all the innocence of theatrical youth," "in powder and patches" (534). "Theatrical youth" is a deliberate oxymoron; "powder and patches"—"cover-up" cosmetics—adulterate artless beauty.

Thackeray obviously contrasts the "knowing" and provocative bawdy stage action and the provoking naïveté of Becky's mawkish lyric. If her "mamma" wants to know the reason for the nightingale's song, "It is because the sun is out and all the leaves are green." "Thus each performs his part, mamma, the birds have found their voices, / The blowing rose a flush, mamma, her bonny cheek to dye" (534). The sentimentalized personifications of the rose and bird are willful misrepresentations—more of the dodges and shams of Victorian morality. The culture's contemporary myths obscure awful truths, unlike the Greek myths, which revealed them. Lord Southdown, whiskers peeping from under his cap, seems "very anxious to exhibit maternal affection by embracing the innocent creature who perform[s] the daughter's part." The salacious behavior is welcomed with "acclamations of laughter by the sympathizing audience" (535). The disjunction of action and words—evident if one looks just a little below the surface of polished manners—exemplifies the corruption of sexual relations and mistreatment of women responsible for turning them into compliant simpletons.

The audience's prurient reaction to the underlying sexual current of behavior is more directly critiqued at the beginning of chapter 64, when the reader is reminded that "There are things we do and know perfectly well in Vanity Fair, though we never speak of them: . . . a polite public will no more bear to read an authentic description of vice than a truly refined English or American female will permit the word 'breeches' to be pronounced in her chaste hearing" (671). But this address to the reader, often interpreted as critical of Becky, is more about the reader than about her. Thackeray needs the Becky- "siren," not because she is the quintessence of corruption in the corrupt world of Vanity Fair but because through her and her "sandy" hair, he is able to redirect his satire back on his readers and, perhaps, free women from the impoverishment of their "chaste hearing."

The rich irony of the Stage Manager's tone is evident in his comment about Becky's "happier days, when she was not innocent, but not found out" (682). Thackeray was a moral relativist like Nathaniel Hawthorne, who suggested in "Young Goodman Brown" that "sin is but a name"[14] and Goodman Brown no different from any other Salem resident. Thackeray, too, means that the word "sin," or "vice," is only a name and not aptly expressive of the complex behavior of human beings. For to be "not innocent" is the inescapable essence of the human condition. He doesn't judge Becky but, rather, the judgmental society in which she lives and us—judgmental readers. In describing Becky, this "siren, singing and smiling, coaxing and cajoling," the author has observed the "laws of politeness."

> Those who like may peep down under the waves that are pretty transparent, and see [her tail] writhing and twirling, diabolically hideous and slimy, flapping amongst bones, or curling round corpses. . . . When, however, the siren disappears and dives below, down among the dead men, the water grows turbid over her, and it is labor lost to look into it ever so curiously. They look pretty enough when they sit upon a rock, twanging their harps and combing their hair, and sing, and beckon to you to come and hold the looking-glass; but when they sink into their native element, depend upon it those mermaids are up to no good, and we had best not examine the fiendish marine cannibals, revelling and feasting on their wretched pickled victims. (671–72)

Thackeray enlists his brightly reflecting irony to turn the "looking-glass" away from the mermaids—all, like Becky, products of their culture—and toward his readers, who catch a glimpse of their own reflection, yet smugly view themselves as members of a different species. The chaos beneath the waters against which he warns, he seems to say, is one of our own making. Our prurience (looking "ever so curiously") causes us to lose our balance and "accidentally" tip in. How else could the mermaids' victims have gotten to the bottom of the sea? We suffer from Goodman Brown's spiritual arrogance, refusing to recognize that "vice called by its proper name" is the medium in which we all live.[15]

But does this argument let Becky off the hook? Thackeray makes no bones about Becky's thoroughgoing involvement in this world; her sexuality *is* her art, her coquette's impersonation. The Manager's rhetoric suggests their interchangeability and interdependence: "At first no occupation was more pleasant than to invent and procure (the latter a work of no small trouble and ingenuity, by the way, in a person of Mrs. Rawdon Crawley's very narrow means)—to procure, we say, the prettiest new dresses and ornaments" (521). Here are invention and procurement, art and sex, with the emphasis on sex, not merely through the second mention of "procure," but with the parenthetically insistent "we say." And if there's any doubt about the implication of "procure," we've only to wait for the moment of Rawdon's discovery of his wife and Lord Steyne in a compromising "attitude" to realize that Thackeray intends the pun.

Rawdon finds this personage (Becky's Aegisthus) "hanging over the sofa on which Becky sat. The wretched woman was in a brilliant full toilette, her arms and all her fingers sparkling with bracelets and rings; and the brilliants on her breast which Steyne had given her. He had her hand in his, and was bowing over it to kiss it" (554). In his rage, Rawdon "tore the diamond out of her breast, and flung it at Lord Steyne" (555). The jewel is the focus of his energies as in the happier time of courtship her "famous frontal development" (190) had enticed him and many others. However, despite revealing the provenance of the gems and of her money (Lord Steyne), the Stage Manager keeps a metaphorical dagger out of Becky's hands: "What *had* happened? Was she guilty or not? She said not; but who could tell what was truth which came from those lips; or if that corrupt heart was in this case pure? All her lies and her schemes, all her selfishness and her wiles, all her wit and genius had come to this bankruptcy" (556). The Stage Manager should know the answers to these questions but claims he's "in the dark."

How can such a "wretched woman" be the heroine of a novel whose subtitle is "A Novel without a Hero"? The answer lies in Thackeray's realism, in his belief that she's no worse than the rest of us. Indeed, she's also capable of gratuitous acts of generosity. Her estimate of Dobbin and efforts to engineer the union with Amelia he so deserves and desires show she can "be a good woman" (436) even without the incentive of "five thousand [pounds] a year" (436). "She admired Dobbin; she bore him no rancour for the part he had taken against her. It was an open move in the game, and played fairly. 'Ah!' she thought, 'if I could have had such a husband as that—a man with a heart and brains too! I would not have minded his large feet,' and running into her room . . . she wrote him a note . . . [saying] she could serve him with A." (708). Becky's opinion of George Osborne—"that gaby of a husband—dead (and served right!) these fifteen years" (720)—reflects Thackeray's own judgment in a letter to his mother of July 1847: "Amelia's [humbling] is yet to come when her scoundrel of a husband is well dead with a ball in his odious bowels" (*Letters* 309). Like Thackeray, Becky displays animus only against those who deserve it. Her occasional retreats from the values of Vanity Fair enable Thackeray to dramatize his criticisms; she's just too complex and various to be named. And aren't we like sandy-haired Becky, a jumble of competing feelings and actions, changing from one period of our lives to another or, in the same season, different in different circumstances?

Thackeray's commitment to realism is like his desire to make his readers feel "the reality of sentiment." Although we may not experience the self-forgetfulness that caused a contemporary reviewer of *Jane Eyre* to write "we for-got both commendations and criticism, identified with Jane in all her troubles, and finally married Mr. Rochester about four in the morning" (quoted in Iser 43), Thackeray draws us into the reading experience by forcing us to judge his characters. The Stage Manager then rudely awakens us from our complacent self-regard by reminding us that he and we are like those we've been judg-ing, desiring our own portion of roast beef. So we "come home" from the Fair—shut up the book—to find that Thackeray has succeeded in making us "perfectly miserable in private." We're left with the reality of sentiment that links the contemplation of our own compromised lives with the bittersweet pleasure of reading this book. "Which of us has his desire? or, having it, is satisfied?" (730).

He was a profound skeptic. Gordon Ray tells the story of Thackeray's re-marking, on leaving one of John Newman's "lectures on Anglican difficul-ties": "It is either Rome or Babylon, and for me it is Babylon" (121). Many of his letters reveal his religious doubts and reaffirm his fierce attachment to "the Seen World." He wrote to Jane Brookfield in August 1850: "I don't know about the Unseen World, the use of the Seen World is the right thing I'm sure. . . . How'll you make yourself most happy in it? . . . by despising today and looking up cloudwards? Pish. Let us turn God's to day to its best use. . . . By Jove, I'll admire . . . the wing of a cocksparrow as much as the pinion of an archangel and adore God the Father of the Earth earthy first, waiting for the completion of my senses and the fulfillment of His intentions towards after-wards when this scene closes over us" (*Letters* 690–91). He similarly refuses to judge Becky by the values of Gothic Christianity. Rather, he insists on consid-ering her from the terrestrial perspective, which approaches the feminist. He won't find her guilty as charged because he recognizes the complexity of "the full rotundity" of the "Earth earthy." A girl who "must be [her] own mamma" (87) has a difficult row to hoe in a world that circumscribes women's lives and aspirations—tacitly recommending their virtual enslavement—which causes "the best of women" to be "hypocrites." In our fallen world, "We accept this amiable slavishness, and praise a woman for it: we call this pretty treachery truth" (167). His transgressing blonde, far from being an avatar of the fatal woman, is his realistic response to institutionalized female servility.

The Stage Manager reports that "a very strong party of excellent people consider [Becky] to be a most injured woman. She has her enemies. Who has not? Her life is her answer to them. She busies herself in works of piety . . . and is

Virtue rewarded; A booth in Vanity Fair

Fig. 2. Another of Becky's successful "female impersonations." (By permission of the Rare Books Division, The New York Public Library, Astor, Lenox and Tilden Foundations)

always having stalls at Fancy Fairs for the benefit of . . . hapless beings" (729–30). The last illustration of his book (figure 2) tells the story of this successful female impersonation. There's ambiguity even in its title—"Virtue Rewarded; A booth in Vanity Fair" (731). But what or who is virtue, and who is rewarded? Dobbin, Amelia, and their children have "found themselves suddenly before her at one of these fairs" (730). Dobbin frowns, Amelia looks to Georgy for protection, and little Janey wonders at her mother's startled expression. Only Becky, resorting to an early-developed habit, "cast[s] down her eyes demurely and smile[s]" (730). Why is she serene while happiness eludes the others, despite the blamelessness or merely common selfishness of their lives?

Robert Lougy believes that the family, as an institution, "can withstand the onslaught of Vanity Fair" (80). Yet Amelia, who jealously thinks her husband is fonder of their daughter than he is of her, "fonder even than of his *History of the Punjaub*," and Dobbin, who, like Ivanhoe, has been disappointed in the prize he has spent his life pursuing, make the family an unlikely redoubt. On the other hand, Becky's indomitability, her multifarious performance, in the absence of alternatives, seems a more successful modus operandi, capable of "radiat[ing] outward and transform[ing]" this world (Lougy 80).

His last sketch and its position illustrate Thackeray's admiration for Becky's ingenious impersonations, her chameleon's strategy for survival. He envisioned Rebecca, empowered by the creative energies of her artistry, continuing "until [her] going hence." For this *latest* role of Becky's, churchgoer and small-time philanthropist, cannot be, as Lougy argues, her "inevitable last role" (78). Despite the real and figurative closures of the book—"Come, children, let us shut up the box and the puppets, for our play is out" (730)—Thackeray means us to imagine her, trying on new costumes, new impersonations forever. In a gesture that strengthens the postmodernist claim that texts only *seem* to have the last word, he placed the ambiguous illustration of blond Becky, mistress of mimicries, smiling serenely, on the final page of the novel. And it's this image of her that we remember. Becky, the performer, recognizes that the "show must go on." She is Thackeray's promise that there will come a time when, for other women, if not for this dauntless and talented player, the stage will be different.

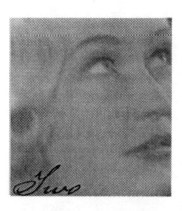

Brontë and Eliot

Blond Transformations

We unite, in the details of our plan, rest, recreation,
and philanthropic work. We seek, also, to give
ourselves training in the eminently useful, but rare, art
among women, *of thinking together* . . . to bring into
relations of sympathy and of service the women of
thought, experience, and of earnest purpose . . . and
by methods free from the formalities and constraints
of ordinary social intercourse . . . to displace these
exacting and exhausting formalities, and so re-act
for good upon our whole social life.
—"Letter from the New England Women's Club to
the English Women's Association and Gatherings,"
The Englishwoman's Review, new ser., no. 10 (April
1872)

In *Pride and Prejudice* of 1813, Jane Austen simply described Elizabeth Bennet as "pretty" but didn't offer a physiognomic portrait—the shape of her nose, the arch of her eyebrow—as later novelists might have done. All the principal characters, none more warmly than Elizabeth herself, agree that she isn't as beautiful as her older sister, Jane, who is also, unlike her, praised for her fairy-tale goodness and docility. Although Mr. Bingley declares Elizabeth "very pretty," Darcy first pronounces her "tolerable; but not handsome enough to tempt *me*" (10). While he changes his mind, later discerning "a fine pair of eyes in the face of a very pretty woman" (19), the reader has from the start been quite satisfied with Elizabeth's face with "hardly a good feature" (21). The heroine makes up for her failure to occupy the first ranks of physical beauty with her satiric wit and provocative plain-speaking.

Austen guessed her readers would happily trade all of Elizabeth's face for one feature: her intelligent, clever mouth. She was one of the first novelists to sever beauty from a heroine's intrinsic worth. However, for Elizabeth, the divorce wasn't final; she falls far to the right side of the great divide separating the attractive from the homely of the earth.

In 1847, only thirty-five years later, but in a vastly different world, Charlotte Brontë went much further. The heroine of *Jane Eyre* is very plain as well as plainspoken. Although Brontë's negative self-image may have been the motive-force for Jane's character and appearance, the importance of her original heroine was that she spoke to others similarly circumstanced. What a liberating experience *Jane Eyre* must have been for thousands of less-than-beautiful women readers who believed they would never marry. And Brontë's truth-telling, matched by her heroine's, was soon seen elsewhere in print. An archly humorous argument concerning women's education as limited to the preparation for marriage and maternity, first appearing in the *Pall Mall Gazette*, suggests the attitude Brontë helped to spark:

> WIVES AND MOTHERS.— . . . To stand still on the road of life waiting to be chosen, in the full knowledge (if statistics are worth anything) that only two out of three can be called, may be an edifying spectacle of patience and humility, but not one calculated to promote self-respect, or even ordinary cheerfulness and content, in the breasts of those who expect, and yet expect in vain, the summons to perform that which they are taught to believe is their duty. It may be very good fun for No. 1 and No. 2, but how about No. 3? Christian resignation is an admirable and saintly virtue, but good Pagan self-assertion is worth something after all. (quoted in the *Englishwoman's Review*, no. 1 [1866]: 36)

Old maids or "redundant" women of the middle or upper classes, as they were called—those who would never marry because there simply weren't enough men to go around—were likely to be plain.

Brontë's decision to disregard the long-standing novelistic convention of pairing heroines with beauty subtly altered the shape of the marriage plot. Of equal interest, despite the fair woman's iconic power in the culture, was Brontë's representation of the blonde—especially in contrast with the spiky heroine she had invented. In her preface to the second edition of *Jane Eyre,* she wrote that she regarded Thackeray "as the first social regenerator of the day, as the very master of that working corps who would restore to rectitude the warped system of things" (36). Her dedication acknowledged his spiritual kinship. The "Greek fire of his sarcasm," the "levin-brand of his denunciation" (36)—those she also found ready to her hand. To work, in her way, to change the world's warped regard for women and women's for themselves, she deliberately "warped" the representation of the blonde, that "pattern of correctness," altering her previously smooth and fruitful domestic course.

And Brontë wasn't unique. In this period, when women were emerging as a dominant force in the writing of novels, we can see a radical transformation in the representation of the blonde, who, no longer submissive, was beginning to serve as a different kind of foil—unlike her character in Romantic novels—for the dynamic dark-haired heroine.

The destinies of brunette and blonde were being reversed in their novels. In the world of representation, the blonde had been the more marriageable female, seeking her fortune through—or, more accurately, being sought by—an entitled male. By contrast, the brunette, less the image of ideal femininity in a culture actively privileging its Saxon heritage, had to work for her bread, gaining employment as a companion, governess, or teacher; she came close to mirroring the lives of her industrious creators. Yet she also surpassed the blonde in desirability as a mate, not because of her beauty, but because of her intelligence and skills—a new kind of marriage portion and an important reformation of the novelistic color code for hair and complexion.

Mary Elizabeth Braddon and the American Louisa May Alcott would represent the blonde as driven by the values of her less-than-perfect community. However, Charlotte Brontë and George Eliot in their novels took a different tack, sailing before the winds of change by provisionally sketching a new tale of women's empowerment. They erased from the written record a long-standing rivalry by creating an extrafamilial sisterhood of dark and blonde.

After her sister Charlotte's novel appeared in October 1847, Emily Brontë's *Wuthering Heights* was published to less than critical acclaim in December

(*Wuthering* 5). Catherine Linton Heathcliff—daughter of the more memorable, passionate brunette Cathy Earnshaw—seems at first the epitome of the fairy-tale blonde, described by the captivated narrator as having "the most exquisite little face . . . flaxen ringlets, or rather golden, hanging loose on her delicate neck; and eyes—had they been agreeable in expression, they would have been irresistible" (19). But the "sentiment they evinced hovered between scorn and a kind of desperation, singularly unnatural to be detected there" (19). Foreshadowing Melville's portrait of the beautiful but "unnatural" "Cenci" of 1852, the phrases "had they been agreeable" and "singularly unnatural" signal a great change. Catherine's rude rejection of Lockwood's aid—"'I don't want your help,' she snapped" (19)—and refusal to make him tea, "her forehead corrugated, and her red under-lip pushed out, like a child's ready to cry" (19), show that the beautiful blonde is no longer proof against the harshness of life as once the fairy-tale heroine's unfailingly sweet temperament helped her to endure with forbearance whatever harrowing circumstances befell her. Catherine may suffer, but she isn't entirely still. Her story, like her blond aunt Isabella's, implies that environment as well as heredity plays a role in the formation of personality. And the blonde, in the mid-Victorian novel and later, instead of being good as gold, may even be openly acquisitive, loving nothing better than golden ornaments and other things that golden coin can buy.

Although Catherine improves as she and her cousin Hareton fall in love, she's still "no philosopher, and no paragon of patience" (249). Nor must we forget that her spirit of adventure and disobedience originally led her to wander beyond the gates of Thrushcross Grange, into the fallen world of Wuthering Heights, where Heathcliff imprisons her. Daring, once only a masculine characteristic, is now a feminine trait.

The sole blonde in *Jane Eyre* is merely selfish and unruly with no saving graces like Catherine's. The embodiment of all that Jane is not, her cousin Georgiana Reed is an odious child. While her Aunt Reed locks ten-year-old Jane in the "red-room" to punish her for her "violence," the adult Jane writes that Georgiana, above all, deserved this frightening discipline. The difference in their treatment all comes down to beauty—the one thing needful, Jane bitterly recognizes, she lacks: "Why could I never please? Why was it useless to try to win anyone's favour? . . . Georgiana, who had a spoiled temper, a very acrid spite, a captious and insolent carriage, was universally indulged. Her beauty, her pink cheeks, and golden curls, seemed to give delight to all who looked at her, and to purchase indemnity for every fault" (46–47). More than her moral flaws, Georgiana's pink cheeks and golden curls are the mote in Jane's eye. She mentions her own plainness, the incubus that haunts her into adulthood, as early as the first page of the novel; she was "humbled by the consciousness of [her] physical inferiority" (39). Had she been "a sanguine, brilliant, careless, exacting, handsome, romping child" (47), all in the household would have accepted her. But beauty is unjustly meted out, with no regard for merit.

Georgiana makes only two other unflattering cameo appearances. Visited at Lowood School by a servant from Gateshead, Jane masochistically asks: "Georgiana is handsome, I suppose, Bessie?" (122). Bessie answers "Very," and follows with the story of Georgiana's great success in the previous season when a young lord had fallen in love and planned to elope with her. Perversely continuing to focus on a comparison of her own physical inadequacy and her cousin's beauty, Jane remarks that she "perceived that Bessie's glance [at her], though it expressed regard, did in no shape denote *admiration*" (123; my emphasis).

Later, when her dying aunt summons her to Gateshead, Jane sees her nemesis Georgiana in all her ample, slothful flesh. Here the narrator has the opportunity to lambaste the unworthy creature by inverting the Renaissance sonneteer's convention: "fair show" may not be matched by an equally fair heart. Her cousin isn't the beauty she was when a "slim and fairy-like girl of eleven. This was a full-blown, very plump damsel, fair as waxwork, with handsome and regular features, languishing blue eyes, and ringleted yellow hair. . . . the blooming and luxuriant younger girl had her [mother's] contour of jaw and chin—perhaps a little softened, but still imparting an indescribable hardness to the countenance, otherwise so voluptuous and buxom" (257).

The unflattering "very plump" and "languishing," the archaism "damsel," "fair as waxwork," and "indescribable hardness" serve as a partial venting of Jane's (and Brontë's) resentment of the socially favored blonde. She dramatizes Jane's criticism of Georgiana by allowing Eliza to pronounce on her sister's selfish slothfulness: "Georgiana, a more vain and absurd animal than you was certainly never allowed to cumber the earth. . . . if no one can be found willing to burden her or himself with such a fat, weak, puffy, useless thing, you cry out that you are ill-treated, neglected, miserable" (264). Jane as mere scribe can't be charged with splenetic jealousy as she closes the book on her cousin, giving Georgiana her deserved comeuppance.

While she might have used the blonde as a more substantial foil for the brunette, Brontë has little need of Georgiana because Jane's pursuit of her true identity is meant to be a relentlessly self-guided tour. Her later dialogue of self and soul shows her independence: "'Who in the world cares for *you*?' . . . Still indomitable was the reply: '*I* care for myself. The more solitary, the more friendless, the more unsustained I am, the more I will respect myself'" (344). Her childish grief at being un*attractive*—literally her failure to draw others to her—is the beginning of her discovery of who she really is.

In the red-room, Jane sees her mirror image by accident; her "fascinated glance involuntarily explored the depth it revealed" (46). She's irresistibly drawn to the "half fairy" "coming out of lone ferny dells" (46), inverting the aversion of others. Her probing of the "depth," her storytelling, is an archeological unearthing and reconstruction of her history. The "lone, ferny dells" is an interesting precursor of similarly affirming landscapes leading to self-development—but through friendship—in Brontë's third and fourth novels.

In *Shirley* and *Villette,* Brontë created nuanced portraits of dark and blond heroines, friends rather than rivals. Caroline Helstone in *Shirley* is not at all the icy or immobile, two-dimensional blonde of Romantic fiction or fairy tale. In this novel, her friendship with Shirley, "not a blonde, like Caroline," but "clear and dark," her face "pale naturally but intelligent" (211) models the possibility for feminine self-discovery and cooperation in the real world.

Caroline, despondent over her thwarted love for her cousin Gerard Moore but also miserable because she's "making no money—earning nothing" (98)—"I should like an occupation" she says, "and if I were a boy, it would not be so difficult to find one" (98)—is offered an alternative to patriarchal power through a kind of dream-work, a women's space and community. Brontë's language is evocative and lush, evading a strict appeal to the intellect and offering the possibility of transfiguration.

In the chapter "Shirley and Caroline," Shirley rejects the young women of the neighborhood: "If she had had the bliss to be really Shirley Keeldar, Esq., Lord of the Manor of Briarfield, there was not a single fair one . . . whom she should have felt disposed to request to become Mrs. Keeldar, lady of the manor" (217). But she's "glad of Caroline's society" (217). Brontë keeps up the "text" of Shirley's masculinity with this and other banter.

However, the possibility of a homoerotic relationship between the girls should not, I think, be taken literally, as in recent readings.[1] Rather, Brontë's sensual language is meant to promote women's friendships beyond the limits of the family. New institutions like Bedford College in London, founded in 1849 by Mrs. Elizabeth Jesser Reid, permitted young, middle-class women to stretch their minds instead of embroidery canvases. Their friendships at

Queens College and Bedford had more than personal consequences; through mutual encouragement and emulation, women were entering the professions, particularly journalism, and taking active roles in social reform movements and political campaigns. Supplying an apt fictive example of the phenomenon of "sisterhood," Brontë has Caroline insist to Shirley that while neither of them ever "had a sister . . . it flashes on me at this moment how sisters feel towards each other. Affection twined with their life, which no shocks of feeling can uproot . . . affection that no passion can ultimately outrival, with which even love itself cannot do more than compete in force and truth. . . . I am supported and soothed when you—that is, *you only*—are near, Shirley" (265).

Brontë's sensuous language explores the desire for something inclusive of the sensual: female self-knowledge through community. Metaphorically, it suggests potential growth and satisfaction leading to women's meaningful participation in the larger world. She anticipated by one hundred and fifty years Eve Ensler's *Vagina Monologues*. Its value, Gloria Steinem writes in her foreword, is that "readers, men as well as women, may emerge from these pages not only feeling more free within themselves—and about each other—but with alternatives to the old patriarchal dualism of feminine/masculine, body/ mind and sexual/spiritual that is rooted in the division of our physical selves into 'the part we talk about' and 'the part we don't'" (xiv). Brontë's vision, too, is grounded in the body, but, unlike Ensler, who refuses to ask for permission to talk about "the part we don't [talk about]," she translated it into idioms her culture permitted for expressing a woman's exploration of selfhood: those borrowed from nature and heterosexual love.

With masculine assertiveness, Shirley announces that she will "seek and find Caroline Helstone, and make her take some exercise" (218). As the two walk over Nunnely Common, they approach its "brow" and "look down on the deep valley robed in May raiment" (219)—the beginning of an "anatomical" survey of nature. Brontë's language, as a vehicle for the expression of the girls' desires and a description of topography, becomes progressively more sexualized. Blond Caroline's assertion only adds to the reader's rich sense of innuendo as the girls continue their talk: "To *penetrate* into Nunnwood, Miss Keeldar, is to go back into the dim days of eld. Can you see a break in the forest, about the centre?" (220; my emphasis). She then describes the "break," an extraordinary "vagina landscape": "That break is a dell; a deep hollow cup, lined with turf as green and short as the sod of this Common: the very oldest of the trees, gnarled mighty oaks, crowd about the brink of this dell: in the bottom lie the ruins of a nunnery" (221). Her language remarkably resembles that of Victorian erotica: "Her cunt was ravishing beyond all description. The mossy Mount of Venus swelled up into a hillock of firm flesh, surmounted and covered with rich, mossy, coal-black hair, straight and fine as silk" (Anonymous, "La Rose D'Amour" 150). The convention of transforming a woman's anatomy into landscape is an old one, even in the novel. Austen depends on it in *Pride and Prejudice* to surprise Darcy into his belated admiration of Elizabeth, and Scott effectively draws on it in *Ivanhoe* when he describes Rebecca's vest, the top three clasps of which are "unfastened on account of the heat, which something enlarged the prospect" (94). Scott's lingering on the almost-pornographic description of Rebecca's breasts transforms them into a picturesque landscape garden of visual delights through the conventionalized locutions of eighteenth-century landscape architecture. However, Caroline's description, unlike these other examples, is meant to be the production of the feminine imagination, not of the male gaze. And Brontë accomplishes another reversal. Instead of eroticizing the female body, she feminizes the landscape, suggesting the possibility of a women's community, enfigured as the abandoned nunnery and centered in the natural world of the present but with origins in "the dim days of eld." Here is a history of "sisterhood"—a community that patriarchy, on orders from Henry VIII, had destroyed, but that women can reclaim if only they will go back to this "centric part."[2]

This vagina domain is well known to blond Caroline, whose name significantly means "little, womanly one" (Rule 39). She luxuriates in (re)counting the treasures of these woods—their "untrodden glades," "strange mosses," "groups of trees that ravish the eye" (221). When asked by the other girl, she assures Shirley that she would not be "dull with [her] alone" (221), adding that "the presence of gentlemen dispels the charm. . . . If they are of the wrong sort . . . irritation takes the place of serenity . . . one easy to feel, difficult to describe" (221). Once we've imagined a vagina landscape, the erotic subtext of the girls' declarations is hard to dismiss.

This decidedly feminine vision of pleasureful serenity at the center of a woman's being is, of course, only one of a number of possible images of ecstasy. Jane Eyre's orgasmic cry—"I am coming. . . . Wait for me! Oh! I will come!"—in answer to her hallucinatory experience of Rochester's voice calling "Jane! Jane! Jane!" (444–45) is the version of female sexuality that Brontë forsook in *Shirley*. Here there is deliberately nothing like Coleridge's "deep romantic chasm" in "Kubla Khan." The "stately pleasure-dome" built by the

Khan's minions may be the center of his private garden of delights. But the treasure that excites the poet's exclamation—"But oh"—is the vital center of the garden, a force of nature, unstoppable and uncontainable, whose waters flow into a sacred river.

> But oh, that deep romantic chasm which slanted
> Down the green hill athwart a cedarn cover!
> A savage place, as holy and enchanted
> As e'er beneath a waning moon was haunted
> By woman wailing for her demon lover!
> And from this chasm, with ceaseless turmoil seething,
> As if this earth in thick fast pants were breathing,
> A mighty fountain momently was forced
> Amid whose swift half-intermitted burst
> Huge fragments vaulted like rebounding hail,
> Or chaffy grain beneath the thresher's flail!
> And mid these dancing rocks at once and ever,
> It flung up momently the sacred river.
>
> ("Kubla Khan" 523)

Coleridge's vagina landscape is a male's fearful but seductive vision of the violent throes of sexual ecstasy. Savage and haunted but also a wellspring, Coleridge co-opts this feminine image for his poetic riff on male creativity. Caroline and Shirley's ideal of connection and creativity is far quieter and more intimate. Their "private place" is the first real example in a Victorian novel of friendship-without-rivalry of a blonde and brunette (compare the treachery of Becky's flirtation with Amelia's husband, George) and, moreover, of two young women who are very different but equally matched in strength of character. Their idyllic sisterhood in the midst of "mother Eve, in these days called Nature" (316) is, thus, for my history of the blonde's representation, an important moment, even if briefly undermined by Brontë in order to make all things (heterosexually) well by the end of the story. But it was only the opening act for the quirky and unlikely dark/blond friendship she would explore in her next novel.

In *Villette* even more than in *Jane Eyre*, Brontë acerbically examines a woman's lack of beauty—one of the two things needful for success in the Victorian marriage mart. But her story is softened by brunette Lucy Snowe's discovery that economic enterprise can substitute for luck in love. Ironically and doubly blonded by her names (she's the only Lucy or Lucile of many in nineteenth-century fiction with dark hair), she admonishes herself: "Courage, Lucy Snowe! With self-denial and economy now, and steady exertion by-and-by, an object in life need not fail you. . . . be content to labour for independence until you have proved, by winning that prize, the right to look higher. But afterwards, is there nothing more for me in life—no true home. . . . Very good. . . . I see that a great many men, and more women, hold their span of life on conditions of denial and privation. I find no reason why I should be of the favoured few" (450–51).

Remember the words of the *Pall Mall Gazette* article: "It may be very good fun for No. 1 and No. 2, but how about No. 3?" Lucy's is the story of "No. 3." Brontë was charting a new direction for women, away from the domestic and into Eliza Cook's "market-place of Activity and Labour." Lucy's self-questioning when she arrives friendless in London—"All at once my position rose on me like a ghost. . . . What prospects had I in life? . . . What should I do?" (107)—will be answered by her as, later, she meets another "ghost," a spectral nun, because of beautiful, blond, and flawed Ginevra Fanshawe.

The exchange of sexual love for economic self-sufficiency isn't ideal—one would rather have both—but it's a real improvement over the niggardly "want's your portion" (Lawrence, *Rainbow* 65) that characterized the lives of many women. Brontë appropriates "prospects" by "feminizing" it, expropriating "economic opportunity" from the masculine domain.

Lucy's surprising intimacy with the beautiful, yellow-haired, shallow Ginevra takes the friendship of brunette and blonde, begun in *Shirley,* to a new place. The girls are the odd couple of Victorian fiction, unequal and incompatible in every way, yet their attachment is compelling, to them and the reader. Brontë's ambiguous portrait of the blonde may be a gauge of the changes in her feelings about herself, but, more important, it reflected the evolution of economic and social positions of women at midcentury—changes to which her novels contributed.

We've seen that in her other books, complexion and hair color aren't trustworthy tokens of character traits, but in *Villette* they're most unstable. Positive associations with blond or golden hair for women in magazine fiction and novels of the period—the racial legitimation of chauvinist imperialism—make Brontë's materialistic and seductive Ginevra Fanshawe something of a culture shock, especially as Lucy's friendship with her underwrites competing qualities on which we're meant to look favorably. Here is a new, more nuanced representation of female character.

First, the novelist means to destabilize our view of Ginevra; the blonde is consistently inconsistent. Second, Brontë offers many examples of Lucy's preference for and staunch support of her, despite her many flaws; her partiality answers for Ginevra's bona fides. Finally, Lucy's own growth into a self-admiring woman of competence, capable of loving and being loved, and, most important, into an entrepreneur, is partly owing to the blondly beautiful almost-grisette.

Ginevra is no stranger to the mercenary values of upper-middle-class Victorian society. She approves the arrangement for her sisters who "are to marry—rather elderly gentlemen, I suppose, with cash: papa and mama manage that." She adds that her sister Augusta is "married to a man much older-looking than papa," disfigured by yellow fever, "but then he is rich, and Augusta has her carriage and establishment, and we all think she has done perfectly well. Now this is better than 'earning a living,' as you say" (116). Thus, from the beginning of their acquaintance, aboard the packet boat *The Vivid* that transports the girls to Labassecour, the contrast is clear. Lucy, dark, penniless, and plain, must work to feed herself; Ginevra, blond, beautiful, and wealthy enough to attract more wealth, is likely to succeed as her sisters will. Lucy will be aligned with economic self-sufficiency; Ginevra with "trading" on personal attraction. But the stark divisions that seem to rehearse the fates of Romance heroines are complicated by the ambiguities that mark Ginevra's character and the friendship between the two.

For example, Ginevra, although a narcissist, refreshingly takes the measure of her own character, saying to Lucy: "I am far more at my ease with you, old lady—you, you dear crosspatch—who take me at my lowest, and know me to be coquettish, and ignorant, and flirting, and fickle, and silly, and selfish, and all the other sweet things you and I have agreed to be a part of my character" (155). Ginevra's body and soul are incongruous. Despite "her fair long curls reposing on her white shoulders" (149), she's not the perfect fairy-tale blonde. Yet while knowing all her failures, Lucy favors her: "I don't know why . . . if two had to share the convenience of one drinking-vessel, as sometimes happened . . . I always contrived that she should be my convive, and rather liked her to take the lion's share. . . . so it was, however, and she knew it; and, therefore, while we wrangled daily, we were never alienated" (312–13).

And Lucy owes much to Ginevra. Ginevra's "slight sentence uttered carelessly and at random" (121)—"I wish you would come to Madame Beck's; . . . she wants an English gouvernante, or was wanting one two months ago" (121)—determines Lucy to follow the inward voice that bids her "Go to Villette" (121). Her fate is sealed when Lucy accidentally finds herself at the door of Madame Beck's "Pensionnat de Demoiselles." The inner voice, "Providence," that had steered her to Villette, now punningly directs: "Stop here; this is *your* inn" (126). Thus, the door is "opened" by Ginevra for Lucy, now launched on the great adventure of her life.

Strangely, these two young Englishwomen, opposites in beauty, depth of character, self-confidence, and values, will be doubles in the stories of their emerging sexuality. Recalling the "mirror-misery" scene in Germaine de Staël's *Corinne* (about which, more later), Brontë places her heroines before a physical mirror and contrasts the states of their immaterial souls. Lucy is clinically interested to see how much Ginevra's "self-love" "could swallow" and "whether any whisper of consideration for others could penetrate her heart." "Not at all. She turned me and herself round; she viewed us both on all sides; she smiled, she waved her curls, she retouched her sash, she spread her dress, and finally, letting go my arm, and curtseying with mock respect, she said: 'I would not be you for a kingdom'" (214–15). However, Lucy counters, saying she wouldn't give "a bad sixpence" (215) to be Ginevra. Her commercial metaphor keeps alive the relation between beauty and money and Lucy's interior and intrinsic worth.

But Lucy's frequent reflections on her mere shadow-being and her belief that no man as beautiful as Ginevra's admirer Dr. John could do more than look through her prove that she has thoroughly absorbed the traumatic lesson of being plain in a culture that prizes beauty. Anger over her own deficiencies fuels her fury at Ginevra, who prefers the foppish Count de Hamal to Dr. John: "You scorn, you sting, you torture him! Have you power to do this? Who gave you that power? Where is it? Does it lie all in your beauty—your pink and white complexion and your yellow hair? . . . Does this purchase for you his affection, his tenderness?" (218–19). Blond Ginevra, whose name recalls the faithlessness of Queen Guinevere, has the "purchasing" power Lucy lacks. Brontë thus continues her lexical campaign, keeping before us the economic value of beauty in this commercial society by contrasting it with Lucy's far different and developing "earning power."

Although Lucy has had no firsthand knowledge of love, she is not without passion. Brontë never implies that women who don't marry and must earn a living are desireless. Lucy's own submerged, and others' more frankly expressed, sexual desire will emerge in the garret, where she memorizes the part of the "butterfly" lover for the school's play, reads a "kind" letter from Dr. John, and is frightened by the spectral nun.

Madame Beck's Pensionnat had been a convent, set in "such deep and leafy seclusion as ought to embosom a religious house" (172). The garden behind the school is the only vestige of this anatomically caressing, former natural beauty. Now embraced by high walls, "that old garden had its charms. . . . The turf was verdant . . . sun-bright nasturtiums clustered beautiful about the roots of the doddered orchard giants" (173). Lucy's sensuous description recalls the sexualized landscape of Nunnwood, another leafy seclusion with the ruins of a convent at its center. The Nunnwood convent was despoiled in the sixteenth century. But another act of outrage against women, according to tradition, was once committed in this one. Buried beneath "a Methuselah of a pear-tree" (172), so the story goes, are "the bones of a girl whom a monkish conclave of the drear middle ages had here buried alive, for some sin against her vow" (172).

Unlike the live burial in Poe's "The Cask of Amontillado," this interment, it's implied, was probably in punishment of sexual desire. Whether real or "urban legend," the tale is responsible for "the inheritance of a ghost story" (172) with its "black and white nun" (172) said to haunt the premises. Lucy's connection to the "spectra," which she first sees in the garret and later in the garden, reverberates throughout her story.

Her favorite spot in the garden near the pear tree, the "allée défendue," so-called because of its proximity to the boys' college where the girls are forbidden to walk, is a figure for her repressed sexuality. Much like the vagina landscape of Nunnwood, "the walk was narrow, and the neglected shrubs were grown very thick and close on each side, weaving overhead a roof of branch and leaf which the sun's rays penetrated but in rare chequers" (174).

As she sits there, an unknown hand hurls a "billet-doux" through a window of the boys' school, addressed: "Pour la robe grise" (177). De Hamal, we later learn, has thrown it, having mistaken Lucy, dressed in the Quakerish dress worn by the schoolgirls, and despite the differences in their appearance, for Ginevra. The mistaken identity emphasizes the connection with the blonde that Lucy has sensed subjectively, despite the unflattering allusion to her in the letter: "that dragon, the English teacher—une véritable bégueule Britannique . . . revêche comme une religieuse" [a veritable British prude . . . awkward as a nun] (178). But de Hamal's words are unjust; passionate Lucy is nothing like a nun.

The love letter should have alerted Lucy to Ginevra's dalliance. Nonetheless, she defends the blonde when she and Dr. John see the girl at a concert attended by the aristocracy of Villette. In praising her beauty and naturalness, missing in the Labassecourian *jeunes filles,* she remarks that Ginevra's hair "was not close-braided, like a shell or a skull-cap of satin; it looked *like* hair, and waved from her head, long, curled, and flowing" (292). But Ginevra's rare beauty is matched by impudence, materialism, and sexual immodesty. Noticing a "handsome bracelet" (301) gleaming on Ginevra's arm, Dr. John comments: "no grisette has a more facile faculty of acceptance" (301). He has also seen "a look interchanged between [Ginevra and de Hamal] . . . which threw a most unwelcome light on [his] mind" (302). What other blonde, besides Becky, has ever been represented this way? Dr. John persists in his belief that Ginevra's "was a look marking mutual and secret understanding—it was neither girlish nor innocent" (302). But Lucy writes that she believed Ginevra "was honest enough, with all her giddiness" (302). Although Brontë insinuates a venal exchange of body for baubles, Lucy refuses to condemn Ginevra, even when she learns the truth about Ginevra's garret trysts with de Hamal.

The approach of the spectral nun, when Lucy is in the garret reading her cherished letter from Dr. John, seems an obvious reminder of the dangers of desire; the pear-tree nun was buried alive for hers. It certainly checks Lucy's, mistakenly inspired by the merely kind words of the letter, through which she has momentarily escaped into happiness. Her metaphorical figuration of joy is another vagina landscape, but one that she actively alters even as she conceives it. Her image of destruction is, thus, paradoxically more positive than Jane's "visionary hollow" or Caroline and Shirley's "deep hollow cup": "Conceive a dell, deep-hollowed in forest secrecy; it lies in dimness and mist: its turf is dank, its herbage pale and humid. A storm or an axe makes a wide gap amongst the oak-trees; the breeze sweeps in; the sun looks down; the sad, cold dell, becomes a cup of lustre; high summer pours her blue glory and her golden light out of that beauteous sky, which till now the starved hollow never saw" (334). Forcible penetration—by storm or axe blade—suggests a passionate and welcomed sexual awakening, which transforms Lucy's "starved hollow" into "a cup of lustre" receiving the "glory" of the powerful, "seminal" sun instead of merely "rare chequers." However, Lucy's figurative moment in the sun, when the "beamy head" of Dr. John shines on her, is brief; "for what belonged to storm, what was wild and intense, dangerous, sudden, and flaming, he had no sympathy, and held with it no communion" (341). Lucy's nature is all those things.

But not so M. Paul, the domineering and irritable professor of literature, "hideously plain" (197), according to Ginevra. Unlike Dr. John, one of whose "spots of commonness" is to insist that beauty and wealth be matched, Paul is above venal considerations in matters of the heart. Lucy's friendship with him is entangled with the nun of the attic, whom the two see in the garden.

Lucy's phantasmagoric night adventure, late in the novel, in which she experiences a moment of supreme jealousy, is joined with Ginevra's own tale of sexual desire. Influenced by a strong narcotic, she leaves her bed and goes to the city park, where she finds all of Villette in festival mode, "one blaze, one broad illumination" (548). When she sees M. Paul there with his young ward, she has a surprising vision of a "domestic" nature—the existence of her own jealousy—as she watches Justine Marie fondly putting her hand up to Paul's lips to be kissed. The mistress of homeschooling in repression and deprivation, Lucy "knows" that M. Paul's family and Justine Marie's have promised her to Paul on his return from Guadeloupe, where he will look after the interests of the girl's family. Lucy had always accepted her loveless fate; she had believed that without personal beauty she could never be the object of another's interest. But her new conviction that love might be hers for reasons other than physical charms proves how she has silently changed. Self-assertion now defines femininity.

As she returns to the school, Lucy hears the thunderous sound of a carriage and sees that "something white fluttered from that window—surely a hand waved a handkerchief" (568). The door of the school still ajar as she had left it, she knows her adventure will not, therefore, "issue in catastrophe" (568). But a surprise still awaits her—one so powerful that even her retrospective account shifts into the present tense, making it live dramatically for herself and the reader.

What, then, do I see between the half-drawn curtains? What dark, usurping shape, supine, long, and strange. . . . It looks very black, I think it looks—not human. . . . Will it spring, will it leap out if I approach? Approach I must. Courage! One step!—

. . . all the movement was mine, so was all the life, the reality, the substance, the force; as my instinct felt. I tore her up—the incubus! I held her on high—the goblin! I shook her loose—the mystery! And down she fell—down all round me—down in shreds and fragments—and I trode upon her.

. . . The long nun proved a long bolster dressed in a long black stole, and artfully invested with a white veil. . . . Whence came these vestments? Who contrived this artifice? These questions still remained. (569)

Long before, just as she was deciding that "If life be a war . . . another pitched battle must be fought with fortune" and that she had "a mind to the encounter" (381), Lucy had met the spectral nun in the "forbidden alley." Then she had stood her ground, neither fleeing nor shrieking, and had questioned the ghost: "Who are you? And why do you come to me?" (381). Another time Ginevra had asked Lucy: "'Who *are* you, Miss Snowe?' . . . in such a tone of undisguised and unsophisticated curiosity, as made me laugh in my turn" (392–93). "I am a rising character: once an old lady's companion, then a nursery-governess, now a school-teacher" (394), answered Lucy. Her response acquires new significance through the story of the nun. The repetition of the question "Who are you?" which links Lucy and the spectra, is better answered when Lucy, newly empowered, rips the "nun" to shreds. Having been put in her bed by others, the nun is laid to (her final) rest—dis-covered by Lucy. But whereas the nun is all artifice, Lucy proves she's the real thing. She had answered Ginevra's question about her identity not in terms of family or social prominence, the only categories of interest to Miss Fanshawe,[3] but in those of occupation and mettle. The qualities she shows when she sees the "nun" in her bed—curiosity, courage, forcefulness, movement, perseverance—define the successful entrepreneur Lucy becomes with help from her lover and financial backer, M. Paul.

On the night of the festival, some others have been enterprising, in an entirely different way. Ginevra and de Hamal are the two missing from the concert in the park. Snatching the opportunity of Madame Beck's absence, Ginevra has eloped with the Count. Her note to Lucy explains that de Hamal had impersonated the spectral nun, exploiting the school's ghost story to gain entrance to the garret for his trysts with Ginevra. She also writes that hers was the hand waving the white handkerchief from the carriage as Lucy returned to the school. Unmentioned is the detail that she had left the Pensionnat's door ajar, which, as we know, made it possible for Lucy to reenter the school. Thus, the blonde has opened the door for the brunette, not once, but twice.

By providing Lucy with the "body of evidence"—the bolster-stuffed nun's habit and an explanation of the spectral events—Ginevra has emboldened Lucy to take command of her own life. Although M. Paul generously rents a house in which Lucy can live and run her school, Ginevra's desires have advanced Lucy's love and success. The active blonde has traveled far from her immobile fairy-tale roots.

Lucy's transformation into a woman of business maps Eliza Cook's journey from hearth to marketplace. A white-haired Lucy Snowe, writing her story, may never have known traditional domestic happiness, but her life has had purpose and pleasure. Indeed, Ginevra's romantic elopement and marriage, an alternative, and more common, life-plot, has not been bliss.

Like Lydia's marriage to the scapegrace Wickham in *Pride and Prejudice,* Ginevra's to the Count has known the cooling of romantic ardor and financial distress. We aren't surprised that wild Lydia succumbs to her fate, but we don't expect the same for the blonde who has, hitherto in fiction, been exempt from the frailties and fate of other mortals. However, Lucy's final words about Ginevra suggest a significant shift in cultural attitudes toward flawed, fair-haired beauty.

While no longer a heroine, nor even a woman of particular value, the difficult blonde remains firmly within society's pale. Lucy enjoys playing with readerly assumptions, archly explaining: "In winding up Mistress Fanshawe's memoirs, the reader will no doubt expect to hear that she came finally to bitter expiation of her youthful levities. Of course, a large share of suffering lies in reserve for her future" (575). Quite the reverse . . . "Of course," Brontë toys with literary convention. There'll be no punishment for her in a Christian afterlife, nor material penalty in this.

In her favor—and there has always been one for Ginevra—Lucy writes: "I thought she would forget me now, but she did not" (576). Instead, she has continued a correspondence through which Lucy learns that Ginevra has sought help from her "god-papa," M. de Bassompierre; "debts had to be paid . . . ignoble plaints and difficulties became frequent. Under every cloud, no matter what its nature, Ginevra, as of old, called out lustily for sympathy and aid. She had no notion of meeting any distress single-handed. In some shape, from some quarter or other, she was pretty sure to obtain her will, and so she got on—fighting the battle of life by proxy, and, on the whole, suffering as little as any human being I have ever known" (577).

Ginevra doesn't epitomize lust, sloth, gluttony, avarice, or any of the other seven deadlies. Neither is she a victim, a model of patience and passivity, saved by the handsome prince (or Count). She's merely an unexemplary being, exceptionally pretty, but otherwise quite ordinary. She has always had a knack for shifting responsibility onto broader shoulders, leaving hers free of the heavy load of suffering that—had this been a fairy tale—her dubious moral nature would have earned.

Brontë has neutralized the iconic blonde, refashioning her as a woman of merely minor excesses *and* sexual desire. She recognized, long before gender studies were dreamed of, that "the inert force" of the "cold, rounded, blonde, and beauteous" young woman, like "the white column, capitalled with gilding" (287), is merely her public face for the marriage market—a social "construction," hiding the spontaneous and instinctive girl beneath. As M. Paul tells Lucy: "Those blondes jeunes filles—so mild and so meek—I have seen the most reserved—romp like boys, the demurest—snatch grapes from the walls, shake pears from trees" (454). Energy and movement are natural to life. Psychological compulsions are the only demons in Brontë's novels, in which there's no room for embodiments of Christian myth. Brontë anticipated Eliot, Meredith, and James.

Her unmasked and secularized blonde prepared the way for Eliot and others to go even further with variations on this assertive figure. Dramatically, in *The Mill on the Floss* and *Middlemarch*, George Eliot also explored a dark/blond sisterhood, the beginning of women's political and social emancipation.

Brontë is almost as interested in Ginevra's libido as in Lucy's superego. To be a woman in Victorian society, Brontë knew, was always to monitor and contain one's energies. It's difficult to read any of George Eliot's novels without marveling at the variety of metaphors that reveal the depth of her preoccupation with the same issues. In *The Mill on the Floss* (1859–60), her semi-autobiographical novel, and in *Middlemarch* (1871–72), she explores the harmful effects of repression. While she conservatively refrained from endorsing any life-plots (like her own) that might encourage young women to see and do much beyond the socially approved bourne, her brunettes and blondes share life-altering moments that model change through mutual aid and fellowship. Brontë had offered the ancient religious community in Nunnely Common as a metaphor for sisterhood; Eliot began *Middlemarch* with the epic life of Theresa of Avila, who founded a conventual community of women in Spain.

The physical restrictions required by midcentury dress—cumbersome petticoats, voluminous sleeves, and outsize bonnets—had important psychological analogues in George Eliot's novels. Eliot created ardent young women keenly aware of the social impediments to broadening and deepening their knowledge, to effecting change in their communities, or even to moving about their small corners of the world with liberty. In *The Mill on the Floss,* in which she was warming to the task of creating the flawed but natural blonde, she writes of the emotional impedimenta of costume in a comic riff on the necessity of "dress consciousness." "In the enlightened child of civilisation the abandonment characteristic of grief is checked and varied in the subtlest manner. . . . If, with a crushed heart and eyes half-blinded by the mist of tears, she were to walk with a too-devious step through a door-place, she might crush her buckram sleeves too, and the deep consciousness of this possibility produces a composition of forces by which she takes a line that just clears the doorpost" (48–49).

Dress consciousness divides dark Maggie Tulliver and her blond cousin Lucy Deane: "As for Lucy, she was just as pretty and neat as she had been yesterday: no accidents ever happened to her clothes, and she was never uncomfortable in them, so that she looked with wondering pity at Maggie pouting and writhing under the exasperating tucker" (73). Lucy, a "fairy-tale" blonde, is placid and tidy in her emotions and clothes. Maggie is a turbulent soul, "writhing" under the restraints of convention as of dress. Her great-hearted and unregulated loves, both in childhood and young womanhood, her desirous intellect, and her physical energy unfit her for a society that favors a narrow life for women, circumscribed by fashion and domestic possessions.

Herbert Spencer, the evolution theorist and great friend of George Eliot, wrote in his *Autobiography:* "Physical beauty is a *sine qua non* with me; as was once unhappily proved where the intellectual traits and the emotional traits were of the highest" (quoted in Redinger 209). Perhaps, as Sara Blaffer Hrdy, the primatologist, argues in *Mother Nature: A History of Mothers, Infants, and Natural Selection,* Spencer wrote it to prove that he had rejected Eliot's love, despite the appearance that she had thrown him over for George Henry Lewes, her common-law husband from 1852 until Lewes's death in 1878 (Redinger 219, 478). Hrdy argues that Spenser found her unattractive, her exception proving the rule to his theory that the female of the species was designed for breeding, not development of intellect. Eliot then retaliated in her fiction by creating a number of very beautiful but inadequate wives and mothers to prove Spencer wrong about the relationship between beauty and maternal fitness.

Her attention to blond beauty, both in *The Mill on the Floss* and *Middlemarch,* would seem to support Hrdy's claim. Early in *The Mill,* she disparages "pale blond ringlets" in, perhaps, the first full "portrait" in the English novel of the "dumb blonde." "Mrs. Tulliver was what is called a good-tempered person . . . and from the cradle upwards had been healthy, fair, plump, and dull-witted; in short, the flower of her family for beauty and amiability. But milk and mildness are not the best things for keeping, and when they turn only a little sour, they may disagree with young stomachs seriously" (13).

Yet even a minor character like blond Mrs. Stelling proves Eliot's a more nu-anced perspective on the beauty/motherhood relationship. Maggie's brother, Tom, at school with the Reverend Mr. Stelling, "hated Mrs. Stelling, and con-tracted a lasting dislike to pale blond ringlets and broad plaits, as directly asso-ciated with haughtiness of manner, and a frequent reference to other people's 'duty'" (120). "Mrs. Stelling was not a loving, tender-hearted woman: she was a woman whose skirt sat well, who adjusted her waist and patted her curls with a preoccupied air when she inquired after your welfare. These things, doubt-less, represent a great social power, but it is not the power of love" (145). She's Rosamond Vincy of *Middlemarch* waiting to happen. However, this portrait of narcissism evolves into one more complicated when Mrs. Stelling, after Mr. Tulliver has had a stroke, pities the little girl and gives Maggie a basket of food for her journey home. "Maggie's heart went out towards this woman whom she had never liked. . . . It was the first sign within the poor child of that new sense which is the gift of sorrow—that susceptibility to the bare offices of humanity which raises them into a bond of loving fellowship" (159). Eliot's own "power of love," her narrative sympathy, makes us feel even with a minor character a realistic complexity.

Cultural and political shifts in women's experience, after 1847, explain Eliot's absorbed exploration of the restraints on women's lives, not least those imposed on "pattern-card" prettiness. Her friendships with feminists Barbara Bodichon and Bessie Rayner Parkes and the alterations, small as they were at first, that these activists were effecting through their social campaigns were the white noise heard in the background of Eliot's novels chronicling women's social and spiri-tual repressions. While she refused to contribute to the *English Woman's Jour-nal*, hating the "second-rate literature" she found in its pages (*Letters*, vol. 2, quoted in Redinger 358), she added her voice to the chorus for change by cre-ating dark, vibrant heroines whose exertion of physical and emotional energy prove their merit. However, her realistic portrait of blond Rosamond Vincy is a more powerful indictment of her culture's oppression of women.

Maggie is a disappointment to her mother, who compares her to her cousin, an-other of the heavenly blond Lucys who populate Victorian fiction. "Mrs. Tulliver had to look by with a silent pang while Lucy's blond curls were adjusted" (52). She frets: "And there's Lucy Deane's such a good child—you may set her on a stool, and there she'll sit for an hour together, and never offer to get off" (37).

Her aesthetic preference for Lucy's "little rosebud mouth" and "little straight nose, not at all stubby" (52) is unwittingly grounded in the "Saxon" history I've mentioned, with its nationalist and racist foundations. Commenting on the town of St. Ogg's, its "traces of long growth and history like a millennial tree" (98) beginning with the imperial Roman legions who abandoned it, the Danes who pillaged it, and the Normans who conquered the Saxons and stayed, the narrator describes the Gothic structure, "that fine old hall, which is like the town, telling of the thoughts and hands of widely-sundered generations. . . . But older even than this old hall is perhaps the bit of wall now built into the belfry of the parish church, and said to be a remnant of the original chapel dedicated to St. Ogg" (98). By the middle of the nineteenth century, despite such indisputable evidence of Norman culture, historians, as I have said, were securing the foundations of British nationalism by inventing a purely Saxon legacy, uncorrupted by Norman influence. Such edited or selective history, a tribute to nation-myth-making and Francophobia, was a means of erasing the year 1066 and the cultural penetration that followed. In country backwaters like St. Ogg's, rife superstition and scientific ignorance actively coupled with inaccurate history: "The mind of St. Ogg's did not look extensively before or after. It inherited a long past without thinking of it, and had no eyes for the spirits that walk the streets" (100). There "the shadow of the Saxon hero-king still walks" (98); the tuition for young girls is no more "than shreds and patches of feeble literature and false history—with much futile information about Saxon and other kings of doubtful example" (235). Thus, the preference for blondness—the material evidence of an invented "Saxon" lineage. The magical thinking of the mother and aunts who prefer Lucy's coloring to Maggie's dark locks and skin is no surprise. The surname Tulliver is an anglicization of "Taillefer," the name of the Norman warrior and *trouvère*, who, according to medieval chronicles and evidence in the *Bayeux Tapestry*, led the Norman army into battle at Hastings, singing of Roland at Roncesvalles.[4] While such information plays no overt role in the narrative, it's there subliminally, suggesting a "Norman" influence in Maggie's (father's) family tree. Maggie, whose exoticism is manifest in her "brown skin as makes her look like a mulatter" (12), is a literary descendant of the darkly complected Norman Templar Brian de Bois-Guilbert, whose foreignness is racially compounded through association with his black Saracen minions. Norman infection is in the air; Aunt Glegg suggests that Maggie's overabundance of dark hair "isn't good for her health. It's that as makes her skin so brown" (53). But her father defends her in a "racial" argument: "There's red wheat as well as white, for that matter, and some like the dark grain best" (53).

In *Corinne,* the heroine, dressing carefully to confront Lord Nelvil, who has jilted her, looks in the mirror and sees "her black hair, a complexion somewhat darkened by the Italian sun, and marked features whose expression she could not gauge: and always, her [blond] sister's face, light as air, looked back from the mirror" (346). This splendid woman sees herself as marked or wanting. She has learned this lesson too well, as have many others who have looked in mirrors over the ages and have seen, accompanying their own faces, a reminder of their imperfection in the ghostly doppelgänger of the "perfect" blond beauty. The mirror lesson is one of the first taught by Western culture, which has always regarded the blonde as the carrier of ideal genetic material. The tragedy for the individual woman is that she has absorbed the message so thoroughly that she believes herself to be its author.

In a psychological variant of de Staël's mirror scene, Maggie conflates her own and her cousin's image: "Maggie . . . was fond of fancying a world where the people never got any larger than children of their own age, and she made the queen of it just like Lucy, with a little crown on her head, and a little sceptre in her hand . . . only the queen was Maggie herself in Lucy's form" (52). She has conveniently blonded her own image. But in the famous scene in the "Red Deeps" in which Maggie returns the novel *Corinne* to her friend Philip Wakem, she explains: "I didn't finish the book. . . . As soon as I came to the blond-haired young lady reading in the park, I shut it up, and determined to read no further. I foresaw that that light-complexioned girl would win away all the love from Corinne and make her miserable. I'm determined to read no more books where the blond-haired women carry away all the happiness. I should begin to have a prejudice against them. . . . I want to avenge Rebecca and Flora MacIvor, and Minna and all the rest of the dark unhappy ones" (270). When Philip suggests that she may avenge "the dark women in your own person, and carry away all the love from your cousin Lucy," Maggie insists that if she's "jealous for the dark woman . . . [i]t's because I always care the most about the unhappy people: if the blond girl were forsaken, I should like *her* best. I always take the side of the rejected lover" (271).

His prophecy later becomes reality. Maggie "carr[ies] away all the love from . . . Lucy" as Stephen Guest's infatuation turns into love. However, the importance of the conversation about *Corinne,* beyond mere foreshadowing, is its illumination of the plot-pattern that Eliot, Brontë, and Elizabeth Gaskell were eager to subvert. Maggie's explanation—that she would side with the blond girl were she the forsaken one—is not a subordinate clause, to be ignored, as most readers who have concentrated on revenge and competition have done. It underscores feminine fellowship, which women novelists had begun to dramatize.

Maggie's final words—that she cares most about the unhappy people—are a testament to women's desire for community based on mutual affection, trust, and aid. While Eliot approached fellowship in *The Mill on the Floss* in shorthand form because she recognized it as only a future possibility, her friends Barbara Bodichon and Emily Davies would be attempting only three years later to establish an institution of higher education for women with Eliot's financial help. In 1873 their efforts succeeded when Girton College became the first women's college affiliated with Cambridge University.

In 1929, the narrator of Virginia Woolf's *A Room of One's Own* would observe of *Life's Adventure,* a novel by the fictional Mary Carmichael: "'Chloe liked Olivia,' I read. And then it struck me how immense a change was there. Chloe liked Olivia perhaps for the first time in literature. Cleopatra did not like Octavia. And how completely *Antony and Cleopatra* would have been altered had she done so! . . . It was strange to think that all the great women of fiction were, until Jane Austen's day, not only seen by the other sex, but seen only in relation to the other sex" (86). Maggie's friendship with Lucy—never as thorny as Lucy and Ginevra's—is genuine, despite moments of childhood jealousy when Tom favors Lucy. The two girls pass their school days in amity, developing a relationship that in young adulthood is warm and sisterly. Eliot gives dimension to their attachment and Maggie's difficult decision to give up Stephen by developing Lucy's character beyond the culturally resonant but flat image of the midcentury "Angel in the House."

She begins her work by interiorizing Lucy, showing us something of the landscape of her mind and demonstrating that even as a little girl Lucy was willing to violate a mythic prohibition—not to "go out of the garden" (84)—"timidly enjoying the rare treat of doing something naughty" (85). Lucy's sense of adventure hasn't all been destroyed by the useless smatterings of education and repressive upbringing that girls were made to endure.[5]

As a child Lucy may be a "little blond angel-head" (201)—a sweet but diminishing epithet that reinforces the meaning of her name—but as a young woman whose hair has darkened to "light-brown ringlets" (293), she shows enterprise in the literal sense. To make Maggie's life happier, she arranges for Guest and Company to buy Dorlcote Mill from Lawyer Wakem. "Yes, Papa," she says, "I'm very wise; I've got all your business talents. Didn't you admire my accompt-book now, when I showed it you?" (342). By telling Stephen

Guest, "But I know you like women to be rather insipid" (294), Lucy proves she's not.

Maggie's decision to return to St. Ogg's after her romantic flight with Stephen is partly owing to Lucy's merit. But her Uncle Deane indignantly locks the door against Maggie, who is "hunger[ing] for an interview with Lucy . . . to utter a word of penitence, to be assured by Lucy's own eyes and lips that she did not believe in the willing treachery of those whom she had loved and trusted" (411). Now in the "mirror-misery" of her mind, Maggie is "haunted by a face cruel in its gentleness: a face that had been turned on hers with glad sweet looks of trust and love from the twilight time of memory" (411). But then Lucy transforms from ghostly to real presence, once more disobeying a prohibition by secretly slipping out of her house to visit Maggie "as she sat without candle in the twilight" (412).

> Lucy threw her arms around Maggie's neck; and leaned her pale cheek against the burning brow.
>
> . . . "God bless you for coming, Lucy."
>
> . . . "I know you never meant to make me unhappy. . . . It is a trouble that has come on us all:—you have more to bear than I have—and you gave him up . . . you did what must have been very hard to do."
>
> . . . "Lucy," said Maggie, with another great effort. "I pray to God continually that I may never be the cause of sorrow to you any more."
>
> "Maggie," she said, in a low voice, that had the solemnity of confession in it, "you are better than I am. I can't . . ."
>
> She broke off there and said no more. But they clasped each other in a last embrace. (412–13)

The ambiguity of Lucy's fractured sentence, "I can't . . . ," makes her whole. She realistically divorces herself from an impossible womanly perfection—a Christian ideal existing solely in the pages of "Silly Novels by Lady Novelists,"[6] as Eliot called them. This scene of Lucy's forgiveness and Maggie's earnest return, of connection between the imperfect brunette and the imperfect blonde—is Eliot's dramatic rendering of the need to move beyond ourselves through a "last embrace" that defines our humanity.[7]

In writing *The Mill on the Floss,* George Eliot made peace with the child and young woman she had been—passionate, intensely intellectual, impulsive, and sexual—qualities that made a parochial and conventionally religious life unbearable. If she settled any score in writing it, it wasn't with Herbert Spencer but herself. Maggie's death by drowning was not merely a convenient way, as Ellen Moers asserts, to remove her from the scene and redress the balance of a flagrant violation of trust ("Heroinism" 322). It was also the expression of a favorite Victorian theme—baptism by water, or dying into life (Buckley 97–108). In *The Mill*, Maggie reenters the conventional community that had rejected her through Tom's final embrace.

But Eliot never wanted to go back to that narrow society except through imagination. Even in symbolic terms she reconfigured the return as a purely earthly, if redemptive, drama of fellowship—not of faith in a "Divine presence" (*Adam Bede* 430) of the sort favored by the unimaginative people of St. Ogg's and, in her family, by her pious father and brother Isaac. Herbert Spencer wrote that "throwing off her early beliefs left her mind in an attitude of antagonism which lasted for some years" (quoted in Redinger 102). But bitterness had gone by the time she wrote *The Mill on the Floss* (Redinger 102). Her spiritually striving young women would never again drown—though they might come close—as Gwendolen Harcourt does in *Daniel Deronda* (749–50). She would figure their conversions only through water imagery.

Eliot liked to chronicle the stories of "exceptional" young women, different—as she herself was—from those they lived among. In *Middlemarch*, Dorothea Brooke, like Maggie, is a "cygnet" raised among numerous "oary-footed" "ducklings"—whether of the gentry or commercial classes. In England, just before passage of the first Reform Bill in 1832, there was no "constant unfolding of far-resonant action" but only "a meanness of opportunity" (3) for a young woman of high ideals and an abstract desire to do good. But for the different social strata they inhabit, there's a similarity between exceptional Maggie Tulliver, misunderstood and hampered by small-minded relatives and St. Ogg's natives, and Dorothea, who, like Maggie at one time, adopts a narrow evangelical and penitential creed, rejecting her mother's jewels as too worldly.

Yet while there's a genealogical connection between Maggie and Dorothea, Rosamond Vincy traces her origins not back to Lucy Deane but to the minor figure of Mrs. Stelling. Like her, mindful of her ringlets or plaits and the fit of her skirt, Rosamond is consummate Victorian femininity—"with a nymph-like figure and pure blondness which give the largest range to choice in the flow and colour of drapery" (71). Tertius Lydgate, the new doctor in town, is dazzled by her—"so immaculately blond, as if the petals of some gigantic flower had just opened and disclosed her; and yet with this infantine blondness showing so much ready, self-possessed grace" (118). No pupil at Mrs. Lemon's school had "exceeded that young lady for mental acquisition and propriety of speech, while her musical execution was quite exceptional," and she had learned "all that was demanded in the accomplished female—even to the extras, such as the getting in and out of a carriage" (71). We cannot be tone-deaf to the "extras."

However, beyond her many accomplishments, Rosamond's a narcissist, as well. Her blond hair epitomizes both her beauty and character: she "put up her hand to touch her wondrous hair-plaits—an habitual gesture with her as pretty as any movements of a kitten's paw. Not that Rosamond was the least like a kitten: she was a sylph caught young and educated at Mrs. Lemon's" (118). The oldest daughter of Mr. Vincy, a ribbon manufacturer (perhaps a comment on his daughter's decorative but slight substance), Rosamond has what Henry James called "the seeing eye." Although she loves her own image most, reflected either in mirrors or in the eyes of others, whatever else she sees and finds attractive, she also desires—whether the new doctor in Middlemarch or, later, the grand house that Lydgate can scarcely afford. Yet for all their differences about spiritual matters and material possessions—Dorothea, ardent, dark, and Quakerish in her simplicity; Rosamond, coy, capitalizing on her infantine blondness, and the last word in style—both are frustrated victims. The former suffers because of the limits on a woman's knowledge and reformist aspirations; the latter, because of her inability to gain and control wealth and social standing.

Mary Garth, on the other hand, although, like her cousin Rosamond, a product of Mrs. Lemon's school, seems to have escaped (because she didn't get the "extras"?) both the triviality of the course of instruction there and, on the other hand, the uselessness of the tuition, "on plans at once narrow and promiscuous, first in an English family and afterwards in a Swiss family at Lausanne" (6) that had been Dorothea and her sister Celia's educational lot from the age of twelve. She is the "third woman," offering, with her own "rough and stubborn" curly brown hair, a welcome complication to the dark/blond dyad of *The Mill on the Floss* and so many Romantic novels. With her honest self-appraisal, comic sense, and worldly, though not unkindly, cynicism, she's Gordon Haight's nominee for the novel's true heroine and, he thinks, Eliot's own representative ("Heroine" 58–67). In fact, as Mary briefly stands in for Dorothea, Eliot is able to lay another ghost to rest—the ghost that haunts so many nineteenth-century novels: the apparition of the beautiful blond woman in Germaine de Staël's mirror.

Rosamond and Mary . . . stood at the toilette-table near the window while Rosamond . . . applied little touches of her finger-tips to her hair—hair of infantine fairness, neither flaxen nor yellow. Mary Garth seemed all the plainer standing at an angle between the two nymphs—the one in the glass, and the one out of it, who looked at each other with eyes of heavenly blue, deep enough to hold the most exquisite meanings an ingenious holder could put into them, and deep enough to hide the meanings of the owner if these should happen to be less exquisite. . . . most men in Middlemarch, except her brothers, held that Miss Vincy was the best girl in the world, and some called her an angel. Mary Garth, on the contrary, had the aspect of an ordinary sinner: she was brown; her curly dark hair was rough and stubborn; . . . and it would not be true to declare, in satisfactory antithesis, that she had all the virtues. Plainness has its peculiar temptations and vices quite as much as beauty. . . . she said, laughingly—

"What a brown patch I am by the side of you, Rosy! You are the most unbecoming companion."

"Oh no! No one thinks of your appearance, you are so sensible and useful, Mary. Beauty is of very little consequence in reality," said Rosamond, turning her head towards Mary, but with eyes swerving towards the new view of her neck in the glass. (83–84)

Rosamond Vincy, her Christian name suggesting the beauty of the material world and her surname her indomitable nature, is herself caught in Eliot's mirror-portrait. She's simultaneously spectator and object. John Berger observes: "Women watch themselves being looked at. . . . The surveyor of woman in herself is male: the surveyed is female. Thus she turns herself into an object—and most particularly an object of vision: a sight" (47). Berger, of course, is writing about real psychological and social relations. In a novel, we see Rosamond's image reflected back not only to her own and Mary's eyes but also to the narrator's critical gaze. We discern her narcissism and what isn't actually present: her brothers' "home-judgment" that she's not "the best girl in the world." The mirror may multiply her so that she's "two nymphs," but self-love—most on display when she "swerves" "towards the new view of her neck in the glass" and untruthfully tells Mary that beauty doesn't count for much—diminishes her.

But unlike Corinne, whose rival is Lucile, Mary doesn't see blond Rosamond as a competitor, for Rosy's own brother Fred is Mary's ardent suitor.

Corinne is wounded by Lucile's ghostly perfect beauty, but Mary jokes with a charming turn of phrase—"a brown patch"—which delights with its "truth-telling fairness" (84). Neither does she internalize any penalty of plainness: "She had humour enough in her to laugh at herself" (84).

Rosamond, unfortunately, never laughs—neither at herself nor anything else. Because she "was always that combination of correct sentiments . . . and perfect blond loveliness which made the irresistible woman for the doomed man of that date" (198), she isn't her brothers', nor the reader's, favorite. "Think no unfair evil of her, pray: she had no wicked plots, nothing sordid or mercenary; . . . she never thought of money except as something neces-sary which other people would always provide. . . . Nature had inspired many arts in finishing Mrs. Lemon's favorite pupil, who by general consent (Fred excepted) was a rare compound of beauty, cleverness, and amiability" (198). The tart description of Rosamond's "finishing" at Mrs. Lemon's reminds us of who really creates such young woman. Only the independent Rev. Fare-brother thinks her "rather uninteresting—a little too much the pattern-card of the finishing-school" (468). But Mr. Chichely, a middle-aged bachelor, offers the mainstream opinion: "There should be a little devil in a woman. . . . And I like them blond, with a certain gait, and a swan neck" (66). A confirmed bach-elor appreciates, from afar, displays of mild spirit and eroticism. Eliot taps into the popular perception, after the 1862 publication of Mary Elizabeth Braddon's *Lady Audley's Secret,* that the blonde may harbor hidden reserves of subver-sive energy. Rosamond saves hers for her female impersonations: "(She was by nature an actress of parts that entered into her *physique:* she even acted her own character, and so well, that she did not know it to be precisely her own)" (87).

She looks like the traditional heroine—"just the sort of beautiful creature that is imprisoned with ogres in fairy tales" (102). But Eliot's genuine sympa-thy (and ours) for Rosamond, queen of a sort of passive-(sexual)-aggression, despite our intimate knowledge of her maneuvers, is an innovation. Austen in *Pride and Prejudice* comically dramatizes Caroline Bingley's transparent mach-inations.

> "Eliza Bennet . . . is one of those young ladies who seek to recommend themselves to the opposite sex, by undervaluing their own; and with many men, I dare say, it succeeds. But, in my opinion, it is a paltry device, a very mean art."
>
> "Undoubtedly," replied Darcy . . . "there is meanness in *all* the arts which

ladies sometimes condescend to employ for captivation. Whatever bears affinity to cunning is despicable."

Miss Bingley was not so entirely satisfied with this reply as to continue the subject. (29)

Darcy speaks for the author, but Eliot implies that a culture that encourages Rosamond's dreaming and supplies her with no other practical occupation is guiltier than the single girl.

Nina Auerbach mistakenly calls Rosamond "lamialike" (8) because Eliot's portrait is entirely in the realist tradition. Lydgate may look into Rosamond's face and "feel the mystery of a power" (Auerbach 9), but it isn't, as Auerbach asserts, the power "of a woman with a demon's gifts" (9). Ordinary terrestrial, sexual attraction causes Lydgate to turn "a little paler than usual" (87) and makes Rosamond "blush . . . deeply" and feel "a certain astonishment" (87). Medusa, an older version of the serpent-woman than Lamia, turned all living things which looked at her to stone (Bullfinch 925). Yet to be astonished is to be turned to stone (stunned, struck senseless—as the root suggests). Rosamond is equally under the spell of "a mutual fascination" (196), as no lamia has ever been.

Later, during their courtship, when she suspects that Lydgate's interest has cooled, "happily Rosamond did not think of committing any desperate act: she plaited her fair hair as beautifully as usual" (221) and never stopped thinking of "house-furniture" (197). She's just a material girl living in a material world. To incite the crowd at an estate sale, the auctioneer Mr. Trumbull offers a riddle that aptly glosses her interests: "Here is a sample: 'How must you spell honey to make it catch lady-birds? Answer—money. You hear?—lady-birds—honey—money. This is an amusement to sharpen the intellect; it has a sting'" (443), as do the narrator's references to "nymphs" (83) and "waternixies" (475)—"what we call satire" (443)—or her suggestion that Rosamond's desire to lay in a stock of the very material "intricacies of lace edging and hosiery and petticoat-tucking" (257) determines her most important calculations. Lydgate soon learns that his dream of "that perfect piece of womanhood who could reverence her husband's mind after the fashion of an accomplished mermaid, using her comb and her looking-glass and singing her song for the relaxation of his adored wisdom alone" (425) will never come true, and that "affection [does] not make her compliant" (427). Dorothea originally "despise[s] women a little for not shaping their lives more" (397). But what practical options does a girl like Rosamond have for overcoming the restrictions of women's lives? She can rely only on a "quiet steady disobedience" (434), "feminine impassibility" (432), and cunning acts of subversion. Yet Eliot is not without sympathy for this girl whose flaw is that she has learned too well the values of her community. If the historian J. G. A. Pocock argues that property was believed to guard "republican virtue" in the eighteenth century (109), one hundred years later, "mobile property" did the opposite, certifying an individual's wealth and status, which merely inspired the drive for more of the same. Rosamond had plenty of company.

Dorothea and Rosamond, of very different social classes, would be unlikely to have had any relationship or, realistically, even to have seen each other. In so many ways opposites, the two may join in the reader's imagination but are infrequently on the same page. Finally, just beyond the midpoint of the novel, they meet in Rosamond's parlor. We see Dorothea's "grace and dignity" of "limbs and neck"; her dress of "thin white woollen stuff soft to the touch and soft to the eye"; "her simply parted hair and candid eyes" (316). Nurture and nature, by contrast, join to produce Rosamond's "infantine blondness and wondrous crown of hair-plaits, with pale-blue dress of a fit and fashion so perfect that no dressmaker could look at it without emotion . . . and that controlled self-consciousness of manner which is the expensive substitute for simplicity" (316). Fashion is shorthand for the characters of the models. But long before their meeting, which makes natural this "sort of contrast not infrequent in country life when the habits of the different ranks were less blent" (316), Eliot has prepared our readerly imaginations, used to cataloging similarities and distinctions, for the appearance of these very dissimilar women.

Their stories are, for the most part, parallel, intersecting in the "real time" of fiction a mere three times in some six hundred pages. Eliot marries them off early, for in her view as in Thackeray's, matrimony is less a reward for change and growth than an opportunity for displaying the characters' psychology. "Marriage," she says in the "Finale," "which has been the bourne of so many narratives, is still a great beginning" (607–8), but it is only a beginning because "the gradual conquest or irremediable loss of that complete union which makes the advancing years a climax" (608) is the really interesting story.

By the second time Dorothea enters Mrs. Lydgate's parlor, she is "for ever enthroned in [Will Ladislaw's] soul: no other woman could sit higher than her footstool" (344). But there is Will, holding Rosamond's hands, telling her "with low-toned fervour" (568) that he cannot love her. Dorothea hurriedly departs, leaving Will to rant in Heathcliffian manner: "Explain! Tell a man to explain how he dropped into hell! Explain my preference! I never had a *preference* for her, any more than I have a preference for breathing. . . . I would rather touch her hand if it were dead than I would touch any other woman's living" (570). What a shock to Rosamond's system. The fairy-tale blonde isn't used to losing out to her dark sister!

Will's theatricality gives way to some of the finest scenes in the book: Dorothea's tortured night of jealousy resolving into deep concern for the Lydgates and her return to their home to offer Rosamond sympathy and help with her obviously troubled marriage. An impressed Henry James in *The Portrait of a Lady* patterned Isabel Archer's dark night of the soul on Dorothea's tormented vigil. Even better is her next meeting with Rosamond, the emotional climax of the novel.

Eliot expresses the energy of her heroine not only through the intensity of the dialogue but also through metaphors invoking turbulent water, storm, and shipwreck. Lucy and Maggie's reconciliation toward the close of *The Mill on the Floss* is the quiet forerunner of the climactic conversion of Rosamond and Dorothea. Yet reconciliation is too weak a word to describe the moment of mutual recognition and affirmation of Lucy and Maggie—cousins, almost sisters—both of whom have loved one man. Maggie parts with Stephen Guest in the flesh, but her final renunciation is this brief season in which she asks, in earnest speech and eloquent body language, for Lucy's forgiveness.

In *Middlemarch*, the two young women stand in entirely different relation to one another. Strangers, they have seen each other only twice before. Yet here they are now, face to face in Rosamond's drawing room, hands clasping hands. The dark-haired girl makes ardent waves of feeling with words and body that swirl around her and her weaker, more egocentric, companion. The energy of her difficult effort is translated through both the broken and crescendoing rhythms of the dialogue and description that move us as well as the hearts of the two young women. Ordinarily placid Rosamond is inspired by the other woman's "self-forgetful ardour" and the "cordial, pleading tones which seemed to flow with generous heedlessness . . . as soothingly as a warm stream over her shrinking fears":

"How can we live and think that anyone has trouble—piercing trouble— and we could help them, and never try?"

Dorothea, completely swayed by the feeling that she was uttering, forgot everything but that she was speaking from out the heart of her own trial to Rosamond's.

... Rosamond, taken hold of by an emotion stronger than her own—hurried along in a new movement which gave all things some new, awful, undefined aspect—could find no words, but involuntarily she put her lips to Dorothea's forehead, ... and then for a minute the two women clasped each other as if they had been in a shipwreck.

"You are thinking what is not true," said Rosamond, in an eager half whisper. ...

"When you came in yesterday—it was not as you thought. ... He was telling me how he loved another woman, that I might know he could never love me," said Rosamond. (582–84)

The scene unites two separate moments in *The Mill on the Floss*—that between Lucy and Maggie and the dramatic reunion of Maggie and Tom, estranged sister and brother, who embrace before their shipwreck in the swirling waters of the Floss. Especially because their fellowship is voluntary, Rosamond and Dorothea's meeting is cathartic for the reader as it is for them.

Briefly, Rosamond is lifted above the contemplation and cares of self into that sphere of self-forgetfulness inhabited by the generous-spirited heroes and heroines of Eliot's "dramatis personae." There won't be another such chance for candor and confidence between two women of different social spheres, unlikely to meet again. Eliot makes it an exemplary performance of sisterhood, standing for an ideal compact or promise of community between women of different classes—dark, blond, *all* women—despite the confinement of their "nature[s] ... in channels which had no great name on the earth" (613).

What becomes of Rosamond, the weaker, less noble nature? Lydgate's acquaintances "thought him enviable to have so charming a wife." Yet she's continued to be "inflexible" of judgment and "mild" of temper, frustrating her husband by "stratagem." "He once called her his basil plant ... [saying] that basil was a plant which had flourished wonderfully on a murdered man's brains. ... It was a pity [said Rosamond] he had not had Mrs. Ladislaw, whom he was always praising and placing above her. ... But it would be unjust not to tell, that she never uttered a word in depreciation of Dorothea, keeping in religious remembrance the generosity which had come to her aid in the sharpest crisis of her life" (609–10). Even more than Ginevra, this imperfect blonde escapes reproof-by-plot, just as she really would in the world. Unlike Caroline in Trollope's *The Bertrams,* she dodges the Victorian penalty of childlessness, having four daughters and being much loved by her wealthy second husband, whom she marries after Lydgate dies at fifty. What made us dream that Lydgate could comb white hair? Rosamond, not he, is the survivor of life's ironies.

These ironies are far-reaching in their social implications. Eliot, in the spirit of realism, offers only her characteristically mild salinity of comment; Rosamond is no more than the product of her class and culture. Her imperfect values and temperament abet the reader's perception that the blonde is no fairy-tale creature but very much of this world worldly, formed by it, according to her experiences, as is Maggie Tulliver or any other of Eliot's sympathetic dark-haired women. Thus, through her, even more than through Dorothea, who, "like that river of which Cyrus broke the strength" (613), learned to be contented with "incalculably diffusive" effects (613), we see the beginnings of altered plot lines and new attitudes toward women. With Rosamond, who remains mired to the end in materialism, Eliot began a realistic critique of the values and conditions that made women like her react against the limited round of their days.

Advances, whether political, cultural, or technological, are usually incremental. The assertion, notwithstanding my original claim for "punctuated equilibrium," is as true for the changes in women's roles in the nineteenth century as for the next generation of computer chips. Despite their own exceptional circumstances, and as much as Brontë and Eliot might have liked to see a different world for women, their aspirations were limited by contemporary probability, which they could nudge only so far, in and through their fictive inventions. They couldn't, as Ensler does in *Vagina Monologues,* redefine women through the anatomical/spiritual equation, below = within.[8]

What, then, is the appeal of these books, not just in college classrooms but, in their cinematic versions, to movie and television audiences? We sense that as social works-in-progress, they dramatically represented possibilities for women that, still distant at the time, spoke liminally of movement toward our recognizable present. The blonde did her part. Awakened from her beauty sleep, she made an important contribution toward restoring sexuality and personhood to the representation of all women, no matter their hair color and complexion. Contemporary readers turned a new page.

But as may happen in any complex society, a countermovement in fiction and performance art mined a belief in women's "dark" powers. Mary Elizabeth Braddon covertly demystified the cultural bases of feminine prerogatives.

Lady Audley's Secret, which established the literary vogue of the blond vixen, paralleled women's growing social and political strength, apparent in the campaigns of this period for higher education and against the Contagious Diseases Acts (1864) that victimized women who were already the victims of economic injustice.[9] The story, and the male backlash it occasioned, is another chapter in the blonde's and all women's quest for the "unalienable rights" of life, liberty, and the pursuit of happiness.

Dyeing the Blonde a Darker Shade

Femmes Fatales, Foolery, and Fin-de-Siècle Fear

> I'm the lovely fiend of fiction
> With the yellow, yellow hair.
> —W. S. Gilbert, *A Sensation Novel in Three Volumes*

Before 1862 there is ample evidence in British fiction that the Saxon blonde is the prize of the marriage stakes. Consider the deliciously snide comment about Mary Crawford in *Mansfield Park*—a novel, like all others by Austen, exclusively populated by dark-haired young women. The Miss Bertrams admire her "lively dark eye, clear brown complexion and general prettiness. Had she been tall, full formed, and fair, it might have been more of a trial" (77). With amiably barbed irony, Austen fleetingly glances at the world beyond the pages of her story where blondes apparently had the competitive edge. Or there is Thackeray's description of the tradesman's daughter Rose Dawson, that vapid blonde, chosen by Sir Pitt Crawley (who had his pick) and of the wealthy young women, accompanying their parents, who could not be other than "blonde, timid, and in pink." Then, hardly understated, is Maggie Tulliver's determination "to read no more books where the blond-haired women carry away all the happiness." In 1861, Mary Elizabeth Braddon, sharpening her pen in her second full-length novel, *The Lady Lisle,* wrote that the mother of the characterless baronet of her story, when a girl, was only "a pretty, pink and white, blue-eyed, flaxen-haired waxen image." Nevertheless, "people who didn't care an atom for her were dying to marry her. She became as fashionable as a man who had written a novel about the working classes, or been tried for murder" (quoted in Wolff 118).

The dark/blond divide of Romance enforced the belief that domesticity and blondness go together like the now proverbial horse and carriage. The hero might have a youthful fling with an exotic Rebecca or Corinne but later settles down with Rowena or Lucile. Or, in the midcentury realist tradition of Elizabeth Gaskell's *North and South* (1854), in the first chapter, "'Haste to the Wedding,'" blond and kittenish Edith, a feminine "ball" of soft, white muslin and ribbons, takes a postprandial snooze on the sofa while her energetic manager of a mother makes the arrangements for the girl's marriage to a wealthy and handsome young captain. However, the dark-haired heroine, Edith's cousin Margaret Hale, endures economic hardship and other trials before finding happiness with a textile mill owner, not of her class, in the unfashionable midlands industrial city Milton Northern. The beginning of this story, in fact, illustrates an assumption of the domestic novel of the period: the genetically endowed blonde often starts with a generous supply of capital or easily acquires it; the brunette, with strength of mind (beneath the hair), must labor for her ultimate reward.

The connection between intellectuality and dark hair, or outright homeliness, is the overt premise of an antifeminist cartoon sequence published in 1871—Florence Claxton's *The Adventures of a Woman in Search of Her Rights.* In this collection of separate, captioned drawings (figures 3–6), a beautiful blonde, engaged to be married, reads the notice of her fiancé's engagement to "another" in "The Times." The succeeding cartoons tell the story of her metamorphosis into a "strong-minded"—that is, homely—woman. Her long and romantic blond tresses undergo an instantaneous alteration, darkening and frizzing up in an unbecoming bob. But her transformation is also intellectual, for she and her nose, which "assumes strong-minded proportions," go off to Oxford, where, in a revolutionary move, she's "EMANCIPATED!! (*Fifth of November*)," and "She proposes to FINISH her education." A foreshadowing of things to come, "Oxford in 19—" pictures three young woman with beautiful blond curls, and the caption "'Fair girl graduates, with Their (?) golden hair.'—*Tennyson*," implying that girls smart enough to be graduates could not possibly be blondes without the assistance of Alexander Pope's "cosmetic powers" (*Rape of the Lock* 2238). The final joke of the series is that all the pictured events have been only a bad dream, from which, happily, the girl wakes in the morning.

"Adulteration"—hair rats, dyes—in its root meaning, "to make impure or inferior by adding improper ingredients," had begun to surface in narratives of the period (as in Wilkie Collins's *Man and Wife*, 1870) with respect to the part they played in the "business transactions" of the "marriage trade." *"Married Off": A Satirical Poem* by H. B., also illustrated by Claxton, links women's venal hymeneal ambitions and adulterated beauty. The distressed mother, Mrs. Hannibal Goit, laments that in the "mart, for exchanging female commodities," a "sensible daughter, / With portionless beauty,—(a flimsy supporter)— / In this age of Brass, Bank-notes, Bricks and mortar," may wait too long to marry. Daughter Rose shows "Certain symptoms of humanity's doom," that is, the propensity to lose her "bloom," while her sister Miss Tulip "trembled to think, she really must dye! / That is—colour the hair—not sicken and die" (5). The poem humorously skewers both the crassness of the "mart" and the cunning of women intent on snagging husbands.

The vitality of communally sanctioned and blatant antifeminism is also obvious from the span of years between the original and re-publication dates— 1871 and 1900—of Claxton's *Adventures of a Woman.*" The second half of the nineteenth century, as I've said, saw the creation of the "femme fatale" in poetry written by men, about which phenomenon, despite his very thorough examination of the type, Mario Praz mysteriously declined to speculate in *The Romantic Agony.* The femme fatale in the poetry of Rossetti and Swinburne unmasks a primitive fear of woman's power and sexuality. However, the implication that blondes are every bit as aggressive and manipulative as their dark counterparts took on another meaning in the extension of the realist tradition of fiction by women, beginning with the 1862 publication of Mary Elizabeth Braddon's most famous "sensation novel," *Lady Audley's Secret.*

Recent analyses of sensation fiction of the 1860s and '70s have focused on Victorian readers' attraction to the domestic violence and mayhem implied by these stories.[1] Their argument is that women readers were covertly able to enjoy the repudiation in these tales of the domestic cage as their authors "prob[ed] what lies beneath the veneer of the apparently stable upper- or middle-class home."[2] Excessive veneration of the family and home in Victorian culture naturally produced a counter-reaction. Yet another social reality, as

Fig. 3. The beautiful blonde reads in "The Times" of her fiancé's engagement to another in *The Adventures of a Woman in Search of Her Rights* (1871). (By permission of The British Library; Shelfmark: L49/1881)

Fig. 4. Her blond hair darkens and frizzes up (naturally!) as she chooses "emancipation" and education. (By permission of The British Library; Shelfmark: L49/1881)

Fig. 5. Golden-haired girl graduates—a (per)oxymoron? (By permission of The British Library; Shelfmark: L49/1881)

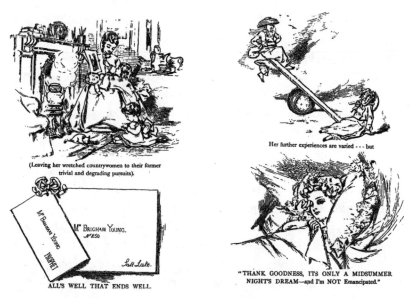

Fig. 6. It was all only a bad dream; thank goodness she's not emancipated, after all! (By permission of The British Library; Shelfmark: L49/1881)

I've suggested, was that many women didn't have the luxury of rejecting domesticity, never marrying because of the surplus female population. Braddon herself, although she lived with and had children by John Maxwell, her publisher, didn't marry until late in their relationship because his wife was alive, incarcerated in an asylum. As her biographer says: "She suffered at the hands of Victorian society and loathed its hypocrisies and cruelties. These she taught herself to satirize so skillfully that her readers need not see her doing it" (Wolff 8). She was subtly critical of the entire arc of female existence—not merely its "marriage portion."

In her tale of bigamy and murder, Braddon turns her readers against the cultural (and racialized) preference for the blonde by unmasking her motives and means. She examines the web of social forces that literally "privileged" her in her effort to avert "redundancy" or, in the words of a British music hall song of a later date, not to be left "on the shelf." Lady Audley is the epitome of blond beauty, but being blond, as Ginevra Fanshawe had shown, does not mean being submissive; it certainly doesn't prevent Lady Audley from conceiving an outrageous plan to achieve economic security. Braddon, following Brontë, continued the image-demolition of the pliant and placid fair girl revered in folk- and fairy tale and cherished in this period of high nationalism. The blonde could be just as rapacious, aggressive, and sinister as the dark antiheroine, Margaret Sherwin, in Wilkie Collins's *Basil* (1856). But she was not the "fatal woman" of the male imagination in which "the exotic and the erotic ideals go hand in hand"—the exotic being "an imaginative projection of sexual desire" (Praz 207). *Lady Audley's Secret* was the beginning of a paradigm shift in realist fiction. While the femme fatale was an exotic figure, already invoked in the poetry of the Pre-Raphaelites, Braddon's model is domestically bred—her aggressiveness not sexual, but commercial, in origin.

Braddon told an interviewer, long after the novel was published, that she had gotten the idea for her book from *The Woman in White* (Wolff vii). Many of her plot details—the incarceration of Lady Audley in an asylum; Robert Audley as an amateur detective; the name of the doctor, Mr. Dawson; and the resemblance between Lady Audley and her maid Phoebe—may come from Collins's novel. However, "idea" means something more elemental.

The connection to Collins had its roots in Braddon's life: her energetic commitment to supporting her mother through acting and, later, through her writing, her common-law husband and her family. A tireless "scribbler," even as she raised Maxwell's children by his wife and then the five children Maxwell and she had together (all but one out of wedlock), she was contemptuous of the materialist aesthetic that determined the destinies of women in Victorian England, for which she had no time—in both senses of the phrase. If she had been thinking of *The Woman in White,* it was to challenge its core assumption that women need masculine protection.

While Collins emphasized the woeful victimization of women who, once married, lost their property to their husbands—indeed, became, themselves, chattel goods without existence in the eyes of the law—even his strong female characters are all, finally, passively dependent on valiant, good-hearted men. In *The Woman in White,* intelligent and resourceful Marian Halcombe needs Walter Hartright; in *No Name,* Magdalen Vanstone requires Captain Kirke to ensure her eventual safety and success. Braddon, the economic mainstay of her family, bridled. In a novel of 1875, *A Strange World,* Justina Elgood complains of the theatrical profession of which she is a member: "Haven't I been told that I've no talent and no good looks to help me, and that I must be a drudge all my life?" (quoted in Wolff 68). But two years later, Justina's "art has grown out of the depths of her own feeling"; her "acting is the outcome of a rich and thoughtful mind rather than the hard and dry result of tuition and study of the mechanical art of imitation" (quoted in Wolff 69). Success for a woman might be the result of "a rich and thoughtful mind" rather than mere "good looks." Such had been true in Braddon's own dramatically rapid rise from obscurity as an actress to an acclaimed and well-paid writer of both penny dreadfuls and "bound" three-volume novels. She was thus determined to unearth and examine the foundation of the imperfect edifice of Victorian sexual relations. While her method, like Collins's, depends on the exaggerated effects of a sensation thriller, her critique of Victorian values is wholly realistic, as is the fate of her golden-haired antiheroine.

Lady Audley's story is one of many secrets. The fairy-tale-beautiful young wife of wealthy Sir Michael has been Helen Maldon, then Helen Talboys, then Lucy Graham. She attempts to murder her first husband, George Talboys; she unintentionally murders Luke Marks, her maid's husband; she's the victim of a supposed hereditary madness (carried and expressed—naturally—in the female line).

Although she begins her story after her character has become "My Lady," living in the "glorious old place" (2), Audley Hall, Braddon offers a retrospective of the conventional rise from comparative poverty—the hypergamous transformation ("marrying up") of the beautiful young woman—that makes possible the "happily ever after" conclusion of fairy tales: "Lady Audley had, in becoming the wife of Sir Michael, made one of those apparently advantageous matches which are apt to draw upon a woman the envy and hatred of her sex. She had come into the neighborhood as a governess in the family of a surgeon living in the village near Audley Court. . . . Her accomplishments were so brilliant and numerous, that it seemed strange that she should have answered an advertisement offering such very moderate terms of remuneration" (4). By naming her Lucy, Braddon consciously inserts her character into what had become, by 1862, a nineteenth-century ritual of heavenly christening. And she interjects the interesting information that Lucy Graham's advantageous match to Sir Michael might well be the basis of "envy and hatred"—an allusion to competition in contemporary society. But we may think of similar instances from fairy tales—Cinderella's stepsisters' jealousy, for example. The attributes of the governess's situation—her unknown origin, extraordinary talents, docility, and patience—are those of the princess-in-disguise, waiting to be claimed by the handsome prince of a distant kingdom. They are all motifs of the folktale. Yet Braddon also undermines such fairy- or folktale conventions by beginning after the point at which such stories conclude: the young woman is already happily married; there's nowhere for Lady Audley to go but down.

Moreover, while her portrait draws on metaphors suggesting the correspondence of beauty and virtue in such stories, Braddon intentionally undermines that harmony. The heroine is *only apparently* as good as the golden beauty of her hair. "Wherever she went she *seemed* to take joy and brightness with her. In the cottages of the poor her fair face shone like a sunbeam. . . . everybody, high and low, united in declaring Lucy Graham the sweetest girl that ever lived" (4; my emphasis). Braddon dedicates most space to Lucy's "sunshiny ringlets" (19) as "the most wonderful curls in the world—soft and feathery, always floating away from her face, and making a pale halo around her head when the sunlight shone through them" (6). Sir Michael Audley is overcome by her "wealth of showering flaxen curls" (5); the association of abundance and blondness is explicit.

But a serpent "troubles" paradise. Her "ringlets were always getting into disorder, [giving] no little trouble to Lady Audley's maid" (52), suggesting moral disarray, as do Em'ly's straying curls in *David Copperfield*. Her nephew

Robert Audley's misogynistic oneiric fantasies are filled with actual reptiles. Lady Audley's "beautiful golden ringlets were changing into serpents, and slowly creeping down her fair neck" (65). His clichéd recurrence to "the horrible things that have been done by women since that day upon which Eve was created to be Adam's companion and help-meet in the garden of Eden" (181) is Braddon's satiric critique of this unexceptional man. Later, mocking his expected disapproval of a woman novelist, the narrator asserts: "Better the pretty influence of the tea cups and saucers gracefully wielded in a woman's hand than all the inappropriate power snatched at the point of the pen from the unwilling sterner sex" (147).

Braddon, especially through his "ventriloquized"[3] diatribe against "noisy" women, exposes Robert's vulgar masculine prejudice. "To call [women] the weaker sex is to utter a hideous mockery. They are the stronger sex, the noisier, the more persevering, the more self-assertive sex. They want freedom of opinion, variety of occupation, do they? Let them have it. . . . but let them be quiet—if they can. . . . I hate women. . . . They're bold, brazen, abominable creatures, invented for the annoyance and destruction of their superiors" (136–37). She thus indicts her young barrister for attitudes that, with minimal shades of difference, he shares with the cultural avant-garde, the Pre-Raphaelites.

The portrait Sir Michael Audley has commissioned of his wife is recognizably of that school. Braddon exposes the antifeminine bias endemic in Victorian culture: in the working class (Luke Marks); the upper-middle class (Robert Audley; Harcourt and George Talboys); the intelligentsia (the Pre-Raphaelites). The violence may be physical, verbal, or visual, but the victim is always blamed.

When Robert and George Talboys wish to view the portrait, they enter Lady Audley's room by crawling through a secret tunnel and emerging through a trap door in the floor (a conspicuous "penetration"). The painting is an indictment of the overt misogyny of the Pre-Raphaelites' fetishized portraits. Repetition of syntactical elements doubles the obsessiveness of the painter's gaze: "Yes, the painter must have been a Pre-Raphaelite. No one but a Pre-Raphaelite would have painted, hair by hair, those feathery masses of ringlets, with every glimmer of gold, and every shade of pale brown. No one but a Pre-Raphaelite would have so exaggerated every attribute of that delicate face as to give a lurid brightness to the blonde complexion, and a strange sinister light to the deep blue eyes. No one but a Pre-Raphaelite could have given to that pretty pouting mouth the hard and almost wicked look it had in the portrait"

(47). Braddon catalogues the rich details of the painting, convincing the naive reader, through the multiplication of similar images, of the apparent hellishness of its subject. While she fastens on the Pre-Raphaelites' hyper-realism, the painting's "hair by hair" verisimilitude or "the exaggerated naturalism [that] seems to be based on a physiognomic accuracy that in turn is an expression of an inner truth . . . at once real and symbolic,"[4] Braddon, I think, is more interested in another tenet of Pre-Raphaelite aesthetics: "the acknowledgement that meaning is always created subjectively, as the projected emotions of the painter himself."[5] Thus she captures the underlying "woman-hating" vision of these painters who, in delving beneath the beautiful exteriors of their subjects, exposed their own distorted, fear-inspired fantasy of powerful females. The massive, muscular women these painters preferred as models don't resemble Lady Audley, but the impassive or vacant stares of these "beautiful fiend[s]," the sense of their demonic (read sexual) somnambulistic possession, is insinuated in the folds of her dress that look like flames, "the red gold gleaming in the yellow hair," and the exaggerated attributes of the delicate face. The hint of Lady Audley's covert licentiousness in the pouting lips (bee-stung lips being a favorite with these painters) suggests the sexual seductiveness of the siren, dangerous to the unwary male.

On the other hand, Lady Audley is deliberately selling an image, which the men are buying. A "heartless little coquette" (69) has learned, like Becky Sharp, what the market will bear. Yet what alternatives does she have, also like Becky, without a "mamma" to protect her? Moreover, Lady Audley has been deserted by her husband and virtually abandoned by her dipsomaniac of a father. There are, then, environmental justifications for her behavior and no simple answers.

Braddon asks the reader to consider how she would feel if her husband abandoned her for the gold fields of Australia, as Helen Talboys's husband has done. Retrospectively, George Talboys's excuse is financial; he admits to no crime in relying (without seeking his consent) on his feckless father-in-law to provide protection and support for his young wife and infant son. Lady Audley, of course, has an alternative perspective. Finding herself a virtual widow, she resented the desertion "by hating the man who had left me with no protector but a weak, tipsy father, and with a child to support. I had to work hard for my living . . . and what labor is more wearisome than the dull slavery of a governess?" After three years with no word from him, she believed she had "a right to think that he [was] dead or that he wishe[d] me to believe him dead" (232–33). After how many years must a woman continue to assume her husband is alive if she's had no word? But Robert Audley has no problem with his friend George's treatment of his wife. Braddon wonders if there's a double standard that protects men from paying for crimes against women.

She assumes we will blame Lady Audley for her impersonations, bigamy, and attempted murder of George Talboys while planting enough clues for the discerning reader to see that any conclusions about Lady Audley's "crimes" may be read in more than one way. However, she reserves her harshest criticism for feminine artifice—the culture of beauty that drives both commerce and the marriage market. Her censure is implicit in the narrator's ironic appeal to the reader to imagine the unimaginable: "Imagine all the women of England elevated to the high level of masculine intellectuality, superior to crinoline; above pearl powder and Mrs. Rachael Levinson [sic];[6] above taking the pains to be pretty . . . and what a drear, utilitarian, ugly life the sterner sex must lead" (147). As usual, her satire is double-edged. It raps the pretensions of "masculine intellectuality" by suggesting that "the sterner sex" is secretly attracted to feminine deception but simultaneously faults women for their devotion to those cumbrous crinolines and ghostly white pearl powder, a favorite with women of the demimonde.

Braddon was later more overt in her criticism of cosmetics, especially pearl powder, in *Rupert Godwin* (1867) and *Dead Sea Fruit* (1868). In the earlier novel, Violet Westford, a young girl looking for work in the theater, is warned by the wardrobe mistress that she shouldn't "let any of the ballet ladies persuade you to plaster your face with *blanc de perle,* or *blanc Rosati,* or *blanc de* somethings, as most of them do until their faces have about as much expression as you'll see in a whitewashed wall" (quoted in Wolff 63). Lucy Alford in *Dead Sea Fruit* is deprived of a role by Ida Courtenay, a kept woman, who arrives at the theater, "as handsome as rouge, pearl-powder, painted lips, painted nostrils, painted eyelids, painted eyebrows, and a liberal supply of false hair could make her" (quoted in Wolff 67). Braddon's belief that she herself had "no good looks to help [her]" (quoted in Wolff 68) in her acting career—reminiscent of Charlotte Brontë's complaint—only partly explains her anger over the artifice of makeup. She genuinely hated the fakery that debased the acting profession, which she loved, and the hypocrisy of British morality that would mount a French play but change the plot so that demimondaines in the original had become schoolgirls in the adaptation (Wolff 66–67). Such contrivances, both off and on the stage, were grist for her satiric mill. Perhaps in *Lady*

Audley's Secret, Braddon was archly suggesting adultery with the name of her antiheroine. An anagram of "Audley," with minimal metathesis and omission, is literally "taken *in* Adul(t)e(r)y."

Women were not merely victims. Braddon unmasked the aesthetic/ethic in which both men and women fully participated and which she believed diminished both sexes. She wanted an alternative for women—lives that relied (as did her own) on intellect and hard work rather than on cosmetics and fashion fakery to lure men. Hints of adulterated beauty, created through cosmetics and preparations for the purpose of attracting a husband, "darken" the golden ringlets of the blonde. Perhaps they're more perfidious to Braddon than Lady Audley's adulterous bigamy. "My Lady" indulges in a little "girl-talk" with her maid, Phoebe (ironically meaning "bright one")—whose beauty is marred by "an absence of color . . . not one glimmer of gold or auburn relieved the dull flaxen of her hair" (17)—advising the use of "transfiguring" products: "My hair is pale yellow shot with gold, and yours is drab. . . . Your complexion is sallow, and mine is pink and rosy. Why, with a bottle of hair-dye, such as we see advertised in the papers, and a pot of rouge, you'd be as good-looking as I, any day, Phoebe" (39). A "bottle of hair-dye," not merely its representation in the papers, may well grace Lady Audley's toilet table. Has her skin been touched by the brush of the rouge pot? Braddon hints that "My Lady" is a cosmetics "adulteress." Her ironic dramatization requires a revision of most of the readings of sensation fiction: that the sensation novelists' chief purpose was covertly to endorse their villainesses' disruptive duplicities. Braddon may have been critical of the domestic cage, but she understood the complexity of the social relations that also implicated women's strenuous efforts—through adulteration, if not adultery—to enter it and secure the lock behind them.

Indeed, Robert Audley finds his first indisputable proof that Lady Audley is Helen Talboys through a "dis-covery" that depends on her overly developed interest in fashion. Early in the story he detects feminine fraudulence in her handwriting. "It is the prettiest, most coquettish little hand I ever saw. . . . Yes, here it all is—the feathery, gold-shot, flaxen curls, the penciled eyebrows, the tiny straight nose, the winning, childish smile; all to be guessed in these few graceful up-strokes and down-strokes" (43). He later finds an album of fashion plates inscribed to George Talboys in the same hand and, equally incriminating, "a bright ring of golden hair, of that glittering hue which is so rarely seen except upon the head of a child—a sunny lock, which curled as naturally as the tendril of a vine" (103). The "ring of golden hair," like "the tendril of a vine," and the handwriting of the last inscription, with its feathery "up-strokes" and "down-strokes" are doubles—each a snare, encircling Lady Audley with a tightening noose of evidence.

Further proof of Lady Audley's past, also the result of Helen Talboys's being a "slave to fashion," is a hat box left behind by Lucy Graham at Mrs. Vincent's establishment, where she got her teaching experience. Robert Audley discovers that a label has been "pasted over another" (157) on which are her former alias and married name. Like the "yellow lock," which Robert places "in a sheet of letter paper" (103), he secures this label between "two blank leaves." Braddon also secures the hair and the hat box label between sheets of paper—her novel—showing that authorial plotting is "smarter" than fashion sense.

"Fair tresses man's imperial race ensnare," wrote Pope in *The Rape of the Lock* (2239). Braddon "plots" her story and makes use of Lady Audley's "fair tresses," first to "ensnare" "man's imperial race," but finally one lone woman. However, while Pope's verses are misogynistic—he blames the woman's "single hair" for "drawing" or ensnaring "us," that is, men—Braddon's meaning encompasses the complex social "plot" that damages "us," the inclusive pronoun representing both men and women. Lady Audley may have inadvertently supplied evidence that incriminates herself, but Braddon's finger points in all directions of the compass. The murder of the wife-beating Luke Marks, who dies in a fire set by My Lady, isn't as compelling to Braddon as the sins of commerce in beauty and beauty in commerce, endemic in her world—the promise in Rachel Leverson's advertisement, "Beautiful for Ever," or the capital necessary "In this age of Brass, Bank-notes, Bricks and mortar" for "exchanging female commodities" in the marriage "mart."

When Lady Audley confesses her full history to her husband, before disappearing into a place where she "will have ample leisure to repent the past" (252)—a *"maison de sante"* (253), or as she herself uneuphemistically calls it, a "madhouse" (254)—she explains that she has inherited her mother's own "disease transmitted to her from her mother, who had died mad" (230). Elaine Showalter argues that "Lady Audley's real secret is that she is *sane* and, moreover, representative" (*Literature* 167). She is like all other "women confined to the home and denied legitimate occupations" (168). Extending her argument, Showalter says elsewhere that the popularity of sensation fiction in the 1860s "came from its exploitation of repressed sexual fantasy and covert protest against the restrictions of domestic respectability" ("Desperate Remedies" 2).

In other words, thus the character, so the readers. Lady Audley, to extrapolate from Showalter's reading, is mad in the other sense of the word—angry. Although I agree that her pathology isn't a disease carried by the "XX" chromosomes, its environmental provocation probably antedates the married state.

Showalter and others focus on "domestic murder" by women in the novel and then the larger question of "middle-class women's fascination with violent crime" (*Literature* 169) as a displacement for their own domestic anger. But Braddon seems more interested in understanding a universal complaint, expressed through her Ladyship's former schoolgirl expectations. After all, most women (then and now) don't really fantasize about doing their husbands in.

Braddon addresses cultural culpability and its comprehensive damage to men as well as women[7] through young Helen Maldon's assumptions about her future. The premise that drove Charlotte Brontë, who denied a monolithic standard of excellence in women, to create Jane Eyre and Lucy Snowe is here, too: beauty should not solely determine a woman's success in life's race.

Lady Audley's tale, unlike plain Jane Eyre's, implicates beauty, but from a vastly different perspective. Never could Helen have said, as does Jane at the beginning of her story, that the world would have treated her better had she been a "handsome, romping child." On the contrary, Helen had too much admiration. "As I grew older," she explains, "I was told that I was pretty—beautiful—lovely—bewitching. . . . I began to think that in spite of the secret of my life I might be more successful in the world's great lottery than my companions. I had learnt that which in some indefinite manner or other every school-girl learns sooner or later—I learned that my ultimate fate in life depended upon my marriage, and I concluded that if I was indeed prettier than my school fellows, I ought to marry better than any one of them" (231). She calls herself "selfish and heartless" (231), but who could wonder that egotism is the leitmotif of an existence founded solely on the superiority of personal charm? In her culture (and no less in ours), beauty often equals wealth equals success. Naturally, self-absorption is a necessary virtue in the "husbanding" of physical capital.

Beauty is her stock in trade; her not-unreasonable hope had been that with it she would accumulate more capital in the form of a husband's wealth. While this aspiration was thwarted in her first bout, she is rewarded in her second match to the wealthy Sir Michael. Thus, she's overwhelmingly fixated on the loss of her beauty with age: "Shall I ever grow old, Phoebe? Will my hair ever drop off as the leaves are falling from those trees, and leave me wan and bare like them? What is to become of me when I grow old?" (71). And so her probable reliance on the products promoted by the likes of Mrs. Rachel Leverson, who promised what all advertisers of beauty products have since promised—"Beautiful for Ever" and (implied) the bigger reward, love.

But beauty cannot save Lady Audley. In hindsight, we should read all the "spectacular" attention that Braddon lavishes on her early in the novel—the narrator's obsessive gazing (and, therefore, necessarily, ours) at her beauty and blond ringlets—as an ironic gesture. For in the end, unsurprisingly, as with the perverted Pre-Raphaelite portraitist, a man, not her charms, controls her fate.

Although the French doctor calls Lady Audley "beautiful devil" (256), Braddon's novel takes no supernatural excursions, remaining well within the neighborhood of domestic fiction. Here is the aristocratic family in need of protection against the scheming of a beautiful but poor woman, not unlike the Bertrams in Austen's realist novel *Mansfield Park,* who must be spared contamination by the fortune hunter Mary Crawford. Indeed, Henry James, in a contemporary review of Braddon, argued that "*The Woman in White* had inaugurated a quite new species of the 'literature of horrors' by introducing 'those most mysterious of mysteries, the mysteries which are at our own doors.'" Collins's and Braddon's "thorough-going realism" was responsible for their fame (quoted in P. D. Edwards 10, 30). Lady Audley's incarceration in the "*maison de sante*" is completely realistic, the prerogative of patriarchal power. Braddon depicted the world as it is—not as she wanted it to be.

Instead of repenting, Lady Audley screams:

> "Has my beauty brought me to *this?* Have I plotted and schemed to shield myself and laid awake in the long deadly nights, trembling to think of my dangers for *this?* I had better have given up at once, since *this* was to be the end. . . ."
>
> She plucked at the feathery golden curls as if she would have torn them from her head. It had served her so little after all, that glorious glittering hair, that beautiful nimbus of yellow light that had contrasted so exquisitely with the melting azure of her eyes. She hated herself and her beauty. (256–57)

Braddon becomes overtly didactic, exposing the way women have relied on beauty, not least, golden locks. But although the novel devolves into a strident morality tale that jars after its defter ironies, the historical interest of Braddon's story transcends any local inadequacy. Its hammer blow to blond beauty was another dent in the Victorian icon.

Lady Audley's Secret had potent appeal for contemporary readers. The audacious blonde had arrived, and readers loved her. The beginning of an article
in the *Englishwoman's Domestic Magazine* of 1871 indirectly tells the story of
the novel's and the aggressive blonde's cultural impact. The review of W.
S. Gilbert's *A Sensation Novel in Three Volumes* (figure 7)—his operetta of
January 1871 (one of the last before his collaboration with Arthur Sullivan
began)—hints at the stir Braddon had created. "In the centre of what, viewed
from the front, looks like a handsomely-bound volume, is one of those sensational woodcuts familiar to the readers of the Railway and Parlour Libraries,
representing a lady with the bright yellow hair with which, since the date of
Lady Audley, it has been the fashion to endow the wicked heroine of the novel,
standing in a most tragic attitude, dagger in hand, over the figure of the good
young man of conventional notoriety" (10, no. 76 [1871]: 222). By 1871, Gilbert knew that the "lady with the bright yellow hair" had taken up residence in
the culture's mythic imagination. But through the magic of his special "topsy-
turveydom," he determined to transform her into an older, revered, and safe
type.

Summoning the Spirit of Romance to ask for help in beginning the second
volume of his novel, the "Author's" incantation is a catalogue of the clichéd
"business" of sensation novels:

> Lynch pin, fallen from a carriage,
> Forged certificate of marriage,
> Money wrongly won at whist,
> Finger of a bigamist,
> (10, no. 76 [1871]: 222)

et cetera, et cetera . . . The Spirit appears and informs the Author that the characters of his "penny-dreadful" "are accepted types, and you can't get on without them" (Gilbert 133).[8] He adds: "They are all creatures who, in their mortal
condition, have been guilty of positive or negative crime, and they are compelled to personate, under my direction, those stock characters of the sensation
novelist which are most opposed to their individual tastes" (Gilbert 133). The
anonymous reviewer writes: "First comes the weird beauty so often of late
described in the pages of romance, with glistening yellow hair and panther-
like step—the Lady Rockalda, personated in her usual artistic style by Mrs.
German Reed" (10, no. 76 [1871]: 222). The visual and verbal humor of this
"assumption" or role was that by the time she played Rockalda, Mrs. German

Fig. 7. Poster for *A Sensation Novel in Three Volumes* (1871). The "lovely fiend of fiction with the yellow, yellow hair" about to stab Herbert, the "good young man." (Courtesy of the Victoria & Albert Picture Library)

Reed was middle-aged: thus the joke of the exchange between Rockalda and the far-more-youthful Herbert, for whom Rockalda is inexplicably a nonpareil of beauty. In their mortal existence devoted lovers, they've been forced by the Author to play antagonists. The outrageously punning dialogue undercuts the tensions of real "sensation fiction."

ROCK. Well, I don't complain, only it was too bad to make a girl of twenty of me.

HERBERT. A girl of twenty! You're a girl of a thousand. (Gilbert 138)

However, the real joke about this "villainess," whose odious business in the Author's novel is to "lure [Herbert] to the limekiln, with [her] panther-like movement and the lurid fascination of [her] yellow hair" (Gilbert 142), is that her "mortal" sin for which she deserves her novelistic fate was to have been "the indulgent mother of five unruly boys, an easy-going peace-loving mother . . . [who] allowed them to have their own way" (Gilbert 135). Her song begins:

> Like a motherly old lady,
> With demure old-fashioned ways,
> In a cottage snug and shady,
> I should like to spend my days.
> Through the village I could toddle,
> To relieve the old and lame;
> I would be the very model
> Of a motherly old dame.
>
> But my tastes and inclinations
> Must be hidden out of sight;
> Oh! Forgive my lamentations,
> I am miserable quite.
> For propriety's affliction
> Guilty deeds I must prepare;
> I'm the lovely fiend of fiction,
> With the yellow, yellow hair.

Perversely, she's doomed to "wheedle, coax, and fascinate, / Then murder, rob, assassinate / Mankind at large" (Gilbert 135–36).

The sincerest form of flattery is probably not imitation but satire. Through the hyperbolical plot turns we expect in his operettas, Gilbert satirizes the already embellished twists of the voguish sensation novel, a genre in which women writers were having considerable success. But while the deconstruction of the silliness of this sort of novel provides the major amusement, the relationship between the stock character of the yellow-haired fiend and her "crime" of indulgent motherhood provided Gilbert with richer, if subtler, ground for social criticism. With his genius for taking the cultural temperature, he understood that "The virtuous young woman has so often been married to the good young man that the public must begin to tire of the incessant repetition" (145). Thus the "rage" for the sensation novel—which took the domestic novel to an extreme—with its exaggerations of ordinary behavior. Gilbert's own method was also to push the limits of probability to defang and declaw his subject. And so, in his spoof of sensation fiction, he arranges even more "sensational" details—the absurd proof, for example, that the Lady Rockalda is not the daughter of the Duke of Ben Nevis because her yellow "back hair" in the form of a "ducal coronet" comes off in his hand (150). "Merciful powers!" says Herbert, "then that mass of yellow hair is —." "A considerable portion of it, false!" admits Rockalda (150)—her honesty about her dishonesty a delightfully disarming rejection of the machinations of the femme fatale she's forced to play. Gilbert's spoofing of the sensation genre and criticism of gender (the devious, sexual woman) comically converge.

Her admission of the false yellow hair is Rockalda's renunciation of the role she's been forced to assume. The "fiend with the yellow, yellow hair" is far from her true identity. Everything about Rockalda, as she speaks in her "real" nature—the "peace-loving," indulgent mother—is a repudiation of the wired, murderous, and erotic woman with the "lurid yellow hair" of sensation fiction. Gilbert, through his topsy-turvy, paradoxical world, ingeniously turns the "vamp" (shortened from "vampire") on her head. By negating the sexual woman, he affirmed the cult of motherhood that flourished so successfully to contain women from the 1840s to the end of the century despite increasingly vocal feminism in the political and social arenas and, by the 1860s, criticism from "feminist" novelists, whose specialty was the energetic female protagonist of sensation fiction.

Rejecting the sexual woman was the "proper" business of Victorian culture. But, paradoxically, it was its proper business to enshrine motherhood (the Victorians were adepts at overlooking this biological contradiction). Jules Michelet, in his 1859 book *Woman,* wrote: "From the cradle woman is a mother, and

longs for maternity" (quoted in Dijkstra, *Idols* 18). The "insanely exaggerated
. . . middle-class desire for visible evidence of domestic harmony" (*Idols* 20),
adjunct to the cult of motherhood, required the woman to be not merely the
"angel in the house"—hard enough, but then angels are reputed to be sexless—but also the "resident nun in the bourgeois family" (*Idols* 11), harder
still, for renunciation, one might argue, is more difficult than desirelessness
for weak human nature. John Ruskin in *Sesame and the Lilies* (1865) asserted
that woman should "be enduringly, incorruptibly good; instinctively, infalli-
bly wise—wise not for self-development but for self-renunciation" (quoted in
Idols 13). While Rockalda's "snug" cottage is not quite the domestic convent,
Gilbert reminds the audience of the desirable norm and of the sensation novel's outrageous departures from it. Thus, by the end of the operetta, he restores
the blonde, now "the very model / Of a motherly old dame," but with much
less luxuriant/erotic hair than when she romped through sensation fiction, to
her "proper" domestic sphere.

Louisa May Alcott's copycat story—the comic sensation novella "Behind a
Mask, *or* A Woman's Power"—borrows some elements of Braddon's novel:
the blond governess, her remarkable talents, her hypergamous union, *and* her
use of adulterating makeup. However, with its more overtly feminist perspective, it swerves toward a far more positive conclusion. Following the advice of
Gilbert's Spirit of Romance, Alcott used an "accepted type" because she could
not "get on without [her]" if she wanted to attract a readership. However, she
could and did subvert it, even as she created it. Written shortly after *Lady Audley,* it was, like Braddon's story, the fruit of personal experience, but fruit more
bitter than Braddon's. She had gone out to hard service at nineteen, much as
her heroine does in "Behind a Mask." Yet except as grist for her imaginative
mill, her ordeal did not end as profitably as her character's.

Her heroine Jean Muir is "small, thin and colorless," "with yellow hair, gray
eyes, and sharply cut, irregular, but very expressive features" (6). Like Lady
Audley, Jean immediately impresses her new employers with her large range
of talents: her alarming ability to eavesdrop on conversations; her expertise in
making tea; and her admirable, but perhaps suspicious, theatrical ability. Miss
Muir is polymorphous, if not perverse.

A fainting fit provokes Gerald Coventry, the not-yet-enamored young master, to say cynically to his cousin: "Scene first, very well done" (7), to which
uncanny Jean Muir, on the other side of the room but having overheard him,

responds: "Thanks. The last scene shall be still better" (7). So Alcott, with her own "addiction to the theater" (xii) behind her plot details, introduces theatrical artifice, deepening the meaning of her title. By the end of the chapter, the theater (Muir's earlier career) is again invoked, transforming metaphor into reality. Appearance can deceive. Who better than actresses know makeup's tricks? In her room, after her successful "first-night" performance, the new governess has a quiet, and quite comic, moment. Muttering "I'll not fail again if there is power in a woman's wit and will!" she drinks an "ardent cordial," "which she seem[s] to enjoy extremely":

> "Come, the curtain is down, so I may be myself for a few hours, if actresses ever are themselves."
>
> Still sitting on the floor she unbound and removed the long abundant braids from her head, wiped the pink from her face, took out several pearly teeth, and slipping off her dress appeared herself indeed, a haggard, worn, and moody woman of thirty at least. . . . She had been lovely once, happy, innocent, and tender. . . . she *half uncovered her breast* to eye with a terrible glance the scar of a newly healed wound. (11–12; my emphasis)

Samuel Taylor Coleridge wrote of Geraldine in "Christabel":

> . . . she unbound
> The cincture from beneath her breast:
> Her silken robe and inner vest
> Dropped to her feet, and full in view,
> *Behold! her bosom and half her side—*
> A sight to dream of, not to tell!
> And she is to sleep by Christabel.
> ("Christabel" 481; my emphasis)

Geraldine, too, drinks a "cordial wine" ("Christabel" 480). And like Geraldine, Jean Muir is "a most uncanny little specimen" (9), a "Scotch witch" (28). As the literal "charmer" or "fair-haired enchantress" (40) of the Coventry family, she's like her supernatural forerunner, who entrances Christabel and her father, Sir Leoline. However, Alcott writes in the realist tradition, later revealing that Jean's "mysterious" wound was self-inflicted for theatrical effect.

Even more significant is the way this scene replicates Alcott's title. "Behind a Mask, *or A Woman's Power*" literally places the word "Power" "behind," or after, "a Mask." Now, in a virtual performance of the word order, Alcott takes off Jean Muir's mask to reveal the power behind it: her superior intelligence and resolve. She needn't, as Braddon does, denigrate beauty as a woman's enemy. Rather, she shows that a woman's friends are her "wit and will." Muir isn't beautiful, yet she's "more interesting than many a blithe and blooming girl" (6) and more compelling. To be "smart," Alcott implies, is alluring and sexy.

While Jean's hairpiece is as yellow as her own skimpy hair, its counterfeit luxuriance detracts from the picture of blond innocence. But Alcott dismisses blondness and delicacy as feminine requisites, allowing us to see what we can only guess at in Lady Audley's case. Muir's secretive drinking of the strong cordial—like Lady Audley's probable secret smoking of cigars (79), an "unladylike" appetite—suggests a masculine (read powerful and courageous) affinity. While Braddon implies that Lady Audley is familiar with hair dye, the reader knows that Jean Muir is neither as much of a blonde nor as demure as she pretends to be. But we don't care; in fact, we rejoice in Muir's victory over pretentious, class-bound patriarchal propriety.

The "dark" side of Jean's powerful nature is revealed in the theatricals at the home of Sir John Coventry, whose grand estate is next door to that of the cadet branch of the family. In a scene that raises the ghost of Becky's triumph as Clytemnestra in the entertainment at Gaunt House, as well as suggesting the "martial" nature of the campaign that little Muir wages, Alcott reveres the chameleonlike mutability of the gifted impersonator of Judith, about to strike the drunken Holofernes. The woman was

robed with barbaric splendor. . . . fillets of gold bound her hair, and jewels shone on her neck and arms. . . .

"Who is it?" whispered Lucia, for the face was new to her.

"Jean Muir," answered Coventry, with an absorbed look.

"Impossible! She is small and fair," began Lucia. . . .

Impossible as it seemed, he was nevertheless right; for Jean Muir it was. She had darkened her skin, painted her eyebrows, disposed some wild locks over her fair hair, and thrown such intensity of expression into her eyes that they darkened and dilated till they were as fierce as any southern eyes. . . . Hatred . . . was written on her sternly beautiful face, courage glowed in her glance, power spoke in the nervous grip . . . and the indomitable will of the woman was expressed. . . .

. . . "Good night to Holofernes; his fate is certain," added another. (50–51)

Visibly swarthy skin and dark hair confirm the subjective "orientalist" linking of violence and "dark" "southern eyes." However, the apparent connection of racial markers, power, violence, and morality isn't negative as in *Ivanhoe* or in Mrs. Symonds's story "Blanche D'Aubigné," in which the unsavory suitor "Mr. Norman" of "Moor" Park is denigrated through these obvious, racialized puns. Moreover, Alcott emphasizes the power of a woman who saved her people. The Roman Catholic Old Testament Book of Judith treats this woman as the heroine who saved the Jewish city of Bethulia from sacking by the Assyrian general Holofernes. Meaning to seduce her, he invited her to his tent where his drunkenness gave her the upper hand; she decapitated him with his own scimitar. Male concupiscence and gluttony play no small part in the story of his beheading by a heroic woman, the indirect cause of the now-leaderless Assyrian army's rout. Jean Muir, Alcott implies, is also mistress of "martial arts."

Unlike Braddon, Alcott completely forgives Muir her artfulness, her makeup, and her making up of identities. Proof of her novelistic charity is the outcome she provides for her character's desperate venture. Unlike Lady Audley, Jean Muir doesn't pay a price for her deceptions. Rather, she gains the largest prizes: Sir John Coventry and his magnificent estate.

Thus, all ends happily for Jean, who accepts the Coventrys' "contempt as her just punishment" (104). And it is "*just*" (her only) punishment. Poverty can disfigure, both physically and morally, but good fortune restores a "once honest nature." There is no bar to Jean's acceptance, however grudging, into the bosom of the Coventry family as her own self-inflicted scar on that portion of her anatomy fades.

Alcott asks readers to share her point of view by presenting Jean Muir as the smartest, most accomplished character in "Behind a Mask." Although she hid intimations of feminist revolt behind the scrim of a completely domestic mise-en-scène (but for reasons unlike Gilbert's comic endorsement of tractable motherhood), Alcott's belief in a woman's power and intelligence was far in advance of her male contemporaries'. Securing her place within the domestic order had been Jean's undeviating goal from the moment she first looked (with a buyer's critical eye) at the Coventry home and said to herself: "'Not bad,' . . . as she passed into the adjoining park, 'but the other may be better, and I will have the best'" (13). Her acquisitive spirit merely holds a mirror up to the materialism of mid- to late nineteenth-century American culture.

However, Jean Muir's energies and inclinations range beyond a mansion "snug and shady" and create chaos as she stirs the ardor of every male she meets. She's even the proximate cause of a fraternal knife fight. Her Medusan powers, as she moves in for the romantic kill, are apparent from her choice of a sexier coiffure: "Of late . . . [t]he close braids were gone, and the loose curls dropped here and there from the heavy coil wound round her well-shaped head" (71). The blonde, with wit, will, *and* sexual power is totemic—no longer an individual case. Jean stands for *all* women whose virtue (both in its marketplace meaning and classical sense of "strength") has been denied or suppressed by patriarchal culture.

"Behind a Mask" represents a sea change: the blonde is not only *not* punished for manipulating others, but she also wins *by virtue* of her intelligence and sexual allure. No male writers of the period—not even Thackeray—created such plots. Alcott, with verve and humor, proves that "virtue" *gets* its own reward.

The genre other than humorous satire successfully deployed to contain women's energies was the horror story. As suffragists and other reformers became increasingly visible and forceful, Bram Stoker's *Dracula* arrived to dampen the social, political, and sexual ardor of the "New Woman," who had lately been leaving her father's bed and board to seek employment in business. Stoker, preferring horror to comedy, reminded women of the dire consequences of exchanging compliant domesticity and maternity for aggressive sexuality. Blond Lucy Westernra's story is no joke.

Dracula of 1897 is an odd mixture of the medieval folktale, with its archetypal ogre, and a modern thriller relying on the new technologies of the developing service industry (in which the New Woman might be employed)—shorthand (49), typewriters (228), "kodak" cameras (32), and phonographs (269)—to aid in the solution of the mystery and destruction of the fiendish Count. However, as Jonathan Harker says: "[Shorthand] is nineteenth century up-to-date with a vengeance. And yet, unless my senses deceive me, the old centuries had, and have, powers of their own which mere 'modernity' cannot kill" (49–50). Indeed, the enduring appeal of *Dracula* proves that the power of myth cannot easily be killed by modernity. Fears of all sorts but especially ancient fears of women dominate this tale of horror. Here are Stoker's worst nightmares about the fair sex.

"Nightmares" and the old-fashioned locution "fair sex" have special resonance in this novel. Count Dracula, in his many reduxes, obviously continues to fascinate, but so do his compelling feminine counterparts, the "Dracula brides"—the three "nosferatu" (261), or "Un-Dead" (246), who tenant Dracula's castle—and Lucy Westernra, the most horrific embodiment of Dracula's female victim-accomplices. Stoker grants prominence in his hierarchy of evil to blond or "fair" women: the most aggressive and forward of the brides and Lucy. While these characters undermine the figure of the submissive blonde of fairy and folktale, they reprise her role in even more ancient myth.

Jonathan Harker, visiting in the Count's castle, is warned by Dracula to sleep in no room but the one he's been assigned. The castle "is old, and has many memories, and there are bad dreams for those who sleep unwisely" (46). However, in obedience to the temptation motif of myth and folktale, Harker wanders into another room, where, naturally, he falls asleep and has a nightmarish experience. Three "ladies" approach him: two brunettes; the other a truly "ravishing" blonde. She "was fair . . . with great wavy masses of golden hair and eyes like pale sapphires. I seemed somehow to know her face, and to know it in connection with some dreamy fear. . . . All three had brilliant white teeth that shone like pearls against the ruby of their voluptuous lips. There was something about them that made me uneasy, some longing and at the same time some deadly fear. I felt in my heart a wicked, burning desire that they would kiss me with those red lips" (51). Of the three, the blond vampire is the most aggressive, shaking "her head coquettishly" while the dark women urge her on. "One said:—'Go on! You are first, and we shall follow; yours is the right to begin'" (51–52). Harker's ambivalence, especially his reaction to the blonde— "some longing and at the same time some deadly fear" (51)—the "agony of delightful anticipation" (52) as she approaches, is Stoker's evocation of the White Goddess—the "lovely, slender woman with a hooked nose,' deathly pale face, lips red as rowan-berries, startlingly blue eyes and long fair hair" (Graves 24). She is the feminine "ancient power of fright and lust" (Graves 24) like Coleridge's sexually aggressive "Life-in-Death." "The reason why . . . the skin crawls and a shiver runs down the spine when one writes or reads a true poem is that a true poem is necessarily an invocation of the White Goddess, or Muse, the Mother of All Living" (Graves 24). Just so with Harker, who describes the women's laughter as "the intolerable, tingling sweetness of water glasses" (51) and the breath of the blonde as "sweet . . . in one sense, honey-sweet, and [it] sent the same tingling through the nerves as her voice, but with a bitter underlying the sweet, a bitter offensiveness, as one smells in blood" (52). The blonde and her dark companions are the erotic aspect of the "Threefold" goddess, "the female spider or queen-bee whose embrace is death," and who, along with the Gods of the Waning and Waxing year "are so much a part of our racial inheritance[10] that they not only assert themselves in poetry but recur on occasions of emotional stress in the form of dreams, paranoiac visions and delusions" (Graves 24).

The aggressive blonde is, of course, happy to oblige Harker by "kissing" him—aka sucking his blood. He anatomizes the sexual thrill of the encounter (made more exciting through the insinuated threat): "There was a deliberate voluptuousness which was both thrilling and repulsive . . . as she arched her neck she actually licked her lips like an animal. . . . Then the skin of my throat began to tingle as one's flesh does when the hand that is to tickle it approaches nearer. . . . I closed my eyes in a languorous ecstasy and waited—waited with beating heart" (52). Harker descends into the darkness of a sexual initiation perilous to life.

But as his oedipal death wish is about to be fulfilled, the Count, the other persona in the "family romance" (here, the perverted father figure) appears, ending the dream: "I was conscious of the presence of the Count. . . . I saw his strong hand grasp the slender neck of the fair woman and with giant's power draw it back, the blue eyes transformed with fury, the white teeth champing with rage, and the fair cheeks blazing with passion" (52).

To return from the Freudian to the Jungian mythic model for the Count, Graves points out that "The weird, or rival, often appears in the nightmare as the tall, lean, dark-faced bed-side spectre, or Prince of the Air, who tries to drag the dreamer out through the window, so that he looks back and sees his body still lying rigid in bed, but he takes countless other malevolent or diabolic serpent-like forms" (Graves 24), as indeed does the Count; Harker sees him emerge from a castle window, headfirst, slithering down "as a lizard moves along a wall" (48). The Count insists that he must wake Harker up—that is, "drag" the dreamer out through the window. But although Dracula's anger is impressive, the women's behavior is more horrifying; a bag containing their night's meal, "a half-smothered child" (53), attracts their attention.

The blond vampire is the hyperbolic case of all women—"You are first, and we shall follow," says the dark-haired vampire. She's the threatening variant of Gilbert's "lovely fiend of fiction with the yellow, yellow hair." If Rockalda wishes to be the "motherly old lady," this blonde is sexualized to the exclusion of the maternal. Child cannibalism is the antithesis of maternal self-sacrifice, the latter prompted, ordinarily, by the "selfish" gene to ensure its continuation through the next generation.

Destroying the child by sucking its blood is also the monstrous inversion of childbirth, of which the "Un-Dead" voluptuaries are incapable. Lucy Westernra, the last blond Lucy of the nineteenth century, is another such invert, kept from maternity through her untimely victimization by Dracula but also, apparently, by her flirtatious sexuality. Harker's report, that he "seemed somehow to know [the blond vampire's] face," is, as Leonard Wolf, the editor of *The Essential Dracula*, says, "a major mystery in the book. Whose face is it? There is the smallest hint that this blond beauty may have something in common with Lucy, whom the reader will meet later. If so, then the plot is very thick, indeed" (51). But Harker's knowledge of the female vampire's face, his "dreamy fear" of it, seems rather a tribute to the "racial memory" of the White Goddess because he has never seen Lucy. The plot is "very thick, indeed," but, as Graves suggests, it's the plot of a cultural myth, not merely of one novel: the male's demonization of the female.

While "Lucy" is a fin-de-siècle reminder of the many heavenly blondes of nineteenth-century poetry and fiction, her strange surname, "Westernra," invoking "Ra," the Egyptian sun god,[11] also points to her golden and racially favored beauty. However, in *Dracula* her names function ironically to suggest a promise of beauty and golden fecundity, reversed or denied. Like many "canonized" blondes before her, the young girl represents quintessential femininity—so ideal that she receives proposals of marriage in one day from three very different but similarly smitten eligible bachelors: Arthur Holmwood; John Seward; Quincey P. Morris. Accompanied by Dr. Van Helsing, Dr. Seward's former medical instructor and intellectual father, they form a sort of glorified boys' club, a contemporary *posse comitatus*, fighting—not soon enough to save Lucy—to rid the world of the vampire.

Much has been made of Lucy's flirtatiousness and avid polygynous proclivity (as if such behavior merited her fatal anemia), implied in her rhetorical question to her friend Mina: "Why can't they let a girl marry three men, or as many as want her, and save all this trouble?" (78). Although Quincey Morris tells her that she's "an honest-hearted girl" and "clean grit, right through to the very depths of [her] soul," (78) Stoker is more conflicted about Lucy and women, in general, than the ventriloquized voice of the American suggests. He believes in her hidden, dark side, which he implies through her semivoluntary initiation into sexuality and her "Un-Dead" behavior—the dramatically monstrous inversion of motherhood.

Breaking news, quite literally, of Lucy's depravity is the report in the *West-*

minster Gazette of children "straying from home" and claiming to have been with a "bloofer [beautiful] lady." All the children who haven't returned home at night "have been slightly torn or wounded in the throat" (220–22).

Stoker embellishes the news with details of the children's game of impersonating the "bloofer lady," "luring each other away by wiles" (221). "Some of our caricaturists might . . . take a lesson in the irony of the grotesque by comparing the reality and the picture" (221). This enigmatic "diversion" (in both senses) from the implied horror of the story plays on the incongruity of childish innocence and adult evil, central to the children's role-playing and embodied in the "Un-dead" Lucy herself. We are meant to confront the paradox: how could such apparent blond beauty—"a dear, giggling English rose" (221)—be an incarnation of vampirism? Indeed, this was the question that, less metaphorically, many of Stoker's male contemporaries asked about women who were active socially and politically. From their perspective, the "New Woman" was "a lesson in the irony of the grotesque." Stoker's novel was an unsubtle reminder of the damage if women were "lured" by suffragists and other reformers from their proper domestic sphere.

Lucy's vampirism becomes increasingly grotesque. After she dies, Van Helsing leads the group of brave adventurers to her tomb to prove that she is a vampire. Stoker deploys images miming aspects of sexual congress that imply male violence against the female. Van Helsing examines the coffin plates, "holding his candle" made from spermaceti extracted from sperm whales so "that the sperm drop[s] in white patches which congeal" (242) as they touch the metal of the coffin. Opening the lid is "as much an affront to the dead as it would have been to have stripped off her clothing in her sleep whilst living" (242). The act, recommended by Van Helsing as the only way to "free" Lucy from the horror of her unrestful, Un-dead state—driving a stake into her heart, which Arthur "str[ikes] with all his might" (262)—symbolically completes the brutal penetration anticipated in the language of the earlier visit to her mausoleum.

But violence is justifiable. Another night, Lucy—or, at least, the distorted Un-Dead Lucy—is seen by the men as she carries off an unfortunate child for her midnight banquet of blood. Differences in her appearance from the live woman's are striking—especially her hair color: "We saw a white figure advance—a dim white figure, which held something dark at its breast. The figure stopped, and at the moment a ray of moonlight fell between the masses of driving clouds and showed in startling prominence a dark-haired woman, dressed in the cerements of the grave" (256). Leonard Wolf cites Charles Berg and Phyllis A. Roth on the question of Lucy's hair color.[12] No readers believe that Stoker simply made a mistake, forgetting he'd already suggested that Lucy's hair, with its "sunny ripples," is blond. Berg, who points out the relationship in European folklore of blond hair and "child-like purity" and black hair with "pure animal sexuality," argues that Lucy's blond hair might be "an example of *coincidentia oppositorum,* a symbol which contains within it its opposite," as would be true of "the pale blond vampire bride with her 'great wavy masses of golden hair'" (256). Roth similarly suggests that "the conventional fair/dark split, symbolic of respective moral casts," reveals Stoker's unconscious "ambivalence aroused by the sexualized female." However, neither reading accounts for the many dark-haired heroines of mainstream domestic novels, nor how Mina, the heroine of *Dracula,* is then also dark-haired. Stoker, the antifeminist, has apparently reverted, briefly and uniquely, in the matter of Un-Dead Lucy's hair, to the Romantic prototypes of the fair and dark woman. *All* women are collectively embodied by the blond and dark "nosferatu." Now blond Lucy, whose "dark side" has been outed, is herself all women—her new corporeal darkness paralleling the allegory of her aggressive, sexualized behavior.

The Un-Dead figure holds "something dark at its breast." Ordinarily the preserver of the infant's life, the breast ironically becomes the site of its destruction. A racialized narrative underwrites the vampiric act as the "something dark" is discovered to be "a fair-haired child" (256). Lucy's behavior is the antithesis of the maternal instinct; the victim is the doubly precious Saxon child. The darkly sexual Un-Dead woman is like the "dark" marauders of the Indian Mutiny who brought death to "Babes Asleep on sleeping mothers' breasts!" (*English Woman's Journal* 1, no. 3 [1858]: 163). A woman who refuses the role of "motherly old dame," by Stoker's logic, must be capable of social and sexual aggression, just as a girl who had wanted to marry three men challenges patriarchal control and order.

The men's encounter with the blond/dark Un-Dead is a blatant excavation of the sexually rapacious woman. Lucy's now-darkened hair is not a "deceitful disguise." Women, from out of the depths of their undomesticated "unconscious," simply show their "true colors." Yet this picture, much like the Pre-Raphaelite paintings of massively powerful women, is more revealing of the male psyche than of the dark "roots" of untrustworthy feminine sexuality. The Un-Dead, blocked from reentering her tomb, where she would have taken her midnight meal, is an interesting illustration of the primitive belief that the erotic woman must be a distortion of a sunny and transparent femininity. Lucy's physical disfigurement betrays her moral deformation.

Like the Dracula brides, the Un-Dead Lucy "seem[s] like a nightmare" (260). The "diabolically sweet" (257) tones of her voice remind Dr. Seward of the "tingling of glass" (257) as the Un-Dead brides' laughter reminded Harker of "the intolerable, tingling sweetness of water glasses" (51). The nightmare is Lucy's sexual arousal-cum-sadism. As the men "recognize . . . the features of Lucy Westernra" (256), they are horrified by the change: "The sweetness was turned to adamantine, heartless cruelty, and the purity to voluptuous wantonness" (256). "Voluptuous" is repeated in subsequent descriptions: "She still advanced . . . with a languorous, voluptuous grace" (257); "the pointed teeth, the bloodstained voluptuous mouth—which it made one shudder to see—the whole carnal and unspiritual appearance, seemed like a devilish mockery of Lucy's sweet purity" (260).

Her voluptuous mouth might as well be painted with lip rouge, confirming the relationship of sexuality, adultery, and cosmetics. The mouth is, of course, particularly prominent in *Dracula* as the organ that fatally damages the vampire's victims. Stoker's fullest description of the Un-Dead draws ineluctable attention to the hair, mouth, and eyes, as does the Pre-Raphaelite portrait of Lady Audley with her "pretty pouting mouth," made "hard and almost wicked" (47); "the brows were wrinkled as though the folds of the flesh were the coils of Medusa's snakes, and the lovely, blood-stained mouth grew to an open square, as in the passion masks of the Greeks and Japanese. If ever a face meant death—if looks could kill—we saw it at that moment" (258). Stoker's "oral fixation" transforms the mouth, and, thus, the face, into a theatrical "passion mask"—the metaphor actively deployed in Alcott's novella but to very different effect. Here, with the passion mask fronting for her features, Lucy is all but unrecognizable, as is her voluptuous, sexualized behavior.

But Stoker's most potent and classical analogue for Lucy is Medusa, whose "sunburst hair" (258) was turned into snakes by Athena because the beautiful young woman welcomed Poseidon's sexual embrace in the middle of her temple (258). He imagines serious consequences for the woman who has forgotten her procreative purpose and enjoys sex for its own sake. By comparison, Mina Murray Harker, like Lucy, also a victim of Dracula's bloodthirstiness, successfully withstands the vampiric disease. Her motherhood by book's end is less a reward for heroism than proof that she has always been different from Lucy. Before her marriage to Harker, she had been "an assistant schoolmistress" (71) yet much preferred to be with her friend Lucy "by the sea, where we can talk together freely and build our castles in the air" (71)—or, at least, a "cottage snug and shady." She scorns the "New Woman," whom both Lucy and she "should have shocked . . . with our appetites" (119). Mina means to suggest an unhealthy neurasthenic—too slender and, thus, unfeminine (for which, read unmaternal)—who also has a "perverted" interest in sex and a desire to topple the "social order." She adds: "Some of the 'New Women' writers will some day start an idea that men and women should be allowed to see each other asleep before proposing or accepting. But I suppose the New Woman won't condescend in future to accept; she will do the proposing herself. And a nice job she will make of it, too!" (120). Mina's "sweetness and loving care" (445), "bravery" and "gallantness" (445) are an embodiment of the self-sacrifice and stoicism of the idealized Victorian materfamilias.

Van Helsing, recounting his hunt for the blond nosferatu's "high great tomb," chooses the maternal, over the erotic, woman, but not before expressing his longing and loss. That "soul-wail of my dear Madam Mina," which prompts him to resume his "wild work" (437) of destroying the vampires, saves him from the "other fair sister," "so fair to look on, so radiantly beautiful, so exquisitely voluptuous, that the very instinct of man in me . . . made my head whirl with new emotion" (437).

The superior position of the blond "nosferatu"—the doppelgänger of the social prerogatives, but also the attractions, of the fair woman—is thus reprised as a final warning. Van Helsing despairs: "Man is weak" (436). He must urgently fight instinct and inclination to escape the clutches (and fangs) of the unnatural, sexual woman. And he was more right than he knew; the seductive vamp was far from finished. She would come to life again just a few years later in early cinema, although not as a blonde until the late 1920s.

While Stoker returned to the figure of the immobile and passive blonde with Lilla in the very poorly plotted *The Lair of the White Worm* (1911), his most blatant antifeminist contribution to the debate about women and their proper domestic role was made through the blondes of *Dracula*. Death and sexuality are intimately linked: one is the inescapable punishment for the other. The blonde (and all others) should not roam at night and ought also to stay home in daytime, attending to domestic duties. These safely check her dark, sexual subconscious. Without maternal aptitude and occupation, woman is a danger—to others *and* to herself. Better, like Mina, to be a mother, repress other instincts, choose life over death.

But Stoker was ignored by women on both sides of the Atlantic, who were mobilizing to gain the vote. In America, Susan B. Anthony and Elizabeth Cady Stanton had been organizing the suffrage movement from as early as 1848, when, at the Seneca Falls Convention, Stanton offered a resolution to the body that demanded women be given the vote. While their English sisters had gotten a later start, in 1897—the year in which *Dracula* was published—seventeen separate groups joined to form the National Union of Women's Suffrage Societies (NUWSS). In 1900, with the death of Lydia Becker, its first president, the organization elected Millicent Fawcett, for whom a still-thriving women's history archive was later named (recently renamed the Women's Research Library). In 1903, the WSPU—the Women's Social and Political Union—was founded by Emmeline Pankhurst. These and other groups of women took to the streets, marching, selling newspapers—*Votes for Women*, *The Suffragette*—and "making a spectacle of themselves" in ways to which Mina Harker would have objected. Their most spectacular demonstration, the Women's Coronation Procession, in which 40,000 marched, was held in June 1911,[13] the year of publication of *The Lair of the White Worm*.

Of course, Stoker's wasn't the only representation of femininity. "Some of the 'New Women' writers" (120) predictably saw their own experience in other terms. They knew that domesticity and maternity could not be the pattern for all women's lives; other drives—the political, the creative—must be expressed. And the maternal and sexual need not be incompatible.

American writers, no less than their British sister-novelists, were strong advocates of a woman's right to liberty and happiness. How she fulfilled her aspirations should be her decision. Yet while real freedom to choose was still a distant dream, their imaginings were themselves important agents in creating for their readers a feminine manifest destiny. Kate Chopin's Calixta was among the pioneers.

Although best known for *The Awakening*, Chopin's sad tale of a woman's "liberation-by-drowning," two of her short stories returned the blonde to the sun's healthy light, showing that sex and motherhood needn't be antithetical. Calixta, a blond Acadian, refreshingly swims against the current and gains the shore in "At the 'Cadian Ball," published in *Bayou Folk* in 1894, and "The Storm," written in 1898, the year before *The Awakening*.

Alfred Lord Tennyson wrote in "A Dream of Fair Women" of "A daughter of the gods . . . most divinely fair" (*Poems* 445). Calixta, a variant of Kallisto, from the Greek, meaning "fair-crowned" (Eilberg-Schwartz and Doniger

107), is also "divinely fair" but otherwise unlike Helen, who "brought calamity" to both the Achaeans and Trojans. There's no catastrophe in either "At the 'Cadian Ball" or "The Storm." Quite the opposite: romance, sex, and domesticity combine to produce the greatest good for the greatest number; a "felicific calculus"[14] marvelously regulates events.

Chopin anatomizes Calixta's beauty and provenance.

> Calixta's slender foot had never touched Cuban soil; but her mother's had, and the Spanish was in her blood all the same. . . .
>
> Her eyes,—Bobinôt thought of her eyes . . . the bluest, the drowsiest, most tantalizing that ever looked into a man's; he thought of her flaxen hair that kinked worse than a mulatto's close to her head. . . .
>
> There had even been a breath of scandal whispered about her a year ago, when she went to Assumption. . . . "C'est Espagnol, ça," most of them said with lenient shoulder-shrugs. "Bon chien tient de race," the old men mumbled over their pipes. (179)

Although her eyes are the bluest and her hair flaxen, she's first an animal. She may never have seen Cuba, but her "dark" Latin blood outs in her drowsy sensuality and the kink of her hair.

"Blood," in the sense of lineage, has been held responsible, whether metaphorically or physically, for the mysterious transmission of sexual and social infection as far back as Leo Africanus's *Geographical Historie of Africa*. From late eighteenth-century American women's Indian captivity narratives, to Fenimore Cooper's portrait of the mixed-blooded heroine Cora in *The Last of the Mohicans*, to the mid-nineteenth-century middlebrow literature of English women's magazines, all with their conscious or unconscious racist and chauvinist agendas, the demonstration of the racial/moral superiority of whites and the home country is a priority. But Chopin's story is unlike those in the *Englishwoman's Domestic Magazine* or Stoker's *Dracula*.

Calixta is different from maternal Adèle Ratignolle in *The Awakening*, who, with her procreative zeal, resists any sexual interest she might provoke. But she's also unlike provocative Becky Sharp, known for her "famous frontal development" (190), who self-consciously plays her attractions for social advantage. The fifty years since *Vanity Fair* had altered what a writer was willing, even eager, to say about sex. Bram Stoker's dangerous blond eroticism doesn't exist in Chopin's stories, told from an American feminist perspective. Calixta is an entirely new species—not merely an incitement to male desire, but a willing confederate, responding in kind and with equal pleasure—and celebrated by the narrator.

In "At the 'Cadian Ball," the wealthy young planter Alcée Laballière makes love to Calixta. He touches her hand, her hair, until "Calixta's senses were reeling; and they well-nigh left her when she felt Alcée's lips brush her ear like the touch of a rose" (186). Chopin's report of the erotic moment from Calixta's perspective revolutionarily argues for the existence of innocent, unencumbered feminine sexuality—a daring position for a woman at the close of the nineteenth century. This one sentence—naturalizing desire—is of tremendous historical importance. Satisfaction isn't the guilty pleasure of objectifying pornography. Sex is what it is, and that is much!

However, the moment is short-lived, for just as the sexual current peaks, Alcée's servant interrupts the idyll. Despite her sensuality, Calixta is a practical woman, soon agreeing to marry the Acadian farmer Bobinôt, the best offer she may get.

And Alcée will marry the ice-queen Clarisse, his mother's ward. His brief interlude with Calixta is only a memory: "Calixta was like a myth, now. The one, only, great reality in the world was Clarisse standing before him, telling him that she loved him" (188). Thus, the fates of two couples are sealed and the story is over. "At the 'Cadian Ball" registers the social truth that most marriages are class-bound affairs. But sex slips the yoke of restraint as "The Storm," the companion story, shows.

Myths persist in a culture because of their vitality in individual imaginations. In the events of "The Storm," Calixta is no longer "*like* a myth" but one well-remembered. Simile, for Alcée, has been replaced by metaphor that retreats before bodily memory. In this short but powerful story, Chopin, trying something radically new, explores sexual passion as a necessity of being. Couples may be oddly mismatched erotically (Calixta and Bobinôt; Alcée and Clarisse), but, says Chopin, no matter. Life sometimes offers its sweet if fleeting accommodations.

The blonde in this story temporarily makes a choice between the domestic and erotic but isn't fundamentally split. Chopin allows Calixta to be both, doing violence, through a fusion of the two, to a literary and cultural tradition of alienation—especially prominent in the Victorian era. But we know their compatibility in life is more the rule than the exception.

A storm conveniently keeps Bobinôt and the child Bibi from home when

Alcée, riding by, asks Calixta for shelter. She's still the same sensual woman Chopin described in "At the 'Cadian Ball": "She was a little fuller of figure than five years before when she married; but she had lost nothing of her vivacity. Her blue eyes still retained their melting quality; and her yellow hair, dishevelled by the wind and rain, kinked more stubbornly than ever about her ears and temples" (282). Her disordered hair may signal potential sexual excitement but isn't a sign of moral disarray. And the events that follow are as natural and unstoppable as the storm. Calixta's "reeling" senses at the 'Cadian ball are now fully gratified in a sexual coupling. Memory of the flesh is a powerful imperative.

In 1847, the rending of a chestnut tree by lightning figured as the double of the sexually tense, unresolved relationship of Jane and Rochester. "And what ailed the chestnut tree? It writhed and groaned; while wind roared in the laurel walk, and came sweeping over us" (284). The strike that destroys half of the tree symbolically foreshadows the rift and separation of the lovers, following Rochester's almost successful bigamy.

The meteorological event in "The Storm," though an important plot element, doesn't stand in for sexual currents. The lightning, making Calixta fear for her child—"If only I knew w'ere Bibi was!" (283)—is merely the proximate cause of Alcée's catching her by the shoulders. Her nearness naturally awakens "all the old-time infatuation and desire for her flesh" (283) and her lips, "red and moist as pomegranate seed" (283). The lushness of this image is a sensuous invitation to the reader's imagination as, in the narrative, the originals are meant as an enticement to the man.

But the storm that occasioned desire is completely forgotten in the throes of their passionate embrace. Here Chopin's transcription of female sexuality is even bolder than in "At the 'Cadian Ball." "She was a revelation in that dim, mysterious chamber; as white as the couch she lay upon. Her firm, elastic flesh that was knowing for the first time its birthright, was like a creamy lily that the sun invites to contribute its breath and perfume to the undying life of the world" (284). Chopin's choice of the participial "knowing," which deliberately cancels its biblical-metaphorical meaning of male sexual conquest (the patriarch always "knows" the woman), restores the literal connotations of recognition and consciousness—*feminine* consciousness. The woman has an inalienable (birth)right to enjoy "the botany of desire,"[15] the "breath and perfume," the by-products of *her* part in the eternal dance of generation. If a "revelation" to the male, she is first one to herself. Their sex prefigures Lawrencian reciprocity: "They seemed to swoon together at the very borderland of life's mystery" (284).

Desire, however, is ephemeral. Sated passion soon gives way to rationality. Alcée rides off, as "the sun [is] turning the glistening green world into a palace of gems" (285): "He turned and smiled at her with a beaming face; and she lifted her pretty chin in the air and laughed aloud" (285).

But there's also laughter when Bobinôt and Bibi return. Calixta, back in domestic mode, is busily preparing dinner. Her joy is real: "'Oh, Bobinôt! You back! My! But I was uneasy. W'ere you been during the rain? An' Bibi? He ain't wet? He ain't hurt?' She had clasped Bibi and was kissing him effusively" (285). We know just how "uneasy" she's been but also that anxiety literally threw her into the arms of her lover. Maternal care and eros may be serial, but Calixta isn't either/or.

"*J'vous réponds,* we'll have a feas' to-night! umph-umph!" (285), she says, thanking Bobinôt for his present of shrimp. Certainly, her "response" is different from when "Her mouth was a fountain of delight" (284), yet "when the three seated themselves at table they laughed much and so loud that anyone might have heard them as far away as Laballière's" (286). The domestic trinity, in satisfying communion, enjoys a literal meal instead of a "feast" of erotic love. A "daughter of the gods," Calixta is, herself, the goddess of all kinds of plentitude.

"So the storm passed and every one was happy" (286). Chopin's final sentence-paragraph revises traditional fairy-tale endings. Perhaps a momentary respite from the banalities of the quotidian is the most we may hope for. Titian's painting of Diana pointing an accusing finger at her nymph Callisto, who has broken her vow of chastity by sleeping with Zeus, is a very different reading from this celebration of Calixta's sexuality.

In fact, the moral of the tale might be "Desire Rewarded." While Chopin published "The Storm" only "into her desk," not risking the public outrage it most surely would have provoked, her startling reversal of the outcome for the "fallen woman"—not fallen at all but elevated into joy and fulfillment—was a promise that the world would someday be different.

By painting the character of Calixta, an exceptional yet potentially representative blonde, Chopin added something new to the image of the erotic woman that would resurface in popular culture by the late 1920s—after the hiatus of the first years of the film industry. In "At the 'Cadian Ball," Calixta's friend Fronie cattily reminds her of her scandalous behavior the year before. "Calixta swore roundly in fine 'Cadian French and with true Spanish wit, and slapped Fronie's face" (179). The men at the ball praise her: "Such animation! and abandon! such flashes of wit!" (184). Thus, Chopin also endowed her sensuous woman with motion, physical pluck, and "lip"—qualities, blended with eroticism, with which the comic "sirens" of the twentieth century would be endowed. These "noisy," non-fatal femmes and bombshells, like Eva Tanguay, the "I Don't Care Girl," exploded proprieties first on the vaudeville stage but then, more sensationally, in the "movies." The great innovation of motion was joined to the equally amazing one of replication, freeing an individual performance from one point in space-time, a first in the history of the world.

In 1927, *The Jazz Singer,* the first "talkie," was released. Starring Al Jolson, not a blonde but a Jewish man in blackface, and with its nonmainstream subject—a son caught between modernity and tradition, the vaudeville stage and the synagogue—it added the dimension of synchronized sound to the images on the silver screen. With that tremendous technological advance, moviegoers were soon able to appreciate the complete range of a woman's erotic powers. Hair made blonder through modern chemistry than it had ever been before was joined by animation and that most sexual of female organs—a woman's "fast talking, wisecracking, and double entendre"–quipping mouth.[16] The blonde of 1930s cinema would change the American landscape and women's place in it.

Four

Double-Peroxide, Moving Parts, and Mobile Mouths

Movies of the 1930s

Edna: Is she blond or brunette?
Fred: Both.
—Ring Lardner and George S. Kaufman, *June Moon*

Blonder than blond. Flaxen, tow, yellow, gold—none of these was dazzling enough, modern enough—to describe the astonishing hair of the movie stars of the late 1920s and early '30s. It was called platinum, after the jeweler's metal, rarer, even more valuable than gold. Jean Harlow was one of the first to try it, spending Sundays at her hairdresser's, her dark roots lightened to match hair that looked no more real than fairy floss. Its audacity was an example of the new confidence of women in the motion picture industry. They didn't need male impresarios. Their images and careers were theirs to make and manage.

There were many inferences to be drawn from platinum's absolute brightness, which, with the darker, natural color beneath, formed a bodily palimpsest of psychological and cultural curiosity. In the medium of black-and-white film, in which most objects register as halftones, it was dramatically apparent. Even a naive audience would have questioned the possibility of Harlow's or Mae West's hair—perhaps imagining these actresses as they were "before," with darker roots that would "grow out" without the weekly administration of peroxide.

Why would women subject themselves to hours of treatments to create this effect (not that they haven't always been willing, for beauty's sake, to submit to the rack)? Was there a symbolic freight that dark hair carried and blond hair erased? Or was there an added fillip created by the nonpresence of the dark roots? Did knowledge of the cover-up add pleasure to their performances? The new representation of women in popular culture, suggested by these questions, was technically possible by 1927 when innovations in lighting and panchromatic film stock made blond hair appear lighter than it had with the older orthochromatic stock (Bordwell, Staiger, and Thompson 281–85). But something else, less obvious at first, had also changed the way these women appeared. A moment in Jane Austen's *Emma* of 1816, about a willful, energetic, and narcissistic girl, not very different in temper and talent from some of the quipping heiresses and working girls of the comedies of the 1930s, illustrates my point.

Late in the novel, Frank Churchill proposes a game to enliven the picnic at Boxhill. One must say "one thing very clever . . . or two things moderately clever—or three things very dull indeed" (287). Good-natured but silly Miss Bates jumps in where most angels fear: "Oh! Very well, . . . then I need not be uneasy. 'Three things very dull indeed.' That will just do for me, you know. I shall be sure to say three dull things as soon as ever I open my mouth, shan't I?" (290). Emma, never one to curb her tongue nor hide her light, "could not resist." "Ah! Ma'am, but there may be a difficulty. Pardon me—but you will be limited as to number—only three at once" (290). Her brief moment of verbal triumph—one that might be imported, unedited, into a film script—is a tribute to Austen's almost two-hundred-year-old genius for witty and realistic dialogue. But Mr. Knightley is not amused. The community's bulwark of wisdom and social responsibility seriously reproaches her. If Miss Bates were "a woman of fortune," he says, "I would leave every harmless absurdity to take its chance, I would not quarrel with you for any liberties of manner. Were she your equal in situation—but, Emma, consider how far this is from being the case. . . . Her situation should secure your compassion. It was badly done, indeed!" (294). Emma's great timing and well-aimed barb notwithstanding, he sees the defect in her wit: she's turned it against one who isn't her equal in intelligence, wealth, or social standing. Her gibe isn't the stuff of *good* humor—ripostes exchanged by evenly matched sparring partners. Would we applaud a heavyweight, inequitably paired with a bantamweight, on his knockout punch? Rather, true comedy, as George Meredith wrote in 1877, midway between *Emma* and the "talkies," depends on the equality of the players.

Meredith was making an even more comprehensive point in his "Essay on Comedy and Uses of the Comic Spirit." Observing a larger division than that of age or social class, he argued that there must be equality between women and men for the comic spirit to flourish—indeed, for evolved civilization to prevail. Comedy thus verges on the political. Meredith compellingly makes the case that women's best interests are served by Thalia:

> But there never will be civilization where comedy is not possible; and that comes of some degree of social equality of the sexes. . . . [I want the] cultivated women to recognize that the comic Muse is one of their best friends. . . . Let them look with their clearest vision abroad and at home. They will see that, where they have no social freedom, comedy is absent: where they are household drudges, the form of comedy is primitive: where they are tolerably independent, but uncultivated, exciting melodrama takes its place, and a sentimental version of them. Yet the comic will out, as they would know if they listened to some of the private conversations of men whose minds are undirected by the comic Muse: as the sentimental man, to his astonishment, would know likewise, if he in similar fashion could receive a lesson. But where women are on the road to an equal footing with men, in attainments and in liberty—in what they have won for themselves, and what has been granted them by a fair civilization—there, and only waiting to be transplanted from life to the stage, or the novel, or the poem, pure comedy flourishes, and is, as it would help them to be, the sweetest of diversions, the wisest of delightful companions.[1] (32)

This magnificent claim for comedy's socioevolutionary issue is at the heart of my discussion of blondes in the movies. The actresses who starred in the enlivening comedies of the early 1930s were fortunate to have come along at a time in history when women had already won the right to vote (in England by 1918, for women over thirty, and by 1928 for all women; by 1920 in America), when more women were working outside the home than ever before, and when reliable methods of birth control were becoming available, freeing them from unwanted pregnancies and enabling them to enjoy sex for *their* own sakes.[2] They had reached maturity in a world starting to take seriously the truth of Meredith's consequential words. The giving-as-good-as-the-verbal-getting, the hilarious counterpunches of screwball and romantic comedy are proof of a new age for women and the world. We might take the ability to transform their hair with the application of peroxide as a metaphor for their new free-doms—biological and social.

And something else, just shy of a cultural revolution, had also occurred. For the first time in history—despite Virginia Woolf's assertion that "wit deserted beautiful lips about the time that Walpole died" (*Jacob's Room* 68)—exquisite women were willing to be not just witty but really funny, to make their audiences laugh out loud, to shatter the silent reverence hitherto accorded the exceptionally beautiful. The platinum or less extreme blonde who took charge of her image was asserting that attractiveness was hers to define *and* that immobility—so long the interpretive guide to astonishing feminine splendor, as is evident in Victorian portraiture and in the popular fin-de-siècle genre of "sleeping women" paintings like Frederick Leighton's *Flaming June* (figure 8)—was meant to be broken by taking her comic pratfalls and opening her funny, wisecracking mouth. Physical, even broadly slapstick, comedy—the only kind imaginable in the "silents," before Carole Lombard's appearance in Mack Sennett's late '20s bathing-beauty/college-athlete comedies and Jean Harlow's featured appearance in Hal Roach's *Double Whoopee* (1929)—was reserved for the obese and the unattractive, like Marie Dressler, the "Queen of Comedy," who starred in 1914 with Charlie Chaplin in the first "feature film" (thirty-eight minutes), *Tillie's Punctured Romance*. But the grossly overweight, rump-kicking, gut-slamming Dressler, whose parodies of delicacy defined her as unfeminine, was nothing like the attractive blond Lombard, who stops in the middle of her race against the "Primpmore" girls (in *Run, Girl, Run*) to powder her nose. She may lose momentum, but her gesture reminds us of her immutable femininity.

The blonde's brash appearance was body language for "Look at me! Enjoy my audacity, and love me for it!" Inventing a new idiom for grace, she said: "Go ahead! Feel free to laugh at what I say and do!" She encouraged "the volleys of silvery laughter," the blithe corrective to all that is "out of proportion, overblown, affected, pretentious, bombastical, hypocritical, pedantic, fantastically delicate"—in short, the essence of Meredith's "Comic Spirit" (48). She had discovered that the novelist, essayist, and poet spoke reliably: the Comic Spirit was her excellent friend. The new sound technology let her audience hear as well as see her performance of his truth.

Gilda/Miriam Hopkins in Ernst Lubitsch's adaptation of Noel Coward's play *Design for Living* (1933) certainly embodied the point. In the wonderful set speech she delivers to her artist and playwright boyfriends, she announces: "A thing happened to me that usually happens to men. You see, a man can meet

Fig. 8. A sleeping beauty. *Flaming June* (1895) by Frederick Leighton. (By permission of the Bridgeman Art Library)

two, three-a, even four women and fall in love with all of them. And then, by a process of interesting elimination, he's able to decide which one he prefers. But a woman must decide purely on instinct, guesswork—if she wants to be considered nice. Oh, it's quite all right for her to try on a hundred hats before she picks one out." When one of her two prospective beaux asks her which "chapeau" she prefers, she answers: "Both!" (figure 9). With her explanation and one-word answer, which question the fairness of contemporary sexual mores, she defined an era of gender equity in film, lasting from approximately 1932 to 1942, in which the "feminine" attributes of coyness or coquettishness, vamping, and sexual treachery were put on hold. They were replaced by candor and a cheerful willingness to be comically compromised in the name of improved relations between men and women. What had been exhortation for Meredith became, for a brief season, a reality of the cinematic landscape.

However, the Comic Spirit had not been the reigning deity in, literally, the projection of women on the silver screen before the "talkies" transformed motion pictures. History, remarks Karl Marx in "The Eighteenth Brumaire of Louis Bonaparte," repeats itself—the first time as tragedy, the second as farce. The film industry, as it grew up in the teens of the twentieth century, in its serious dramatic productions, seems to have been compelled to imitate the representation of women in nineteenth-century Romantic fiction. With their essentially religious vision of women as ennobling or condemning their sexual opposites, films like D. W. Griffith's *Birth of a Nation* (1915) and *Way Down East* (1920; re-released 1930) modeled the fair heroine as a figure of Christ-like self-sacrifice, endurance, and passivity for the sake of a man while showing

Fig. 9. Gilda/Miriam Hopkins choosing "both" *"chapeaux,"* Frederic March and Gary Cooper, in *Design for Living* (1933). (Courtesy of Photofest)

that dark women, like Lydia Brown, the mulatta housekeeper of Radical leader Austin Stoneman (in *Birth* . . .), ruined men by reducing them to unrestrained beasts. A variant of the type, also of 1915, was the dark-haired and vaguely non-Western Theda Bara,[3] who, with her kohl-encircled eyes, played an exotic "vamp" in *A Fool There Was* (she was the first to utter the still-famous but misquoted line: "Kiss me, my fool!"). She demonically controls the American (Anglo-Saxon) businessman, who is defenseless against her spell. By contrast, blond actresses like Mary Pickford, ("America's sweetheart"), Mae Marsh, and Lillian Gish, D. W. Griffith's favorite star, were innocent victims of men's (in *Birth of a Nation*, black men's) sexual rapacity. These girl-women were stalwart defenders of a sexless, self-denying domestic ideology, reprising Victorian attitudes about home and women.

From the Lambs of the Silents to the Golden Fleecers

Grainy footage rolls. The title *Birth of a Nation* appears, followed by the cast of characters. White letters, inside an ornate Victorian frame, cover the black screen: "If in this work we have conveyed to the mind the ravages of war to the end that war may be in abhorrence, this effort will not have been in vain." So begins D. W. Griffith's, and the fledgling movie industry's, first twelve-reel movie. Griffith chose for its subject the conflagration of the Civil War and the rise of the Ku Klux Klan during Reconstruction, when blacks briefly gained political power. But the narrative, based on two overtly racist novels by Thomas Dixon, *The Clansman* and *The Leopard's Spots*,[4] now seems less about the abhorrence of war than the reassertion of the "Aryan birthright" (the words of an intertitle) brought low by "abhorrent" miscegenation (another intertitle reads: "Passage of a bill, providing for the intermarriage of blacks and whites"—passed, that is, by the disproportionately black South Carolina Legislature during the 1871 session).

The second intertitle—"The bringing of the African to America planted the first seed of disunion"—is the film's real preoccupation. While apparently grounded in an agricultural metaphor, the assertion, covertly but potently, plays on the biblical metaphor for insemination. The film is openly sympathetic to the white southerners during Reconstruction, endorsing the Klan as the defender of their "unadulterated" bloodlines and encouraging the conviction that the true conflict between North and South is over "the [southern] white man's burden." The North, by contrast, dangerously fails to recognize the hypersexuality of the black man, whose sole object is forcing (blond) white women into offensive sexual union.

In Piedmont, South Carolina, "life runs in a quaintly way that is to be no more." Slave children lark and black elders are conscientious as kindly Dr. Cameron and his family sit on their porch with their puppies and kitten, a portrait of domestic harmony. Into this pastoral idyll intrudes the disastrous abolitionist Stoneman, who champions the slaves by furthering the political career of his mulatto protégé Silas Lynch (his surname a recommendation for appropriate punishment). Stoneman intends to "crush the white South under the heel of the black South." But Lynch shows the impossibility of changing his "leopard's spots" when late in the story he sexually threatens Stoneman's daughter, Elsie, played by blond Lillian Gish (figure 10). Even for Stoneman there are limits to black prerogative.

But he is far from abhorring all miscegenation. His housekeeper, Lydia Brown (Mary Alden in blackface), provides the dark counterpoint to the blond heroines, Elsie and her cousin, Flora Cameron/Mae Marsh (figure 11). In an early scene, Lydia, interrupted by a visiting senator in her "ambitious dreaming" (a euphemism identifying her as "uppity"), works herself into a fit of passion—spitting, ripping her shirt, cramming her fist into her mouth—in a display of her repulsively primitive (read "black") nature. When Stoneman discovers her, his tender, then salacious embrace (she shows her triumph only to the camera) and the accompanying intertitle—"The great leader's weakness that is to blight a nation"—are the sexual predicate of the scene. Griffith's phobic vision of miscegenated sex extends beyond the particular coupling to the destruction of the vast collective—the nation.

But the script manufactures horror of the "blight" more directly through the fate of the blond women who, unlike Lydia, are portrayed as delicate, innocent, and victimized. Flora Cameron is strikingly blond as a child in the first scenes and is still fair-haired by the time her brother Ben returns home after the Civil War. Exceptionally lively, she frisks and primps to make herself beautiful for the war hero by placing strips of woolly cotton—"southern ermine," in the words of the intertitle—on the bodice of her dress. Small coded messages like this one are meant to create sympathy for the South—beaten, impoverished, but still regal and unbowed.

Despite the film's being a "silent," Griffith was able to make the comparison of the women through sound as well as sight. Joseph Carl Breil's original musical score, played at the film's New York premiere in March 1915,[5] augmented

Fig. 10. Lillian Gish as Elsie Stoneman in *Birth of a Nation* (1915). Orthochromatic film stock and the position of the light source account for the variation in Gish's hair color. (Courtesy of Photofest)

the visual contrast between "brown" Lydia's bestial tearing of her dress and blond Flora's adorable capering and decorating of hers.

Two of the musical themes accompanying Flora's adult appearances were based on contemporary popular (and erotic) dance rhythms—the tango and "hesitation waltz" (Marks 149). Although they may explain the attraction of

Fig. 11. Mae Marsh/Flora Cameron in distress, as usual, in *Birth of a Nation*. (Courtesy of Photofest)

the black renegade soldier Gus, who follows Flora and proposes marriage as she walks in the woods, Martin Miller Marks offers a subtler reading. They repeat earlier musical themes that function as leitmotifs for Stoneman and Lydia, associating Flora with these "miscegenates."

The link to Stoneman establishes the connection between his Reconstruction policy of promoting black political power and Flora's death. Gus's daring to approach a white girl (so goes Griffith's argument) is unmistakably a result of the leader's encouragement of the law legalizing intermarriage. To escape the black man's apparently determined pursuit, she jumps from a stone cliff. The frames showing Flora's expiring form are captioned by the fulsomely sentimentalized intertitle: "For her who had learned the stern lesson of honor, we should not grieve that she found sweeter *the opal gates of death*." The gender-reversed "Pietà" tableau—Ben Cameron cradling his dead sister in his arms—is the first visual association of the virtuous and self-sacrificing blond woman with Christ. Lydia Brown's tango theme, labeled "Lust and Passion" in Breil's score,[6] much like Flora's second theme, creates another aural link between these contrasting characters. While dark-skinned Lydia aggressively manipulates men, fair Flora's innocent sexuality has made her the victim of a black man's "lust and passion."

Lighting also illuminates Griffith's thematic material. When Ben, the heroic "little colonel," carries Flora back to the family's war-ravaged home, he walks onto the set, supporting her lifeless body in his outstretched arms. His eccentric, U-shaped route takes him past an (offstage) open-flame, carbon arc light,[7] which literally "highlights" the film's message about women. We realize that a powerful light floods the set, for Flora's hair is brilliantly illuminated—suddenly more brightly blond than in any earlier footage.

The surprising glare is probably not an accident of primitive lighting technology. In *Birth* . . . hair color changes, depending on whether scenes were shot outdoors in natural light or on sets illuminated by klieg lights. Slight variations in the orthochromatic film stock, purposely tinted differently from scene to scene, also altered hues. However, the startling illumination of Flora's hair could have been eliminated had the effect been unwanted. Its brightness was used by Griffith to confirm that the "angel," once more back "in the house," is the epitome of blond fairy-tale immobility.

Richard Dyer similarly notes that "The white woman as angel was . . . both the symbol of white virtuousness and the last word in the claim that what made whites special as a race was their non-physical, spiritual, indeed ethereal qualities. It held up an image of what white women should be, could be, essentially were, an image that had its attractions and drawbacks [as in dead Flora's case!] for actual white people" (*White* 127). In 1813, Jane Austen, clear-eyed as always, had comically arranged for Mr. Collins to hoist himself with his own spiritual petard by condoling Mr. Bennet on Lydia's elopement with Wickham:

"The death of your daughter would have been a blessing in comparison with this" (*Pride and Prejudice* 220). The "blight" for "the nation" in 1915 was that Griffith and the culture that welcomed his movie had not progressed beyond the un-evolved thinking that Austen had already skewered one hundred years before.

But apparently Griffith felt he hadn't made his point forcefully enough. For Elsie, too, after Flora's death, almost falls victim to a "black" man's "lust and passion." When late in the film Elsie pleads with Silas Lynch to stop the riot-ing blacks, he proposes marriage, as Gus had to Flora. She's outraged by the "affront," but Lynch will not be put off, arranging for a forced wedding. In her anguish, Elsie, more delicately, reprises Lydia Brown's stumbling display of animal passion, tottering helplessly about, her hair and dress becoming in-creasingly disordered.

One of the problems with orthochromatic film stock, used until the late '20s, was its insensitivity to yellow, which darkened blond hair (Gregory 319). For this reason "backlighting on blonde hair was not only spectacular but necessary" (Bordwell 226). However, as Carl Louis Gregory also noted, "the more loosely the hair is arranged the lighter it photographs" (319). He might have been thinking of Griffith's direction of Gish in this scene, for she never looks more blond than when the menacing Lynch is about to overwhelm her, her tousled hair picking up the light. The garland she wears, like Christ's crown of thorns, and her outstretched arms—a convenient blending of cruci-fixion imagery and feminine supplication—suggest, as in Flora's death scene, the connection of the white woman's sacrifice and Christ's. But fate is kinder to her than it was to her cousin Flora as the Klan rides to her rescue. Crucifixion iconography is now only a metaphor for blond, feminine virtue.

In her moment of crisis, Elsie cooperatively swoons. Griffith seems to have adapted a favorite plot device of the mystery writer Wilkie Collins, who proved the helplessness and immobility of even his strongest female charac-ters—Marian Halcombe, Magdalen Vanstone, Anne Sylvester—by rendering them comatose at crucial junctures in his plots. Elsie's faint is an emblem of the angelic, blond woman and her sanctified "white" blood, a reminder that its preservation depends on her remaining immobile and sexless (even her beau Ben Cameron doesn't get a virginal kiss until late in the film) and certainly staying far away from predatory black men.

The movie, of course, ends happily for the whites with all the lovers united in a sunny, pastoral setting. The picturesque pairing of cousins—Elsie and Ben Cameron; Margaret, the surviving Cameron sister, and Elsie's brother Phil—

fades into their vision (as in a cartoon bubble) of destructive war followed by millennial peace. A gigantic Norse god, sword flailing above a crowded field of human combatants, dissolves into an equally colossal Christ, towering benignly over happy white folk strolling through a pleasure ground. There is no sign of blacks in the new heaven on earth.

Racial purity and white supremacy, objectified through Griffith's cinematic representation of the blonde, were promoted by the fledgling industry, concerned for its own reputation. Dyer argues that the glorification of the "southern" "ideal of womanhood" and the "Victorian virgin ideal" represented by Mary Pickford and Lillian Gish were aspects of the effort to make the new film industry respectable when immigration from southern European countries and the northern migration of blacks were altering the ethnic composition of the nation (*White* 127).

However, Griffith, five years after *Birth* . . . , had an ostensible change of heart—not about black men, but white women. With the necessity for establishing the bona fides of the industry no longer as compelling, new social pressures required a reexamination of the "woman question." *Way Down East,* a film he made in 1920, the same year the Nineteenth Amendment was passed, amends his portrait in *Birth* . . . of the victimized, sexless, and passive blonde. In this movie, the sexual exploitation of women, covertly sanctioned by society, patterns the story of the blonde's heroic struggle. However, the difference between Anna Moore/Lillian Gish, the simple country girl in *Way Down East,* and Elsie Stoneman in *Birth* . . . is that Anna is conscious of, and belatedly but forcefully protests, the double (sexual) standard, while no one would believe that Elsie had the slightest acquaintance with the expression or its meaning.

The 1930 reissue of the still-silent movie begins with a rationale for Griffith's socially conscious intention—to promote women's "human rights" after they had been granted the civil right to vote. Times, he recognizes, are still difficult for them, despite the "ideal of one man for one woman," "because not yet has the man-animal reached this high ideal—except perhaps in theory." Sex is no longer the subtext as in *Birth* . . . but the declared subject of this weeper-turned-comedy.

The plot exposes the cad Lennox Sanderson, who deceives the beautiful, blond, and destitute Anna Moore. Tricked into a mock marriage and then suffering her infant's death, this twentieth-century Cinderella coincidentally meets up with her betrayer after she's found domestic work on a farm. Adding insult to injury, he tells her she can't remain in a neighborhood where he has his "reputation" to maintain.

Her depression occasions a scene in which Griffith takes full visual advantage of the figure of victimized blond womanhood. In a rare escape from her chores, Anna sits on the shore of a nearby lake, gazing mournfully at the beckoning water, perhaps with suicidal thoughts. At the least, her Romantic posture and the natural scenery combine to suggest a *tableau vivant* of innocent blond affliction. While Griffith had little control over lighting outdoors, he was able to moderate the effect of the orthochromatic film stock he used. Anna unfastens her luxurious hair, running her fingers through it. The separated strands pick up more light and appear blonder than in any previous scene, emphasizing Anna's position in a long genealogy of persecuted fairy-tale blondes. But Griffith soon departs from the traditional script for such characters, relying on two modern plot twists.

Through the town gossip, her employer learns that Anna has had a child out of wedlock. At a dinner party at the farm attended by Sanderson (a hardly believable crossing of class lines), the farmer publicly confronts Anna as she waits at table, ordering her, despite his wife's and son's protests, to leave his home (figure 12). But before she goes, Anna exposes Sanderson as the man who has compromised her. In an impassioned (though silent) speech aided by exaggerated and unmistakable body language, she asserts that he, not she, is the guilty one.

What happens after—Anna, ill-clad and desperate, losing her way in a violent snowstorm, stumbling onto an ice floe in the river, lying spent on the block as it hurtles toward the rapids, then being rescued by the farmer's young and handsome son—is all unexceptionally in keeping with traditional male heroics in the service of the distressed damsel. But Anna's shouting the English equivalent of "*J'accuse!*" and the son's marriage to the "fallen (but blond!) woman" represent a significant plot turn, not only for this film but for real women's lives. Sex unsanctioned by marriage vows no longer precluded a future chapter of worldly happiness and respectability. Griffith was a force for progress by denying the moral legitimacy of George Eliot's censorious and conservative "world's wife." That collective creature would fault Anna, no matter the circumstances in which she'd been "sullied," while forgiving the man for "sowing his wild oats," as, indeed, she did Stephen Guest in *The Mill on the Floss.* Thus, Anna's character, which came to moviegoers' attention twice—through the original and rereleased film—was an important way station between the

Fig. 12. The farmer orders the disgraced Anna Moore/Lillian Gish to leave his home in *Way Down East* (1920; 1930). (Courtesy of Photofest)

passive or repressed figures of blond womanhood in *Birth* . . . and the pleasingly sexual, pleasantly aggressive blond stars of the early talkies.

A figure that occupied a different place in the middle ground between the sexual victim and the woman who actively enjoys sex was the blond "vamp" of the late '20s. More commonly known as the "gold digger,"[8] the vamp's avatar in an era of conspicuous economic success, she helped to complete the arc of the blonde's early movie career (up to 1942), paralleling her novelistic migration from innocence, at the beginning of the nineteenth century, to a Blakean higher innocence, or "organized experience," by its end. This migration, in less metaphoric terms, meant the blonde's passage from the pastoral countryside (as in *Birth* . . . and *Way Down East*), in which she embodies an idealized and treasured precapitalist, near-mythic past, to the dynamic urban econoscape, where use and exchange value are beginning to be demystified. In the former films, the woman's natural blond hair invokes the traditional virtues of femininity reflected in folk- and fairy tale. More broadly, it nostalgically enfigures the virtue of a lost agrarian culture (seamlessly sutured onto the "fallen" present through the magical medium of film). By comparison, the gold digger's chemically acquired, counterfeit blondness (advertising her aggressive embrace of personal marketing strategies) in the films of the late 1920s signals women's newly active participation in the social and political economy of "money power, individualism, [and] entrepreneurialism" (Harvey 348). The firmly established film industry no longer feared "gilt" by association with the gold digger and thus felt free to represent this blonde as a force to be reckoned with, as were her counterparts of the previous century—Becky Sharp, Lady Audley, and Jean Muir—arbitrageurs who traded sex (or the promise of sex) for hard specie. Although these heroines played against physical type, the moviegoers' knowledge that the gold digger's blond hair came out of a bottle amplified the deliciously comic dissonance of her figure. Yet while such examples of feminine resourcefulness or enterprise were largely controlled by the male-dominated studios, they were hardly the sinister images of antifeminine propaganda that Bram Dijkstra, in *Evil Sisters,* asserts they were. True, the gold digger never got around to asking Mae West's hilarious second question; she was merely content to know if there were something in the man's pocket (preferably, which she might remove). But in a culture in which wealth and luxury were prized, she was far from unique in her economaniacal focus. Audiences were well aware of the large company she kept; her sins were merely ven(i)al.

Lorelei[9] Lee (named after a siren in Germanic legend who lured sailors to their deaths), the best-remembered gold digger of the 1920s, mounted the Broadway stage by 1926 after her celebrated appearance in Anita Loos's satiric novel. But the blonde, whom "gentlemen preferred," was not immortalized in celluloid until Marilyn Monroe re-created her in 1953.[10] Marie Skinner was another such digger for a stranger's gold in D. W. Griffith's late-career silent *The Battle of the Sexes* (1928). She was played by the platinum-bobbed Phyllis Haver, who, five years before, in her avatar as a dark-haired comedienne, had been featured as Buster Keaton's romantic interest in the goofily humorous *The Balloonatic.* An unprecedented departure from centuries-old images of femininity that linked long tresses and fertility, the "bob" freed women from the laboriousness of washing, combing, brushing, and styling abundant hair. Bound breasts and raised hemlines—creating the new androgynous look—also contributed to the freedom of both blondes and brunettes, who had more time to have fun.

As in both *Birth . . .* and *Way Down East,* Griffith's theme in this movie is sex. But whereas the male, black or white, had been the aggressor in the earlier films, the "flapper" or "fast" woman of the Jazz Age, in a role reversal that dominated popular culture in the late '20s, was now the sexual predator—a displacement onto the "sexual Other" of responsibility for materialistic excess that conveniently avoided an uncomfortable (male) self-indictment. The sexual woman, freed by reliable birth control, was out of the closet and would soon turn her representation to "account." The only surprise was that she was often a blonde. Although the meaning of blondness has continued to "float" from the late '20s to the present, the blonde has invariably thwarted cultural expectations, paralleling her performance and reception in the second half of the nineteenth century.

The opening shot of the movie is a close-up of the gold digger's legs, sexily crossed and ending in a pair of leopard-skin pumps—the first hint of her carnivorous nature. The camera underscores this suggestion with a contrasting shot, panning screen-right, to the legs and prim black shoes of a dark-haired manicurist. The polite smile, frank look, and firm shake of her head "no"—the hand maiden's answer to the lecherous overture of her male customer—signals the difference between this "working" girl, who plays it straight, and Marie. The camera then returns to the owner of the leopard pumps, but this time to her upper body and, surprise!, her blond bob being cut and styled, emphasizing its importance (figure 13), as she energetically chews her gum and chuckles over her book. Amusingly, in this story dominated by Marie's worldly manipulations of the wealthy real estate developer William Judson, she's reading Louisa May Alcott's *Little Women.* Her obvious delight in the book and the jaunty music that accompanies the scene set the tone for the movie, as does the quipping intertitle: "Marie Skinner wasn't as hard as most gold diggers—she was harder." This story will not be a tragedy, no matter what Marie does. Actually, nothing about Phyllis Haver is much darker than her platinum bob.

Judson, in the next chair, is being congratulated by his barber on the real estate deal he's just closed—reported in the paper he's reading. Marie is tantalized; comically, her head moves sideways on the stalk of her upright neck in the stylized movement of a Hindu dancer, the better to overhear their conversation and catch a glimpse of the headline. Her pupils have practically morphed into dollar signs.

Cut to the happy Judson home, where wife and grown children, daughter

Fig. 13. Marie Skinner/Phyllis Haver getting her blond hair "bobbed" in *The Battle of the Sexes* (1928). (Courtesy of Photofest)

and son, wait expectantly for "Daddy" to celebrate "Mama's" birthday. Daddy's last of many presents to his devoted, grateful (and middle-aged) spouse is the most opulent. Although the diamond bracelet brings tears to her eyes, we know that the best present is Judson's heartfelt embrace. But Mama's failure to blow out all her birthday candles transparently signals that her wish for life to continue in this happy way won't be granted.

Indeed, the rest of the story—driven by Marie's gold lust—unfolds as expected. With the help of her partner-in-crime, the unscrupulous "Jazz hound" Babe Winsor, Marie entices the real estate tycoon into her rooms and a purely mercenary affair. Sanctimoniously defending his right to pursue life, liberty, and happiness, Judson leaves his wife for the gold digger. His despairing spouse, standing on the roof's ledge, is saved from a suicidal leap by the daughter. The long vertical camera shot down to the street, with its busy traffic, underscores the amoral power and energy of the modern metropolis.

But this synopsis paints Marie as much worse than we feel her to be. Haver's caricatured portrayal of femininity, like Becky Sharp's female impersonations, gives her gold-digging a humorous spin. The lighthearted musical score determines our mood, as does Marie's comic attempt to plan her "vamp attack" on Judson. Her sultry pose, wrecked by the appearance of a tiny mouse, and the swimming strokes she practices in her new bathing suit while lying on the floor are too droll to be seductive. As Babe Winsor, "Mr. Cool-As-a-Cucumber," leaves her apartment, self-parodying Marie theatrically despairs: "Such a man—perfumed ICE!" And she's inherited Becky Sharp's generosity, truthfully telling Judson that his daughter (found in Marie's bedroom in Babe's embrace) had not come to her apartment for "that Jazz hound" but because she had wanted to save her father. Griffith, with laughing gas for analgesic, performs oral surgery on the vampire's canines.

In the end, Judson must buy bonds to keep the blackmailing Winsor ("the wrong answer to a maiden's prayers") from spreading "unpleasant publicity" about him. We don't doubt for a moment that this self-deluded man richly deserves this minimal financial penalty, considering the pain he's inflicted. Babe, who has pocketed the real estate developer's check, reclines on Marie's lap (holding "Babe" will be as close to motherhood as Marie ever gets) while she applies soothing (cucumber?) lotion to his eyes after his strenuous extortions. In an allusion to the first great vamp film, *A Fool There Was* (meant as a wink to the audience),[11] Marie says to the languorous Babe: "You're a fool, but you're MY fool," which she then proves by deftly removing Judson's check from his breast pocket and slyly tucking it into the top of her knee-high stocking. There may be love, or at least desire, but no honor, between these thieves! But we think, Good for Marie! She's far more appealing than Babe, and she's certainly worked harder for financial "success." In fact, the film is far more critical of the men than of her. Judson's vanity, his ridiculous exercise routine and elastic corset, expose his narcissism, as does his selfish "free will" ("I have the right to live as I want"). In this movie, it isn't the woman who primps but the egotistical male. Both Judson and the coldly calculating Winsor have gotten their just desserts.

Marie's patronymic, "Skinner," implies damage but only of the superficial, cutaneous, sort. Yes, this blond vamp is undeniably venal. But although she may go after her victim's money, she doesn't try for his life's blood, as did Theda Bara with her insidiously draining kiss in *A Fool There Was*.[12] And we forgive Marie because the Judson family members recover from their wounds by movie's end. In a repetition of the film's opening, the repentant husband returns home, a year later, as his wife's "surprise present" during Mama's birthday celebration. Supported by the saccharinely sentimental musical score, strings dominant, the domestic lesson is inescapable: love, not diamonds, in this hard-edged, glittering urban culture, brings true happiness.

The Battle of the Sexes doesn't endorse extramarital sex, but neither does it condemn it. What's sauce for the gander is equally sauce for the goose. When Judson finds his daughter in the arms of Babe Winsor, he shouts: "You—you here with that jazz hound. You're disgracing the whole family." But she won't let him get away with the sexist cliché: "It's too late for that, Daddy. You beat me to it. I'm just following in your footsteps." As he retreats for support to the double standard ("That's different—I'm a man."), she heroically counters: "Yes—well, I am a WOMAN!"

So should we imagine the sequel to Marie Skinner's gold-digging life, we might picture her making her way up the social food chain, enticing other Mr. Judsons—in a mercenary but not entirely unsympathetic way, getting even with all the men who, over the centuries, have taken advantage of women and then cast them onto the dust heap when their charms were no longer fresh or the affair convenient. Her "work" can be viewed in the light of an income-redistribution scheme—a sort of capitalist five-year plan for the American "material" girl that displaces the traditional marriage plot. However, the film industry's actual "sequels," the movies made two or three years after *Battle* . . . , particularly in the four-year period of the pre-Code era but even into the early 1940s, show the blonde (and occasional brunette) doing and being better than any Marie.

In the early days of the Depression, the liberated blonde of cinema was no longer a heartless gold digger, only partly because there were, in the real world, fewer Mr. Judsons on whom to prey. After 1929, the culture of Hollywood was necessarily in dynamic with the undeniable change in the nation. In the context of instant poverty for many, the blonde once more became a lightning rod for economic and social anxieties, serving to ground the fears of struggling moviegoers, who sought relief for a few hours as they sat in the safety of darkened theaters. They could forget their worries as they escaped into the glamorous world she inhabited, or, if her life too closely resembled theirs, they might take comfort in her intrepidity. Whatever had happened to the world, she, at least, was a survivor.

The bold blonde in films of this period was a new figure of strength and determination. If she weren't an heiress, she was working as hard as men to support herself. Her economic independence but also biological freedom (only implied, of course) was bound to alter her sexuality, as well. She would no longer accept being on the receiving end of a relationship but, rather, would insist on an alliance of equals (as does Gilda in *Design for Living*). Neither did she require it to be institutionally sanctioned by church or state. Thus, the representation of sex in pre-Code movies was "naturalized," portrayed as benignly pleasurable. The blonde, as easily as her male counterpart, might take it if she wanted it, and no one blamed her. With her mouth now capable of producing sounds, she made her own excellent case for equality and sexual freedom as she never would have, or could have, before.

Goodbye, Vamp . . . Hello, Camp!

Mae West, along with Jean Harlow, one of the first to go platinum, was a slow-drawling, self-dramatizing, outsize female impersonator who, by 1933, was the single biggest box-office attraction in the industry. Maria DiBattista in *Fast-Talking Dames* (93) excludes her from the "sisterhood" she celebrates—those mile-a-minute mouths in the beautiful heads that topped the slim, athletic, fast-moving bodies of the '30s stars—Miriam Hopkins, Claudette Colbert, Barbara Stanwyck, Myrna Loy, Jean Harlow, Carole Lombard, Katharine Hepburn, Jean Arthur, Irene Dunne, Ginger Rogers, and, later, Rosalind Russell. West, in fact, in her delivery went against the general cultural phenomenon of clipped and rapid speech. (Men, as well as women, spoke in an accelerated tempo as Walter Burns/Cary Grant brilliantly demonstrates in *His Girl Friday* of 1940, speaking much faster than Hildy Johnson/Rosalind Russell. She comically cuts off his rapid-fire, nearly incomprehensible delivery with the tobacco auctioneer's wind-up—"sold American!")

But while she drawled, West was "fast-talking" in the slanging sense of "fast" or "racy." With her very ample hourglass figure, she was unique among '30s actresses in her version of femininity. But she was also distinctive in another way, testing the limits of what might be said before the camera, making the representation of sexual desire, especially of feminine sexual desire, possible. There was barely ever a kiss in her movies, even in those before 1934, which has something to do with another West initiative—the estrangement of desire and sex from love. Yet in the stirring of her viewers' imaginations through what she said, all was not innocence, *and* it was great fun! In *Night after Night* (1932), when the hatcheck girl, noticing Mae/Maudie Triplett's sparkling jewelry, remarks, "Goodness, what beautiful diamonds!" West quips: "Goodness had nothing to do with it, dearie!" This single sentence opened a vista of bedrooms and embraces that had never been shown on-screen nor would be until the amended Motion Picture Production Code of 1930—first seriously used as a yardstick for measuring "decency" in films in July 1934—was laid to rest in the socially and politically liberating '60s (Doherty 1). But in another sense, when we consider her screen persona and those of the other actresses of the '30s, her assertion was incorrect. Goodness had much to do with the revision of the way women, especially blondes, were meant to be understood by the audience; "goodness" and sex were new bedfellows. With her platinum hair, West canceled the myth perpetrated by whites about whites, particularly about white women: that they are defined, as Richard Dyer argues, by "non-physical, spiritual, indeed ethereal qualities."

The motion picture, with its technology of duplication,[13] is truly the first "mass" art form in the history of culture—viewable, as I've said, simultaneously by hundreds of thousands, theoretically, millions, of people. Nor does it depend on literacy. The box-office "take" has always been a good measure of what makes pulses beat fast, so, as Thomas Schatz points out in *Hollywood Genres*, moviegoers influenced plot elements, character types, and stories that would be repeated and conventionalized by studios into recognizable genres. West's early movies were cross-genre stories, drawing, in the early years of the Depression, on the rage for the gangster film, with its anarchic crew of bad boys (exploding bullets and each other but finally brought to justice by the forces of law and order), and the equal appetite for the love story, which provided another kind of relief from the misery of life outside the movie theater.

Her appearance as Maudie, the tough-speaking but warmhearted ex-girlfriend of Joe Anton/George Raft, owner of a high-class speakeasy in the

Raft–Constance Cummings romantic vehicle, provides comic relief from the gangster and romance plots, both very thin. Maudie good-naturedly barges into the place, smacks Anton on the lips, and befriends his diction coach/current events teacher, the elderly, stout, and very refined Miss Mabel Jellyman/ Alison Skipworth, who is all atwitter over being in a speakeasy. The two become chums as Anton leaves them to their own devices—drinking themselves into a champagne stupor.

When Miss Jellyman, still in the speakeasy, wakes up the next morning with a terrible hangover, she laments that she'll lose her job, having failed to show up for her teaching duties. "Why, dearie, you're wasting your time. Why, a gal with your poise and class, why you'd make thousands in my business. . . . it's one of the best paying rackets in the world," says Maudie. The humor of this exchange depends on our remembering that Maudie was sporting diamonds that had "nothing to do with goodness." Trying to be diplomatic but also realistically thinking herself disqualified for the "profession," Mabel answers, out of her Victorian past, that Maudie's "business" "has been a great factor in the building of civilization. And of course, it has protected our good women and thereby preserved the sanctity of the home. . . . But m' dear, don't ya think I'm just a little old?" Maudie registers the insult: "Say, what kind of a business do ya think I'm in? . . . Say listen, dearie, ya got me all wrong. I've got a chain of beauty parlors!" Like Miss Jellyman, Maudie is an honest working woman. "Goodness" really does have something to do with it. When she offers Mabel a job at a salary of one hundred dollars a week as hostess in her new beauty salon, the diamonds-sex connection is reduced or, really, elevated to a spot of good humor.

George Raft, probably thinking of this scene among others, wrote in his autobiography, "In this picture Mae West stole everything but the cameras" (quoted in West, *Goodness* 157). By 1935, she was the highest-paid actress in Hollywood (she reported $480,833 in earnings for that year) so that, as she said, "With this kind of income I was even paying for my own jewels—sometimes," although she couldn't keep from adding a trade(re)mark: "I have always felt a gift diamond shines better than one you buy for yourself" (*Goodness* 186).

Following her success in *Night after Night*, West again dangled one foot into the underworld in her next two films, both starring vehicles for her: *She Done Him Wrong* (1933) and *I'm No Angel* (also of 1933, with screenplay and dialogue credits assigned to West herself). Her characters in both, like Maudie Triplett, are on the "up-and-up" despite the company she keeps. As in a number of the films of the period, in which the occupations of the leading ladies reflexively comment on entertainment, West's characters are performers. In *She Done Him Wrong* (Paramount's remake of West's 1928 Broadway hit, *Diamond Lil*), she's Lady Lou, a singer in Gus Jordan's saloon (with an elaborate boudoir on the upper floor,[14] but that's another story) on the Bowery during the "Gay Nineties"; in *I'm No Angel*, set in present time, she's Tira, a carnival peepshow vamp and then circus lion tamer. As a woman who stands her ground with men as well as lions, West was a surprising and comic inspiration for women who had to support themselves and their families in the first years of the Depression. You would safely bet she took no enemies prisoner.

But she was also a refreshingly and unabashedly sexual being, who salvaged the reputation of desire. She wrote: "The great acceptance of me as a woman character, who expounded the most liberal sexual ideas on the screen was an amazing thing . . . freeing the sexually shy from their binding emotional blocks and repressions" (*Goodness* 169–70).

In *She Done Him Wrong*, Lou arrives in a carriage, dressed, as always, to accentuate her curvaceous figure, making her grand entrance into the saloon, where Gus introduces her to his "business associates"—"Russian Rita" and her boyfriend, the handsome (and, apparently, three-timing gigolo) Serge Stanieff.[15]

But Lou knows how to handle Stanieff. Although with her voice of experience she counsels Sally, a young girl in distress, that "men's all alike, married or single. It's their game. I happen to be smart enough to play it their way," she really plays it her own, as her quip to Stanieff proves. When he tries to sweet-talk her with the compliment "The men of my country go wild about women with yellow hair," she answers: "I'm glad ya told me 'cause I wanna keep straight on my geography." Her wit eclipses the woman-as-sex-object, proclaiming her agency, as, indeed, everything about West's over-the-top physical manner and verbal foreplay does. Her smart repartee puts her in the driver's seat despite her preference for blues like "I Wonder Where My Easy Rider's Gone," which depict women as victims of faithless lovers. Her secret is to be cynical about romance; she's never starry-eyed and sentimental about a man. Love, she should have said to the hatcheck girl, has nothing to do with it.

But we love Lady Lou, just as West's public did in 1933. We relish her one-liners, which cut through masculine pretension and expose the bankruptcy of the sexual double standard. They float through popular culture even today, unmoored from their original cinematic origins. When the suicidal Sally (revealed much later to have been "ruined" by Stanieff) asks, "Who'd want me after what I've done?" Lou retorts: "Listen, when women go wrong, men go right after them." Her effort to find a job for this girl whose "guy done her wrong" ("a story so old it should have been set to music," West twangs) underscored, without belaboring the point, the importance of financial independence for women. She's no gold digger, relieving a man of the "something" in his pocket.

We also like her frank appreciation of men as sexual companions. Her invitation, both to Stanieff and Captain Cummings—"Why doncha come up some time and see me?"—her best-remembered and most-quoted line—was a hit even with audiences in the conservative farm belt. Her elegant boudoir above Gus's saloon—the "up" of her invitation—is her natural habitat, in which much of the film's action takes place.

West is also a great social leveler. When her maid, Pearl (Louise Beavers), calls her for her bath, interrupting the beginnings of a beautiful relationship with "warm, dark, and handsome" Captain Cummings, Lou wittily drawls: "You take it—I'm indisposed." Even her joking put-down in the following dialogue has something to recommend it.

LOU: Oh, Pearl, Pearl!

PEARL: I'se comin'. I'se comin'!

LOU: Yeah, you'se comin'! Your head is bendin' low. Well, get here before winter.

The exchange recalls Stephen Foster's "Old, Black Joe" (1860). This "secular hymn," meant to celebrate "the beauty and dignity of a black man," was the first such song in American history.[16] West's "Well, get here before winter" and her camaraderie with Pearl do much to cancel the inequality inherent in the relationship.[17] Her performance on the saloon stage acknowledges in a public space her admiration of black culture. The excited faces and swaying bodies of the patrons during her songs "Easy Rider" and "Frankie and Johnnie" show they like these blues much more than the saccharine "Silver Threads among the Gold" sung by an Irish tenor.

The lady/maid connection, also given prominence in other West movies, undercuts the reality of the separateness of the races and the limited possibilities for female friendship by approximating, if only in the boudoir, the cross-race bonding of men in the adventure film of the same period (figure 14). West, who frequented Harlem's nightclubs, was rumored to have had black lovers.

Fig. 14. Tira/Mae West with her maid in *I'm No Angel* (1933). (Courtesy of Photofest)

She certainly did much to mainstream black music and performance style by taking them for her own, emphasizing the black/white relationship as one of connection rather than contrast.[18] She specifically mentions her interest in black culture in her autobiography when she writes that Howard Merling, an actor friend, had told her "some startling things about what went on in that section of Manhattan [Harlem]. Negroes had become the rage of society. Artists and critics like Covarrubias[19] and Van Vechten had taken them on" (*Goodness* 141). Merling, she writes, advised: "Mae, maybe you ought to do a play on the subject. Mixing the black and white theme together" (*Goodness* 141). Although he wasn't referring to *I'm No Angel*, the entertaining impromptu number she breaks into in that film, with her black maids as backup singers (who imitate her strut and gestures), is both a virtual demonstration of cross-race companionship and her interest in the crossover musical idiom for which she became famous.[20]

Lou's brushes with the underworld—with her ex-boyfriend, Chick Clark/

Owen Moore, now a Sing-Sing jailbird; with Gus Jordan, of whose criminal activity she's ignorant; even her accidental killing of Russian Rita (who attacks Lou with a knife, jealous over Stanieff's attentions to the woman with the "yellow hair")—leave her untarnished in our estimation *and* Captain Cummings's. Once he's convinced that Lou had no idea she was getting a "job" for young Sally in the white slavery trade he's been investigating, Cummings does more than forgive her. Russian Rita, when first introduced to Lou, had uttered the platitude, "I've heard so much about you." Lou had demolished the cliché by responding, "Yeah, but ya can't prove it." Her comedic touch always forces her audience to face the meaning, usually sexual, that lies just beneath the surface of her words. Such honesty of spirit, which contrasts with the hypocrisy of all around her, must attract Cummings. In the privacy of the carriage in which the two ride—Lou believes to the police station, where she expects to be booked—he slips a diamond engagement ring on her finger. Despite her reputation, this straight-arrow law man (who affectionately calls her "bad girl") wants to make her his wife. Like Lou, he knows the worth of a diamond—even if it's in the rough.

Another song Lou sings in *She Done Him Wrong* expresses West's idiosyncratic version of Einstein's equation, $E=mc^2$; her energy was equal to her shapely mass times the square of that Westian constant "sex." "A guy what takes his time, I go for anytime. / I'm a fast-movin' gal who likes 'em slow." With this song (another borrowed from the repertoire of "race" music, her instructor's guide to the female pleasure principle, and the first of its kind on the silver screen), which plays on the paradoxes of pleasure, she announces her interest in sexual satisfaction. In *I'm No Angel,* West's inimitable trademark hips-and-shoulders-swinging walk, in the vocabulary of body language, suggests a self-conscious staginess that has much to say about her attitude toward sex and, ultimately, love. The medium shots of her frequent poses in three-quarters profile, one hand on hip, lips parted in a semi-ironic smile, breasts and platinum, marcelled waves prominent, do more than invite our attention. The "gaze" of the male or female viewer is unquestionably but gratifyingly riveted by the spectacle of her original, forceful, and comic sexuality.[21]

She also achieves dominance by a peculiar move when she's embraced by a would-be lover. As he catches her by the waist, she characteristically leans her upper torso slightly back and away, resting her hands, flexed at the wrists, on his upper arms—firmly resisting him and putting distance between them so that her lips, forming her inimitable words, rather than his kisses, control the sexual exchange. A remark in her autobiography about Tinseltown suggests that she was fully aware of the implications of her position: "Hollywood treated me well after I fought to establish myself, but I always held it at arms' length like a would-be lover one didn't fully trust" (*Goodness* 177).

John Tuska offers an interesting account of the shooting of West's love scenes in *I'm No Angel,* in which she cleverly used technology to create attitude:

> The most tempestuous love scenes between Cary and Mae were filmed individually and edited together for the work print. Mae would sit on her lounge chair, face the camera, breathe her words of soft romance, emote, melt the lenses, rise, and walk to her dressing room. Some time later Cary would come to the set, sit in a chair next to hers, now vacant, and make love, again with the camera in close-up, but no other object within range. It comes off flawlessly on the screen. But it gives Mae's Tira character a "stagey" aspect she very much wanted, because, for all the talk about love in her films, and outside them, Mae is basically cynical about it. (89)

The look in her eyes, sensual but almost as if she's seeing *through* her lover, was achieved by his actually being thin air (figure 15). The effect resonated with West's belief that men could be depended on only for pleasure—always transient, at best.

The flip side of her self-reliance is the outsize funniness of her sexuality. Ashton Stevens, drama critic for the *Herald and Examiner,* got the point.

> Never have I seen a woman kiss on the stage as Mae West kissed on the Apollo stage [playing in *Diamond Lil* in Chicago] Sunday night. Never have I seen an actress pawed from hip to buttock as Miss West's avid leading man pawed her in that bedroom set with the golden swan bed.
>
> When the rain began to fall on the bedroom window, I reached for my hat, for Diamond Lil certainly did not play cards. And then my own laughter saved me. . . . I saw that the embraces in *DIAMOND LIL* are much the same funny, fiendish exaggerations that the obscenities are in *The Front Page* [Ben Hecht's play about newspapermen]. They belong not so much to Sex as to Humor. (quoted in *Goodness* 131)

Edward Elsner, who directed West's play *Sex,* offered a more discriminating analysis when he told her: "You have a quality—a strange amusing quality, that I have never found in any of these other women [directed by him in

Fig. 15. Tira "looking through" her lover, Jack Clayton/Cary Grant. (Courtesy of Photofest)

other productions]. You have a definite *sexual* quality, gay and unrepressed. It even mocks you personally" (quoted in *Goodness* 84). She recognized this "self-mocking sex quality" as "just my vaudeville style" (*Goodness* 85), but "few people knew," she says, "that I didn't *always* walk around with a hand on one hip, or pushing at my hairdress and talking low and husky. I had created a kind of Twentieth Century Sex Goddess that mocked and delighted all victims and soldiers of the great war between men and women. I was their banner, their figurehead, an articulate image, and I certainly enjoyed the work" (*Goodness* 163). Her on-screen parody of sexuality was a deliberate move, the physical expression of her philosophy "that a woman has as much right as a man to live the way she does if she does no actual harm to society" (*Goodness* 94). While West's moral autonomy doesn't trivialize sex, her manner and actions divorce it inalterably from both romantic love and the havoc it was presumed to wreak on its male victims. As Parker Tyler, the great cinema theorist, argues, she parodied the sex goddess/vampire—that destroyer of men who had reigned from the teens through the '20s in cinematic representations of female sexuality: "Her unique blend of sexiness and vulgar comedy . . . was the screen's first sterling brand of conscious sex camp" (*Sex Psyche* 22).

But if she were a "slayer" of men, she used only her wit as weapon, and it was solely their pretensions that suffered injury. While other actresses and actors perform to create the illusion of reality or naturalness, West drew attention to artifice (as does a female impersonator). The period costumes, the platinum hair were all part of the act, deliberately chosen by West to make her audience understand the elaborate performance at the heart of sexual coupling.

Added to the paradoxical physical embodiment of humorous availability but detachment is West's intellectual strength, which appears most obviously—aside from her devastating one-liners—in the trial scene in *I'm No Angel*. She demolishes Jack Clayton/Cary Grant's male character witnesses, testifying on his behalf in Tira's breach-of-promise suit against Clayton (he's broken off their engagement, believing that she's been seeing other men). She proves she's a "fast-movin' gal" in wit as well as sex, exposing their lies and real immorality with her flawless logic (figure 16). The courtroom, including Clayton, who is happy to be proved wrong about her "infidelities," breaks up in laughter. Dumbness had nothing to do with it!

In 1853, eighty years before *I'm No Angel,* Charlotte Brontë invented the character of Ginevra Fanshawe. Ginevra, we remember, is a sexually active blonde, trysting with her lover in the unlit garret of a girls' boarding school. But that was in another country—really, in another world—without electricity and oil and all the inventions and freedom their harnessed energy would make possible. I have argued that Brontë's decision not to condemn the schoolgirl, nor punish her for her behavior, beyond awarding the usual wages that go to the unenterprising, represented a consequential shift in the characterization of the blonde and, by extension, of all women. With the enormous box-office success of *I'm No Angel,* Mae West had become a national icon who would be linked with another in her next film, *The Belle of the Nineties,* when she appeared as the Statue of Liberty (figure 17). The drama critic George Jean Nathan, taking a leaf out of West's book of wordplay, said she looked more like "the Statue of Libido" (Tuska 89). Rather than merely going *un*punished, West was being nationally celebrated for bringing "sex out in the open" and making it "amusing" (*Goodness* 162). Despite the Catholic Church and the Hays Office's displeasure, the public adored her. If Brontë helped to bring about important

Fig. 16. Tira, a "fast-movin' gal" in wit, acting as her own attorney. (Courtesy of Photofest)

early changes in the representation of women in popular culture, Mae West's contribution was seismic. She cleared the way for the younger fast-talking blondes of the romantic and screwball comedies, which quickly displaced the gangster film as the most popular genres of the period.

Honest Working Girls

There was hardly an actress who didn't go some shade of blond for at least one of her films in the 1930s. Norma Shearer, Ruth Chatterton, Claudette Colbert, Kay Francis, Katharine Hepburn, and Barbara Stanwyck (although she succumbed in the '40s) were the exceptions. Even Joan Crawford, associated with dark and treacherous roles, went a shade of blond at one time. But a number of women were platinum, or slightly darker, blondes consistently from picture to picture. Their hair was an essential element of their personas—like Bogart's nasal twang or Jimmy Cagney's aggressive gangster patter.[22]

Fig. 17. Mae West in *The Belle of the Nineties* (1934). George Jean Nathan called her "the Statue of Libido." (Courtesy of Photofest)

No one was more identified by hair color than Jean Harlow. Howard Hughes had cast her, when she was only eighteen, as the sexy temptress in his 1930 *Hell's Angels,* a film about her romantic involvement with two brothers, both British fighter pilots. In it she uttered the now-famous line, "Would you be shocked if I put on something more comfortable?" She replayed a tamer version of the vamp in the Frank Capra–Robert Riskin 1931 romantic comedy *Platinum Blonde,* starring Robert Williams as Stew Smith, a reporter, and Loretta Young as Gallagher, Smith's coworker pal. Harlow was cast as the heiress Ann Schuyler, who, with her platinum hair and great figure, temporarily unmans the hard-boiled Stew, making him give up both the newspaper and the friends he loves so he'll fit into her stuffy social-register world. Like the canary in the bedroom assigned to him in the Schuyler mansion, Stew feels like a bird in Ann's gilded or, more accurately, platinum cage. He eventually wises up, realizing that he misses his work, and that his pal Gallagher, always secretly in love with him, isn't just one of the guys but a beautiful woman.

Harlow seduced the moviegoing public, as Ann did Stew, with good results for her career although disastrous consequences for her female admirers. Her sexiness and comedic talents were obvious, but it was her platinum hair that attracted the most attention. As she gained fame, peroxide sales skyrocketed. Botched attempts to look like Jean forced thousands of women to shave their heads, reversing the old saw that art imitates life.

Hollywood producers of the past had consistently cast dark-haired women in the parts of vixens, but Jean emerged as the first star to incorporate the platinum-blond look into her acting.[23] She was another version of the sex goddess, but through her new interpretation, one that, like West's, had no fatal consequences for the men who came under her spell. Or, perhaps, spells had nothing to do with it.

In fact, sexy as she was—the camera, in all of her films, made the most of rear shots of her retreating, wholly feminine form (moving with very un-Westian gyrations) and of her startling blond hair—her comic MO was too self-deprecating to injure the men who eventually came to love her. Although her comedic potential was there in her brief appearance in *The Double Whoopee,* in which she walks grandly into a hotel despite having left the entire rear portion of her dress in the door of a cab, only a hint of it was visible in *Platinum Blonde.* The willingness to be both comic and sexual, I've argued, distinguishes the actresses of this period—finally even the soulful Greta Garbo in *Ninotchka* (1939)—from previous representations of beautiful women.

Harlow, in 1932, as she would three years later in *China Seas,* played an amiable prostitute in *Red Dust.* She arrives at the Indochinese rubber plantation managed by Dennis[24] Carson/Clark Gable, having skipped Saigon to avoid the police. Vantine's tough-but-sweet humor—through which sex is visible under the skimpiest of wraps—is immediately apparent, most memorably when she quips about a tiger, roaring nearby in the jungle. "Guess I'm not used to sleeping nights, anyway" is a comic, self-inflicted put-down that effectively identifies her occupation (pretty easily guessed from her sexy peignoirs and general demeanor). She's attracted to Carson, who first resists her overtures but soon realizes he's been handed a real gift. With self-deprecating humor and emotional honesty, she rejects Denny's offer of money for the month they've cohabited. "No, Denny," she says, "it wasn't that way"—proof that she's already in the Recording Angel's Book of Gold.

Slayers of men aren't in the habit of exposing their own weaknesses. H. Rider Haggard's Ayesha, "She-who-must-be-obeyed," was a raven-tressed, two-thousand-year-old, white African sex goddess.[25] She didn't crack jokes when she opened her mouth, instead making fearless men "positively quiver with terror at her words" (Haggard 144). If goddesses allow themselves "to quip and crank, to suffer interruptions, to talk of ordinary things" (Woolf, *Common Reader* 45), they are realistically reduced to the human level, participating in the give-and-take of relationships. The cinematic conventions of exaggerated, singularly feminine evil of the sex goddess/vampire were already absurd by the end of the silent era. The talkies, especially in their first years, defined by voluble and adroit verbal reciprocity, were the vampire's death knell.

But even before the talkies, Phyllis Haver's gold-digging Marie, as I have argued, illustrates the descent into the truly divine comedy of ordinary things. The impulse of high modernism—of Virginia Woolf's or James Joyce's novels, for example—as well as of the photojournalism and social realist American fiction of the 1930s—to record the quotidian was occasionally matched even by Hollywood's dream merchants. For as well as the consequences of sound production, it was undeniably true that women through the flapper era had changed. Sex, by the end of the '20s, was freer (not least because of the new methods of birth control) and, therefore, jollier than it had ever been. Sex was "It," as in Clara's Bow's "It Girl," and dark-haired Clara Bow was approachable and very human. Perhaps, then, Mae West had nowhere to go but into parody for her representation of sexuality, and Jean Harlow smartly "humorized" the blond goddess.

Their unique styles were very much of their own making. They embodied the revolutionary idea that the role of the vamp assigned to women over the millennia, from Circe on, might actually be a misogynistic exaggeration. Becky Sharp's comedic propensity and flair for impersonation and Calixta's unabashed sexuality were meeting on the screen, and audiences were obviously delighted.

Platinum hair may paradoxically remind the viewer of the potentially dangerous darkness beneath—a memory trace of the Romantic Other. But if so, that meaning resonates with humor and fun because the dazzling color and means of achieving it are so blatantly contrived. Denny, in a moment of rare amity early in the film, appreciatively looks Vantine over and asks: "Was your hair always this color?" "Uh hm, I was always a towhead," she answers, as if he (and we) were born yesterday. But while the platinum may be counterfeit, hiding dark roots, Vantine's good-hearted sweetness is authentic.

Yet Dennis's casual affection doesn't last long. His head is turned by patrician "Babs" Willis, wife of Gary, a young and enthusiastic engineer who's come to Indochina to learn the rubber trade from Carson. But the Willis' tennis racquets in their presses suggest they aren't ready for the steamy and rough life of the jungle. More evidence is that Gary already has malaria, through which illness Carson competently nurses him.

The love plot thickens when an accidental grounding of the riverboat causes Vantine to return. Sensing that Denny has a new interest, she isn't shy about getting his attention. The bathtub scene becomes, arguably, the definitive moment of the old-time sex goddess's demise. Earlier, the Chinese servant Hoi[26] had explained to the dismayed Babs the fine points of bathing at the plantation. In full view of the entire compound, one must ladle water over one's head from the rain barrel, which also holds the only potable water in the camp. As Denny approaches the building, Vantine showers him with water. Then, pausing in her ablutions, she looks fetchingly over the balcony railing, blond hair attractively piled atop her head (figure 18). He's more than a little annoyed to find that she's actually in the barrel. "What's the matter?" she asks, "Afraid I'll shock the duchess? Don't you think she's ever seen a French postcard?" Not amused, Carson tries unsuccessfully to yank her out by her hair. Then, exasperated by Vantine's sweetly sunny belligerence, he pushes her head under water. Even a goddess can't survive an undignified dunking.

But the two love triangles—Babs-Denny-Vantine, Denny-Babs-Gary— are unstable configurations. Gary, recovered from malaria, is more than eager

Fig. 18. Vantine/Jean Harlow before Dennis/Clark Gable plunges her blond head underwater in *Red Dust* (1932). (Courtesy of Photofest)

to prove his toughness by going into a remote jungle area to survey for a new plantation. With him conveniently out of the way, Denny and Babs can luxuriate in their own "jungle fever." As his passion for Babs gets serious, Denny manfully decides to break it to Gary that he's fallen in love with his wife. However, his trek through the jungle leaves the deed undone because he realizes how much Gary cares for her. Carson may be a sinner, just like Vantine, but in the end he's too decent to break up the marriage. He sarcastically tells the golden-hearted prostitute: "You know what I've just been? I've been noble. . . . Little Denny is an angel now, with a big heart and a big round halo." And, somehow, he finds himself seeking comfort with his own kind: "You know about us?" he asks her. "We belong here. They don't, those two." Their affectionate tussling wakes Babs, who finds them in a compromising embrace. Even more shocked by Carson's intentional compounding of his infidelity—he says he was just playing Babs for a good time—she discharges her smoldering passion through the barrel of a gun she's brought along. Fortunately, her aim isn't lethal.

By amazing coincidence, Gary returns from the jungle at this very moment. Although Carson explains that Babs shot him because he "made a pass at her," it's Vantine who really saves Carson's skin and Babs's honor. With imaginative powers we might have guessed she had, she embroiders Denny's six-word "confession" with her own tale: "This bozo's been after her every minute, and tonight he comes in drunk and tries to break into her room, and she shoots him, the way a virtuous woman would a beast like that!" Gary is all too eager to hustle his wife out of Indochina and back to Westchester, where their wooden racquets won't warp.

The end of the movie is a segue into jungle domesticity. Proving her heroism of deed as well as word by pushing the bullet through Denny's back with an iodine swab, Vantine next shows her more feminine side. When she first arrived at the plantation, she had demonstrated maternal inclination by trying to get a depressed and angry Denny to eat, rather than drink, his dinner. Now the mothering instinct expresses itself energetically as she entertains the recovering Carson by reading the "Children's Corner," the only feature left to read in the camp's one newspaper. As she cheerfully animates the animal characters of the story, Carson, ready for more adult entertainment, impishly "tiptoes" his fingers over his blankets to make contact with Vantine's delectable body. But things have changed since their last embrace. Now the "mother" pushes his wandering fingers away, scolding her bad little boy for misbehaving.

These two are nothing like Jane Eyre and Rochester. While Carson's close brush with death may be Hollywood's version of the wages of near-sin (as Brontë arranged for Rochester to be maimed in the fire set by his mad wife, Bertha), Vantine, unlike Jane, is not tending her husband. Rather, this happy "conjungle" union has not been blessed by church or state and, for all we know or care, may never be. For this was 1932, two years before Joseph Breen of the Hays Office would interpret morality for Americans by applying the strict standards of the Motion Picture Production Code to on-screen representations of sexuality and violence. The blonde was still enjoying her freedom.

Harlow, with exceptions like Ann Schuyler in *Platinum Blonde,* was usually cast as lower class, even if hard work, looks, and, in the case of *Wife vs. Secretary,* competence allowed her characters to climb the ladder of success. But the same self-deprecating humor and habitual linking of sex and mirth showed itself in role after role. In *Dinner at Eight,* George Cukor's 1933 ensemble production, she played Kitty, the adulterous, social-climbing wife of an unscrupulous investor, Dan Packard. Lying in bed all day feigning illness and barely clad in sexy negligees, she waits for her doctor-lover to make his "house call." But while she seems to be a dumb blond tramp, she has a conscience, perfectly comprehending that her husband is scheming to ruin Oliver Jordan (to whose home she dearly wants to be invited for "dinner at eight," but that's not her only reason for decency). With no love for her husband (played by Wallace Beery, also Harlow's unsavory "secret sharer" in the shipboard piracy scheme of *China Seas*), she blackmails him to prevent his stealing Jordan's shipping line. The best moments in the film are the closing shots of Kitty going in to dinner with Carlotta Vance, Oliver Jordan's theatrical aunt (played deliciously by that former "Queen of Comedy," Marie Dressler). Kitty announces that she "was reading a book the other day" (Carlotta, overcome), "all about civilization or something, a nutty kind of a book. Do you know that the guy said that machinery is going to take the place of every profession?" Carlotta, looking over Kitty's alluring figure, quips: "Oh, my dear, that's something you need never worry about!" Not that we needed Carlotta's words or pantomime to realize Kitty's physical charms, but the comic association—even by way of contrast—of the blonde with machinery, instead of mystical powers, firmly places her in a brave new world in which the sexuality of woman may be the subject of a joke and—even more important—humor itself one of its attributes.

Harlow next played Lola Burns, a rising movie star, in *Bombshell,* also of 1933. The plot parodies the film industry's well-oiled publicity machine. Space Hanlon, the "PR man," "media-hyping" this blonde "Bombshell," a name he claims to have "dubbed" her with, has invented Lola's sexy image to stimulate box-office sales. The opening frames, like so many other self-reflexive comments in films of the period, are a series of montages: Lola's face and dazzling platinum hair in close-ups on the cover of *Photoplay;* stacks of fan magazines; newspaper headlines ("The Love Life of Lola Burns!" [pun, of course, intended]; "Society Matron Sues Lola Burns"; "Lola Burns Spars With [boxer] Primo Carnera"); Lola doing product placements; fans on trains soaking up the gossip in the magazines and papers; or dreaming about her in movie houses as she passionately kisses Clark Gable on the big screen. The women want nothing more than to be her—the men nothing less than to possess her. The added fillip was hardly an insider's joke—references to Jean Harlow's recent film career. With pre-postmodern *jouissance,* the fiction of Lola and reality of Jean dizzily mix.

The scheming Hanlon/Lee Tracy's embroidering of vulgar stories about Lola drives the thin plot. In a nod to the realities of the Production Code, her maid, Loretta (Louise Beavers—always the maid), wakes her early to film retakes of the bathtub scene in *Red Dust,* "demanded" by the Hays Office for decency's sake.

Frustrated by her exhausting schedule and Hanlon's salacious stories, she decides to end her career and adopt a child, encouraged by Mrs. *Tit*comb of the *Ladies' Home Journal,* who had asked if she didn't have "a longing for the right of all womanhood . . . listening for the patter of little feet." Of the baby she chooses from the orphanage, she says to the matron: "Do you think his hair'll be any lighter when he grows up? Wouldn't it be nice if he were a blond, and then people'd think he was really mine?" However, drawing attention to her chemically treated hair is the real joke.

As soon as Hanlon learns of her plan, he tells Lola: "You can't adopt a baby. . . . The fans don't wanna see the "If Girl" [a play on Clara Bow's "It Girl"—and another self-referential joke about the film industry] surrounded by an aura of motherhood, leanin' over a cradle, sterilizin' bottles!" And to the gossip columnists: "You think I want my 'Bombshell' turnin' into a rubber nipple?" The numerous puns on mammary equipment wouldn't have made it past the censors after July 1934.

Lola and Space's sparring over his wrecking her chance at motherhood and romance is the only tension in this silly story. The head of Monarch studio had even suggested to Hanlon that his efforts to destroy Lola's love life might be motivated by personal jealousy rather than professional zeal. And so it is. But just as Lola finally melts into Space's embrace, another of Hanlon's stooges, who, throughout the film thrusts himself at Lola, pretending to be her abandoned husband, appears once more, popping his head into their car to ask Mr. Hanlon: "How'm I doing?" Lola "burns" again, this time with rage, as the music swells and the words "The End" fill the screen.

Andrew Sarris in *"You Ain't Heard Nothin' Yet"* dates the invention of the "screwball"[27] genre—romantic comedy marked by wisecracks, slapstick, pratfalls, and the like—from 1934, that is, after the censors removed sex from the movies. Dismissing the argument of film critics who believe that the devices in these comedies are equivalent to "frustration" attributable to the "economic crisis" and "the threat of approaching war," he maintains that the frustration is rather a result of the censors' removal of sex, leaving only the substitute of badinage and, when language gives out, pranks and pratfalls (45).

But *Bombshell* of '33 has all the distinguishing characteristics of the screwball genre, minus the heavy hand of the censor (figure 19). Sarris is probably right in rejecting the economy and war threat but fails, I think, to take account of women's changing positions in the early '30s as determining the nature of encounters between potential lovers in film.

I referred earlier to the satisfaction of verbal play between evenly matched sparring partners. The phrase is as much explanation as description of what occurs between men and women in these movies. A woman's desire to engage reveals her transformation from victim to fully armed combatant in the battle of the sexes. She needn't settle for second-best. In fact, she needn't settle at all. Verbal quipping, even physical fighting, is prologue to love—if love is to be at all. In 1941, Virginia Woolf articulated the impulse when she wrote of her hero and heroine in the last pages of *Between the Acts:* "Before they slept, they must fight; after they had fought, they would embrace. . . . But first they must fight, as the dog fox fights with the vixen, in the heart of darkness, in the fields of night" (219). Thus in nature, so with civilized women and men.

But there is also hoary theatrical precedent for the shenanigans of screwball. From the sixteenth century, the clown figures of commedia dell'arte, prefiguring Punch and Judy, swatted and batted each other about, treating audiences to the low-comedy version of love and war between the sexes. Censors had nothing to do with it. With the "playing" field leveled by the Nineteenth Amendment, birth control, and the Great Depression, women, free

Fig. 19. Lola "burns" in movie poster for "pre-Code" *Bombshell* (1933). (Courtesy of Photofest)

to express this aggressive, but not unhealthy, side of human nature, happily joined in the free-for-all. I would, then, replace "frustration" with "foreplay" to define the characteristic behavior in screwball's version of reality.

Carole Lombard's first great comic part—Mildred Plotka, alias Lily Garland—in Howard Hawks's madcap *Twentieth Century*, is very much like Harlow's in *Bombshell*. The 1934 pre-Code movie, released May 11th (Ott 119), is about the ongoing battle between Broadway director Oscar Jaffe (John Barrymore, whom Lombard credited with teaching her to play comedy) and his protégée, a lovely young thing who can't act at all (she had been a lingerie salesgirl) when she begins rehearsals for Jaffe's play[28]—*The Heart of Kentucky*—a trite melodrama about the Old South. But Lily Garland will be his prize pupil—even if it takes a corsage pin, slyly lifted by Jaffe from Lily's coat lapel and jabbed by him into her bottom, to get her to project her voice, in a full-throated scream, to the upper balcony.

Cut to opening night. The theater audience wildly applauds Lily as she takes her curtain call. She's never blonder nor more romantic looking than when she returns to her dressing room, still dressed in her Civil War–period, off-the-shoulder gown. The camera moves in for a close-up of Lily's radiant head and bust, dissolving into soft focus on her expression of fervent gratitude and hero-worship as Jaffe, with exaggerated humility, enters her dressing room to pay his respects to a "great artist" (figure 20). But she humbles herself before him, protesting that her success is entirely his, showing him the now-treasured corsage pin (her memento of her real start as an actress) piercing a satin heart-shaped pillow, fringed with lace. As she holds it up for him to see, the camera dollies in for a screen-filling shot of the pin-pierced pillow, subliminally resembling the exposed female genitalia, anatomically correct, down to the last detail. The blonde and sex are intriguingly united.

But melodramatic romance devolves into broad comedy as Jaffe, always histrionic, asks for the "honor" of kissing the artist good-bye. Yes, the blonde meltingly answers, yes. The camera cuts to his leg and foot, with which Barrymore deftly closes the dressing-room door, but not before we see his eyebrows arch devilishly in anticipation of sexual conquest.

Another fade out and cut represent a jump in time and a further revision of Lily and Jaffe's relationship. No longer the ingenue, she is now an experienced "twentieth-century" woman and his mistress. But she's tiring of Jaffe's possessiveness. As Owen O'Malley/Roscoe Karns, Jaffe's emissary, arrives at her

Fig. 20. Oscar Jaffe/John Barrymore "pays his respects" to a great star, Lily Garland/ Carole Lombard, in *Twentieth Century* (1934). (Courtesy of Photofest)

apartment to let her know that she's driving the great director mad with jealousy, he enters her bedroom, bumping into the black putto that decorates the prow of her gondola bed, eyeing it as if it had offered him a personal affront. This showboat of a bed is a florid affair, as sensational as Mae West's swan bed in *Diamond Lil,* and meant to stand in for the now-worldly Lily's success as an actress. Her current role in *The Bride of Bagdad* [*sic*]—a poster for the play is backstage in the theater—as well as the black putto, darken the blonde, suggesting Lily's transformation into a sexually experienced woman.

Soon after, discovering that Jaffe has hired a detective to tap her phone and tail her, Lily flees New York, boarding a train headed to the irrigated, greener pastures of Hollywood. Jaffe, told of her defection and with his usual flair for melodrama, underscores the visual symbolism of the putto by dashing black paint against the poster of *The Bride of Bagdad,* literally blackening (and obliterating) Lily Garland's name.

Unlike Mae West's vehicles, *Twentieth Century* makes no patent allusions to race except for Jaffe's passing comment on the ludicrousness of his assistant director Max Jacobs's name-change from Max Mandelbaum. The black/white symbolism, overt after the paint-dashing episode, and Jaffe's immediate choice of another female actress, Valerie *White*house, to replace Lily, negatively define the assertive blonde, but the perspective is Jaffe's—not the film's, nor ours. Indeed, that Lily is Jaffe's mistress is not a matter for the morality police; it doesn't challenge the values of the audience in the least.

But Jaffe's anger at Lily is as much economic as sexual. Without his star, Jaffe's own career is in free fall. He must even disguise himself to board the Twentieth Century Limited—the real-life Chicago–New York train that gave the film its eponymous title—to escape his creditors. By coincidence, Lily Garland, dressed in a leopard-trimmed coat and hat (figure 21) and dark sunglasses—no Victorian belle now but a twentieth-century woman—also boards the train. The antic business (figure 22) of the rest of the movie is Jaffe's manipulative effort to get her signature on a contract for a starring role in his next play—his only hope of reviving his once-glorious career. Playing on her distress when she believes he's "dying" of a bullet-grazing, he gets her to sign. When she realizes she's been duped, their dog-fox-and-vixen combat resumes and continues as Jaffe directs her in the first rehearsal of the new play, reprising the movie's opening scene. "Here we go again, with Livingston through darkest Africa," quips the wise-cracking Owen O'Malley. The screen fades to black on their Punch-and-Judy love, just as it had on the warring Lola Burns and Space Hanlon in *Bombshell*.

This movie and *Bombshell* were moments of consequence for women, as were Mae West's films. When Lily was resisting Oscar Jaffe's monomaniacal grip on her life, she screamed to Owen O'Malley: "I'm no Trilby! For three years I've never done anything, read anything [of which he hasn't approved]. That's not love; it's pure tyranny!" She thus invokes the giantess Trilby O'Ferrall in George du Maurier's 1894 novel *Trilby*, in which Trilby falls under the spell of Svengali, mesmerized by him to become a singer of unearthly beauty. While Nina Auerbach reads du Maurier's novel to show how he transforms Trilby into a demonic, double-edged figure, capable of killing men with her great beauty (16–22), Lily's more straightforward interpretation of the character, with whom she compares herself, is that she's the victim of men, not their assassin. She merely claims her equality and right to freedom, which Jaffe has usurped. She will exercise that freedom through her work as a movie star.

Fig. 21. Lily Garland as a twentieth-century woman. (Courtesy of Photofest)

In fact, with romance on hold or redefined as "permanent revolution," both *Bombshell* and *Twentieth Century* focus on the imprimatur on work—women's work. The conflict between the would-be lovers in both films centers on the actresses' productivity, not reproductivity. The question of motherhood never surfaces at all in *Twentieth Century;* in *Bombshell* it's the men who do the discouraging. Jim Brogan, Lola Burns's director on the Monarch Studio lot, says to her: "Say, you can't raise a family and make five pictures a year! You're just in a mood, and you're playing a scene with yourself. I'd like to have a camera turning on you right now. Say, you'd be a sensation! . . . Ah, honey, you just think you want a baby, that's all. Why don't you call up some orphan asylum. Tell 'em to send you over one on a thirty-day free trial." And this just at the time when Nazi ideologues were promoting Aryan domesticity with the Teutonic blonde as the genetic vessel of choice.

Although there are marriage proposals and engagements at the end of *Gold Diggers of 1933* (the Busby Berkeley backstage story/musical with Dick Powell, Joan Blondell, Ginger Rogers, and Ruby Keeler, who, oddly, dons a platinum marcelled wig for her final number), there is no question of the chorus girls' giving up their theatrical careers. Work tops romance. Flimsily, "Old Man Depression" is the inspiration for the musical the chorines perform in and the actual character of the hungry wolf at their door when they're out of work early in the story. But the wish to be active, to fulfill their theatrical ambitions

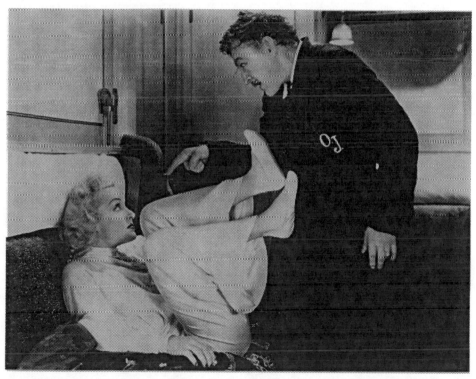

Fig. 22. Screwball love aboard the Twentieth Century Limited. (Courtesy of Photofest)

looms larger than the question of filling their stomachs, as the character played by Dick Powell confirms. He's a talented songwriter-turned-singer, escaping the etiolated life of the rich to work, not for the money (he has plenty from his wealthy relations, who oppose his "disreputable" theatrical career), but because of his creative aspirations. "Were it not the pitifulest infinitesimal fraction of a Product, produce it, in God's name!" wrote Thomas Carlyle, exactly a century before. "Up, up! Whatsoever thy hand findeth to do, do it with thy whole might. Work while it is called Today; for the Night cometh, wherein no man can work."[29] *Gold Diggers* is the updated version of his exhortation.

True, there's an apparent disconnect between the celebration of work in *Gold Diggers* and in many other movies and the scarcity of actual jobs in the 1930s. But these films served as advertisements for the phoenix of capitalism, mystifying economic reality to suggest that individual perseverance would transform the bleak, jobless landscape. The surprise is that women's work outside the home should be the focus in plot after plot.

Regi Allen/Carole Lombard in *Hands across the Table,* Mitchell Leisen's 1935 film about a gold-digging manicurist, openly states her ambition to marry a millionaire. "Oh love," she cynically claims, "I don't want anything to do with it." But her cynicism is of the once-bitten-twice-shy variety—not Mae West's first-strike approach. Regi, however, doesn't live according to her own principles, falling for Ted Drew/Fred MacMurray (figure 23), a penniless ex-millionaire playboy who has lost his fortune in the Crash, instead of the very wealthy, willing, and kindly Allen Macklyn/Ralph Bellamy (who would also play the rejected lover in *The Awful Truth* and *His Girl Friday*), a flyer before he was crippled in another kind of crash. Her choice of men means that work will continue to be an imperative.

The pressure of city life for the working girl is immediately apparent in the first frames of the film. Regi and her girlfriend/coworker are jostled in the crush of commuters as they leave the subway car at Grand Central Station, bound for their jobs as manicurists in the barber shop of the swank Savoy Carleton Hotel. In *The Battle of the Sexes* (remember the manicurist in the opening scene of that film), the city was projected as a glamorous, powerful, modern environment. Seven years later in *Hands across the Table,* the representation of the city is inseparable from the grind of the unglamorous workaday world. "You just try getting up every morning at seven, then jammed in the subway, and then poking at people's cuticle all day, and then jammed back in the subway again at night!" Regi tells Allen Macklyn. Again in 1936,

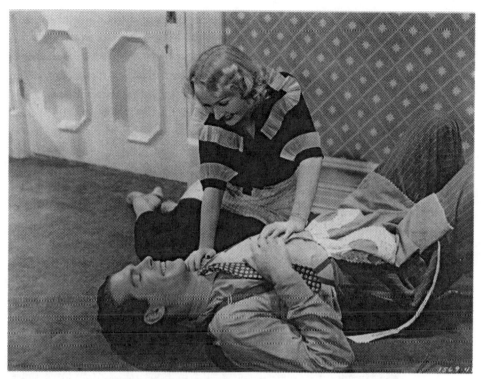

Fig. 23. Regi/Carole Lombard's hands across Theodore Drew III/Fred MacMurray in *Hands across the Table* (1935). (Courtesy of Photofest)

the painted cityscape, the background for the horizontally scrolling credits of Frank Capra's *My Man Godfrey*, would also be inseparable from the even less glamorous unemployed—"the Forgotten Men," living in New York City's dump on the edge of the East River—which painted scene magically morphs into the real as the camera rolls.

But work also acquires meaning through Lombard's style. As both quipping and cynical Regi in *Hands . . .* and dizzily comic Irene Bullock in *My Man Godfrey*, Lombard was the operative definition of the chameleon actor, performing ably in serious drama or pressured, slapstick comedy. In these films, as well as in her screwball performance as Hazel Flagg in *Nothing Sacred* (1937) and, arguably, in her greatest comedic role, Maria Tura in *To Be or Not to Be* (1942), she developed her trademark sighs and audible "mmms"—apparent feminine flutterings, which in the screwball world don't signal romantic acquiescence but are breath-catching moments before the next volleys of silvery laughter—her attack on life itself. The meaning of work gains substance through her energy—even when she plays the wealthy socialite Irene—and the sheer speed and vitality of her speech and movements. She's a life force; something, we feel, must be getting done, being accomplished by this benignly cheerful dervish of activity. And, of course, something is. No matter how silly her behavior, she achieves results, she gets her man: Godfrey/William Powell (her real-life ex-husband), who "butles" for the Bullocks in *My Man Godfrey;* Wally Cook/Fredric March, the reporter who covers her "human interest" story in *Nothing Sacred.*

Early in *Hands . . .* , Regi asks Ted if he's ever considered work as an alternative to the poverty he openly proclaims. No, he answers. There's nothing he's been trained to do except marry a rich woman, thus establishing the symmetry of their aspirations although not of their experience. However, when he falls in love with Regi, he comically complains: "Do you know what she's done? She's wrecked my life! She's got me thinking about looking for a job!" At the end of the film, they ride on an open-topped bus, deciding through a coin flip their order of business: lunch, marriage, or a job hunt: "Heads we get married and tails we go to lunch. If it stands on edge, I'll look for a job," says Ted. But the coin catapults onto the street with Regi and Ted in screwball pursuit—jamming traffic and inspiring a symphony of blaring horns. Indecorously crawling on hands and knees, they discover it, wedged on-edge in a manhole cover. The movie's last words are Ted's capitulation to the new order of "business": "Well, I guess we look for a job."

Like this vertical coin, Lombard's talents were perfectly balanced. She was able to play with verve, humor, and intelligence a great variety of roles but also to project absolute integrity. As the "Twentieth Century Limited" speeds to New York City, Lily Garland, fed up with serving as Jaffe's "meal ticket" and his histrionics, argues with her director and former lover: "That's the trouble with you, Oscar—with both of us. We're not people—we're lithographs! We don't know anything about love unless it's written and rehearsed. We're only real between curtains!" Although she means the comparison as an indictment, Lily might well be paying Lombard a genuine compliment. For Carole Lombard had an aptitude for duplicating characters in Albert Camus' sense of the actor's unique ability to multiply and enrich both hers and our experience. While other movie stars were identifiably themselves in film after film, Lombard despite recognizable mannerisms was something more: she was radiantly various—the real thing each time.

The very quality that arguably caused primitives to fear and distrust the actor—the absence of a discernible and stable identity[30]—was Lombard's great strength. Yet one trait was coincident with all her roles: at core, an intelligent and energetic sincerity. When Regi first meets Allen Macklyn, she admits she's looking for money, not love. Other women, she says, feel the same way, but she's willing to confess it. Or take Hazel Flagg, whose radium-poisoning death sentence, giving her two more weeks to live, has been "commuted" by her doctor (who realizes he has mistaken the lab results) to an ordinary life span. As she says to him: "It's kind of startling to be brought to life twice, and each time in Warsaw [Vermont]." At first she willingly perpetrates a hoax, accepting an official invitation to visit New York City, where her "heroism" in the face of certain death will be celebrated. And wouldn't we be tempted to do the same if we came from sleepy Warsaw, Vermont? However, after a night of carousing in the big city, she wakes up feeling terrible. Her doctor says: "You have, in medicine, what is called a hangover." "I've something worse than that," she declares; "I've got a conscience."

That's the point. All these women have a conscience and its correlate: down-to-earth, middle-class values. In *Bombshell*, Lola Burns expresses her middle-class decency when she learns that her suitor's parents, the blue-blooded "Middletons of Boston," object to her acting career. She asks: "Is it any disgrace entertaining people?—makin' 'em laugh, makin' 'em cry?" Middle-class commitment to honest work, these movies imply, will be the motive force that gets America out of the Depression. Irene Bullock's hardworking "man" Godfrey, despite his (phony) lower social class, was proof that the middle class is the sturdy backbone of American enterprise and morality.

These women, from Mae West on, represent a policy of "full faith and credit" (marriage) or "truth in lending" (a satisfying love affair). Theirs is a kind of economics of morality: what you see is what you will eventually get. This truth even extends to their blond hair . . . well, at least to Carole Lombard's. In *The Princess Comes Across*, King Mantell/Fred MacMurray, acknowledging the current blond vogue, says of the "Princess" Olga's hair: "Hey, did you see that hair? That wasn't bleached. That's what I call a 'royal' blonde!" Of course, Mantell will soon find out that the Princess isn't really a princess at all (or, perhaps, more accurately, she's a fairy tale of a princess) but plain Wanda Nash, an aspiring, so-far-unsuccessful actress from Brooklyn. But it's Wanda who will tell him the truth, explaining the economic necessity for her ruse. No studio will give her a contract if she doesn't erase her plebeian origins by turning herself into an exotic princess from Sweden, home of natural blondes. However, in another sense, all these blondes are the modern world's updated version of "the princess." The "royal blonde" has been transformed—a figure of activity, integrity, spirit, and grit.

And all these women (with the exception of Mae West) are, in fact, "natural" blondes—peroxide notwithstanding. Whatever cunning they use or lies they tell, their freedom of movement, zaniness, or eleventh-hour repentance makes them unique in cinema history. Coy is not a word they're familiar with, even when they're interested in a man. When Regi tells Ted Drew that he's had too many drinks, Ted, pretending to be the uxorious husband, says to the waiter: "Hey, you see what my home life is? Nag, nag, nag!" "But your wife is so pretty," says the waiter. "Pretty? Mmmm, well [sizing her up], I suppose so, in an oriental sort of way. You know [turning to Regi with a thoughtful, considering air], you'd be very beautiful with blond hair." As if in a somnambulistic stupor, she slowly answers, giving equal measure to the utterance of each word: "I . . . have . . . blond . . . hair." "I know it," he simply responds. Despite the others in the noisy restaurant, they're alone, submerged like divers in a silent sea, looking intently into each other's eyes. There is nothing between them but the truth of their emotion; they are falling—if not already—in love.

Ted's heart has really been conquered by the new attributes of Regi's blond hair. She can be silly, have fun, be real, when, for example, both of them break down in laughter as they fight to stop a bout of loud hiccups in an elegant restaurant, or when Regi, following Ted's lead, begins to unbutton her blouse, taking a maître d' at his literal word when he informs them: "I'm sorry, it's the rules. Patrons cannot enter wearing those clothes." Regi, Hazel Flagg, and Wanda Nash, not to mention Jean Arthur's Babe Bennett, the prize-winning and, at first, self-serving and manipulative reporter in *Mr. Deeds Goes to Town* (1936), or her Clarissa Saunders, the cynical Senate aide in *Mr. Smith Goes to Washington* (1941), or Penny Carroll (Ginger Rogers), the hardworking dance instructor in *Swing Time* (1936), are ultimately "natural" in their behavior. I could lengthen this list with many more names. Let Wanda Nash's confession sum up the truthfulness and naturalness of all these women. Beginning in her counterfeit Swedish accent as the Princess Olga, surrounded by admirers at a dockside press conference in New York, she says that this is her happiest moment. But then, suddenly stepping out of that character, losing her accent, and destroying her chances for a Hollywood career, she wails: "No! I've never been so unhappy in my life. I can't go on being a phony. I'm a Brooklyn gal, do you understand? I'm nothing, do you understand, I'm nothing! I've never been to Sweden in my life. I'm a Brooklyn gal. Yeah, my folks live on 15th Street, yeah. They're there right now. Oh, Mom, can you hear me?"

The whole point is not that she's nothing, but really something—something never seen before: a striving, working-class girl with a loud voice, brave, brash, and wily enough to invent and carry through a scheme to garner a studio contract and the work it would mean, and honest enough to admit to the fraud in the moment of "awful truth." Her reward, of course, is that the *real* princess, the "Brooklyn gal" Wanda, gets more than a prince—her "King" Mantell, the band leader, who's risked his life to track down the murderer on their ship. Wanda and her sisters are unlike Scarlett O'Hara, that redhead, whom Parker Tyler describes as a "masterpiece of self-deception, self-bribery: she can go on happily only because, in spite of her failure of character, life has bestowed on her a faculty of isolating desire from its crisis in action—a faculty which makes her the screen's typical heroine of all time and a symbol of Hollywood itself" (*Hollywood Hallucination* 61). Certainly in the '30s, Scarlett was far from the typical Hollywood screen heroine.

Even in times of economic hardship (or war), the public loved and needed comedy—the premise of Preston Sturges's *Sullivan's Travels* (1941). An example was the lighthearted *Roxie Hart* of 1942 (the William Wellman/Nunnally Johnson remake of the play *Chicago* by Maurine Watkins) in which Ginger Rogers, her hair dyed a dark red shade (registering as black in the black-and-white film), did her spirited version of a jailhouse rock—the "Black Bottom."[31] Because Ginger Rogers had achieved stardom as a blonde, dark-haired Roxie creates a sort of double-exposure. We see dark hair; we remember blond. The blonde's dark roots have been unequivocally "outed." With credits rolling, we read the blithely amusing dedicatory words of a protofeminist manifesto: "This film is dedicated to all the beautiful women in the world who have shot their men full of holes out of pique" and "'For that lovely porous skin, try a 38,' Roxie Heart." A montage of newspaper headlines (figure 24) further uncovers the 1930s' assumption about blondes (they're active, sexual, and potentially angry): "'Not Guilty' Verdict in Trial of Blonde Who Shot Her Friend Six Times Accidentally."

This will be Roxie's story, or almost. Convinced that the publicity she gets will be her big break, the wannabe chorine surrenders to the police after they find the body of her agent/boyfriend in her apartment. The reporters assume that her wild behavior is "caused" by "black" music and dance: "Is it true, Mrs.

Fig. 24. "Beautiful Roxie Hart [Ginger Rogers], Black Bottom Slayer" in *Roxie Hart* (1942). (Courtesy of Photofest)

Hart," asks one reporter, "you were swept off your feet by jazz?" and "What about the 'Black Bottom'? Good at it—ain't ya?" When the photographer/Phil Silvers arrives at the jail to find Roxie and the reporters doing the Black Bottom (figure 25), he exclaims: "Well, hush my big black mouth!"—explicitly linking the blonde-turned-redhead and black culture. Yet although the assumptions about the blonde and blackness in this movie may seem a retrograde revisiting of the Dracula brides, Roxie and the other blondes are always found innocent by juries in Cook County—another reason she was willing to go to jail. Later in the movie, when she changes her image to revive the reporters' flagging interest in her story, she's comically transformed into a Madonna, gum-chewing as always (appearing in prison, with her lawyer, Billy Flynn, to announce that she's expecting a little "stranger"). She has a new look: a black, nunlike veil decorously covers her head, and neat bangs replace her tousled curls.[32] At the end of the film, she arrives to collect her husband, Homer Howard, a reporter who had covered her arrest and trial in 1927. Homer has served as the "narrator" of the movie's story, regaling his drinking buddies in a Chicago bar with an account of those long-ago events. Now, fifteen years later, Roxie's a real live mama, her car jammed with kids. Looking frazzled by domestic burdens, she tartly announces: "Darling, I've got some news for you. We're gonna have to have a bigger car next year." This is one of the few comedies—*My Favorite Wife* is another exception—in which the heroine has children. However, in *Roxie Heart* they're merely the film's comic punch line. The dedication of the opening frames cheerfully haunts the end of Roxie's story; women, even those in domestically harmonious unions, might have reason to be "piqued."

In the early 1940s, Hollywood retreated, not from comedy, but cynicism, as in Frank Capra's idealistic *Mr. Smith Goes to Washington,* which put an ideological spin on romance and the blonde's projection as a rounded character. Clarissa Saunders, whose Christian name, "most brilliant one," defines her intellect, is the mover in the hero's campaign to end the corruption of a state political ma-

Fig. 25. Roxie Hart rocks the jailhouse doing the Black Bottom. Publicity still. (Courtesy of Photofest)

chine and its influence in the Senate. The naive hero, Jefferson Smith/James Stewart, can't succeed without Clarissa's intimate knowledge of the Constitution and arcane Senate rules.

But freedom and democracy needed shoring up on the international as well as the national front, and Hollywood willingly played its role. Despite the film's farcical character, preserving these principles is never more important than in Ernst Lubitsch's *To Be or Not to Be.* In this movie, comedic commentary on the invasion of a country and the extermination of Jews is an evolutionary turn beyond Sturges's simple position in *Sullivan's Travels:* the people may need to laugh, but the Comic Spirit can be appropriated for important political work . . . with a blonde to make the case.

Lubitsch, the Jewish emigré who had earned his Hollywood reputation with sophisticated romantic comedies like *Trouble in Paradise* (1932) and *Design for Living,* first turned, in 1939, to a comic critique of Soviet Communism in *Ninotchka* (with a real blond Swede, Greta Garbo) and then of Nazism in his trenchantly funny *To Be . . . ,* featuring the inimitable Jack Benny and Carole Lombard. As Joseph and Maria Tura, stars of a theatrical troupe in Warsaw performing just before and during the German occupation in 1939, they give real substance to Lubitsch's political purpose through their mastery of comedy. He asked his audience to consider the relationship between acting and acting—the necessity for *acting* when *all* the world's a stage.

The plot turns on deceptions of every kind—of political espionage and double agents, of adultery, but also of the aesthetic deceptions inherent in theatrical performance and the medium of film itself. However, the story champions the value to civilization of truth, both sexual and political. In fact, this film elides the two, essentially arguing that the sexual *is* political. Although unlike in character, tone, and genre, *To Be or Not to Be* and Meredith's "Essay on Comedy" arrive at a similar place. There can be no true comedy without sexual equality, the proposition that breathes life into Maria's sparring relationship with her husband and also the wonderful dressing-room interview with her much younger, starstruck admirer, the airman Captain Sobinski/Robert Stack, who, in his mind, has arranged Maria's future without consulting her.

But *To Be . . .* goes further. It makes the claim that comedy *safeguards* equality and freedom not only for women but everyone. Laughing at Hitler is a powerful weapon in the arsenal to ensure that the dictator remain in people's eyes "just a man with a little moustache." However, the film was criticized when it was released in 1942 by some who took offense at Lubitsch's effort to trivialize the evil of the Nazis by representing them as ridiculous blunderers. In other words, they rejected his position on the uses of comedy—an issue to which I'll return.

Although many of the high comic moments belong to Jack Benny and the other male actors, Carole Lombard received top billing, and her Maria Tura has some truly memorable scenes in a movie that is neither a "woman's film" nor a romantic or screwball comedy. The weight of a decade of wonderful roles for women is behind the realization of her part in *To Be*. . . . Maria is physically and morally courageous, willing to risk her life to kill Professor Alexander Siletsky (a Pole spying for the Gestapo), loyal to her husband despite her daytime trysts with Sobinski, and, above all, very, very funny.

The movie is postmodern in its Chinese-box beginning. A little man with a little moustache and German military uniform appears on the streets of Warsaw in August 1939, gathering a large crowd of motorists and passersby as he looks at the storefronts named for their Polish proprietors: Lubiński; Kubiński; Lomiński, etc. "Is he, by any chance," asks the voice-over, "interested in Mr. Maslowski's delicatessen? That's impossible! He's a vegetarian! And yet he doesn't always stick to his diet. Sometimes he swallows up whole countries. Does he want to eat up Poland, too?" Political satire is thus frankly introduced. But how did "Hitler" get to Warsaw? "Well, it all started in the General Headquarters of the Gestapo in Berlin."

Fade out and cut to "Gestapo" headquarters, where Jack Benny, the Gestapo colonel, questions a little boy about his father's loyalty to Hitler. But the interview is interrupted by the excited announcement, shouted from offscreen, that the Führer himself has arrived. As the little man with the brush moustache enters, he raises his arm in the Nazi salute and says "Heil myself!" (A line so good that Mel Brooks "borrowed" it for *The Producers*), thus comically and unquestionably dispelling any possible tension in the moment and, of course, destroying the belief that we're witnessing an incident in Gestapo HQ.

We've been deceived by the technology and aesthetic contract of film into believing in a reality that is altogether different from the reality of the story. The breaching of that contract is conclusive when a disembodied voice shouts: "That's not in the script!" Someone has objected to "Hitler's" speaking implausible words. A switch in camera angles reveals Dobosh, the director, seated at a table and following a script as the actors speak their lines. He disapproves of breaking faith with an ideal (and future) audience, whose wish it would be to continue a self-willed theatrical deception. "But it will get a laugh," argues

Mr. Bronski, the actor playing Hitler. But Mr. Dobosh doesn't want a laugh, emphasizing the distance between his sort of political critique of Nazism and that of Ernst Lubitsch. Mr. Greenberg (the inimitable Felix Bressart), the Jew in the cast whose ambition is to play Shylock in the Rialto scene ("Hath not a Jew eyes?" becomes, in Greenberg's interpretation, "Have we not eyes?"),[33] asks: "Do you want my opinion, Mr. Dobosh?" When Dobosh says "No!" the irrepressible Greenberg adds: "All right, then let me give you my reaction. A laugh is nothing to be sneezed at!" underscoring the political advantage of Lubitsch's comic approach. When Dobosh further complains of a lack of verisimilitude—that Mr. Bronski doesn't look like Hitler—the actor leaves the rehearsal to prove, by walking on the street, that the citizens of Warsaw will be deceived by his impersonation (thus explaining why "Hitler" was standing in front of Maslowski's delicatessen).

Moments later, the point about the power of the comic and its relation to authenticity is replayed when Maria Tura makes her flamboyant entrance—blond, beautiful, and energetically striding directly into the camera's lens—in Lombard's animated style. Maria's movements are entirely different from Lily Garland's in the first scene of *Twentieth Century*, in which she's timid and tentative, from her awkwardly jerking arm down to her trembling fingertips. Full of confidence, Maria's wearing a dramatic satin halter-top evening dress with a sexy slit skirt (figure 26). She interrupts Dobosh, in the middle of explaining to the cast his political interpretation of this "serious play, a realistic drama." How does he like her dress?

DOBOSH: (distracted) Very good, very good. (turns back to cast) It's a document of Nazi Germ—(double take) Is that what you're going to wear in the concentration camp?

MARIA: Don't you think it's pretty?

DOBOSH: That's just it!

MARIA: Well, why not? I think it's a tremendous contrast. Think of me being flogged in the darkness. I scream. Suddenly, the lights go on, and the audience discovers me on the floor in this gorgeous dress!

GREENBERG: That's a terrific laugh!

DOBOSH: That's right, Greenberg! (double take) You keep out of this! (addressing Maria) That a great star, an artist, could be so inartistic! You must be out of your mind!

Joseph Tura now enters, reprimands Dobosh for talking so disrespectfully to his wife, and then joins the director: "Sweetheart, the dress stinks!"—a comment provoking Maria to verbal battery. Her voice rises in irritation: "It's becoming ridiculous, the way you grab attention! You're only afraid I'm running away with the scene. (scornfully) You're the greatest actor in the world—everybody knows that, including you!" She rehearses Tura's competitive narcissism: "Whenever I start to tell a story, you finish it! If I go on a diet, you lose the weight! If I have a cold, you cough. And if we should ever have a baby, I'm not so sure I'd be the mother!" Thus, they go "along, Punch and Judy, attracting each other and repelling, as love must do if it is not to end up as calendar art or a pop tune."[34]

And, thus, a comic battle of the sexes is declared, even in the midst of a tense political moment when the fate of a country—whether it is to be or not—hangs in the balance. Aesthetic deception and sexual politics first meet

Fig. 26. Maria Tura/Carole Lombard interrupting the rehearsal of a "serious play, a realistic drama" about Nazi Germany in *To Be or Not to Be* (1942). (Courtesy of Photofest)

in Maria's dressing room when the starstruck Sobinski tells Maria he's seen her in the newspaper, pictured behind a plow. Where was she? he wants to know. "In *The Chronicle*," Maria answers literally, perplexed that Sobinski believes in a reality other than the publicity shot. After their relationship has developed (she's flown in his bomber), he tells her that he won't let her continue her acting career. "Oh, no! no! I wouldn't let you! That's out!" Maria looks incredulous, amazed at his impervious imperiousness. As if one man like this in her life isn't enough! "You want to live a quiet life," he continues, basing his assertion on an infallible source: "You said so in *The Chronicle*." He then recalls the photo: "You won't have to use that plow anymore. I'll buy you a tractor." Only the maid's agitated announcement that the war has started puts Sobinski off his determined pursuit of the star.

But sex and politics will be joined more intimately, literally at the hip, as the action progresses. Seduction becomes a weapon of choice in fighting the enemy and an element in Lubitsch's aesthetic-political Chinese box: play, inside represented life, inside film, inside the political reality of 1942.

Aesthetic deception stands in for political betrayal. Lubitsch, with his ordinarily light comedic touch, wanted to put art at the service of the political. Overtly connecting art and politics, one of the characters remarks: "Well, we don't have to worry about that Nazi play anymore. The Nazis themselves are putting on a show right now—a much bigger one."

Thus, early on, the actors must stop "acting" (the Gestapo's closing of their theater makes that easy), and start acting for their lives and the lives of their Polish compatriots; willy-nilly they become characters in that Nazi "show." Creating, as Lubitsch did at the beginning of the film, an ironic but pleasurable conflation of representation and "reality," the actors transform their actual theater into a space in which to deceive Alexander Siletsky into believing he's visiting Gestapo headquarters. And their dramatic skills do fool the Nazi for a time. Jack Benny plays Colonel Ehrhardt of the Gestapo ("So they call me 'Concentration Camp Ehrhardt!'" he blusters), to whom Siletsky delivers a list of the names of those helping the Polish underground. But even when their theatrical craft fails (Siletsky eventually realizes the Gestapo chief is Joseph Tura, the actor), they know they still must act. As he tries to escape, he's shot, his body illuminated by a spotlight as he runs across the theater's stage. The moment neatly highlights the relation between aesthetic representation and life: the stage is to performance what shooting is to real-world action.

Maria Tura is actually the first of the troupe to engage with the enemy, plying her craft on the world's stage. Before his visit to "Gestapo Headquarters," Siletsky had summoned her to a grand Warsaw hotel, commandeered by the Gestapo for its important officials and guests. He has obtained her name, among others, from the exiled Polish airmen based in Britain, who had regarded him as a trusted friend of the Resistance. On the pretext of delivering a message to her from Sobinski—a cryptic "To be or not to be" (recalling their dressing-room trysts while her husband played Hamlet)—Siletsky uses the occasion to persuade the beautiful Maria to become a Nazi agent. She performs her most successful role in his hotel room (figure 27), where he's "set the stage" for his seduction.

Over a trolley heaped with edible luxuries unavailable in occupied Warsaw, Siletsky proposes that the wise course for Maria would be to join personal interest to *realpolitik*. In his courtly but minatory manner, he flatters and coaxes:

SILETSKY: Mrs. Tura, you're an actress, aren't you? And naturally, in the theater, it's very important that you choose the right part.

MARIA: Very.

SILETSKY: But in real life, it's even more important that you choose the right side.

MARIA: The right side? But what is the right side?

SILETSKY: The winning side. Life could be made very comfortable for you again, Mrs. Tura.

MARIA: Well, naturally, it's all very attractive and tempting. . . . But what are we going to do about my conscience?

Her tone matches Siletsky's for detached sophistication. But ending on the word "conscience," despite suggesting that its casual disposal is a group project, recalls for the avid Lombard fan that moment in 1937 when Maria's predecessor, Hazel Flagg, also from Warsaw (Vermont) and hardly sophisticated, similarly complained of this problematical organ. When Siletsky invites her to dinner, she says she must change her dress for the grand occasion—a ruse to leave the hotel and report back to her comrades-in-arms. Theatrical deception and truthful acting for the greater good become one and the same; she substitutes *real political* action for *realpolitik*.

Her "return engagement," now dressed in the satin halter-top dress to which Dobosh had objected (another conscious elision of acting and acting),

Fig. 27. Maria Tura playing her greatest "role," seducing the traitor Professor Siletsky. (Courtesy of Photofest)

is her great seduction scene—one in which she does the seducing. She plays up to Siletsky, making him believe she's falling under his spell. When he kisses her, she acts the somnambule, drugged by his sexual power. Artfully, she drops her head backwards as she falls away from his embrace and barely lifts her weakened arm in the Nazi salute. She "involuntarily" whispers "Heil Hitler!" Siletsky is enchanted; for us, it's a comic high point. Then, obtaining the spy's signature through another ruse, she takes the opportunity of his absence (he has been summoned to Gestapo Headquarters) to type a suicide note above his signature. Her plan is to kill him when he returns.

Maria/Lombard's "performance" is possibly the finest she has ever given because, as the saying goes, she's "playing for keeps." Her successful deception of Siletsky serves truth: her loyalty to the Polish Resistance and to the values of democracy and freedom. The Comic Spirit is her best friend and constant companion through the highly serious business of plotting to relieve Siletsky of his incriminating list of Resistance fighters. Knowing that she's endangering herself by going back to the hotel for her "romantic" tryst with the spy, she returns to her apartment to prepare, where, finding Tura and Sobinski, she explains what she'll do. Engaging with Sobinski in a round of comically incomprehensible, vaudeville-inspired double-talk—about Siletsky, spies, lists, and the Gestapo—her account goes right over the head of her mystified husband (and serves him right, too! we think). She proves herself the indubitable past master of the comic moment.

Lombard's part in *To Be . . .* , adapting the words of Mr. Greenberg, is "nothing to be sneezed at." Leaving aside the question that some reviewers objected to Lubitsch's comic treatment of political evil,[35] the film proved that a beautiful woman was equal to a man in her ability to make audiences laugh. Lombard could switch roles with ease, playing aggressively witty Judy to Jack Benny's Punch, or falling into a wonderfully parodic interpretation of the Hollywood "somnambule,"[36] all the while preserving the honesty and freshness that had characterized the blonde in the 1930s.

Along with her mother and twenty-one other passengers, Carole Lombard, returning from a government-sponsored war bonds promotional tour, died on January 16, 1942, when her plane crashed into Table Rock Mountain, southwest of Las Vegas (Ott 39–40). *To Be or Not to Be* was released one month later, on February 15th. Many saw the film as "a fitting tribute to the vital, arresting beauty and personality of the star" (Ott 184). But one might say with justice that *To Be . . .* was an equally fitting valedictory for the representation of all remarkably forthright and energetic blondes of the period. Maria Tura was already a bit of a freak or last gasp, for something was happening to that image—indeed, to the image of all outspoken and candid women in cinema— as the 1940s wore on. The equality that had defined the relationship of Vantine and Denny Carson in *Red Dust* or Ellen Wagstaff Arden/Irene Dunne and her husband Nicky/Cary Grant in *My Favorite Wife* (1938) hardly existed by 1941, when the baby-blond Veronica Lake was cast in the subordinate role of bland sidekick to Joel McCrea's Sullivan in *Sullivan's Travels*. While the hero's importance is made clear from the film's eponymous title, there is no irony intended when, at movie's end, the rolling credits identify Veronica Lake's character merely as "The Girl."

There were exceptions, of course, but in the main, Hollywood was turning women into nameless ciphers, literally into "placeholders," as the action centered in the real "theaters" of war. But worse was to come. After 1941, women would be cast as support staff—nurses and girlfriends—sending their men into battle, cheering them up and on, or as wives, waiting on the home front for heroic husbands. At the end of the war and just after, women's work was no longer critical. Pink slips peeked from paycheck envelopes, and the blond antiheroines of film noir began to occupy a place in the American psyche that had been filled in the early years of the century only by dark-haired vamps. Molly Haskell seconds Freud in *Moses and Monotheism:* "Maternal deities were at their most powerful when the matriarchy was about to be toppled, and the same principle of compensation may account for the rise and fall of goddesses in cinema. Certainly as the forties wore on, the balance tipped first one way, then the other, as women became a more serious threat to the economic hege-mony of men. The questioning was for real, and the films took on nasty, an-tifeminine overtones" (132–33). In 1936, James M. Cain published the murder mystery *Double Indemnity.* He describes Phyllis Nirdlinger, the original plotter of and co-conspirator in her husband's death, as "maybe thirty-one or -two, with a sweet face, light blue eyes, and dusty blonde hair" (5). Playing opposite Fred MacMurray in the 1944 movie, brunette Barbara Stanwyck—one of the few actresses, as I've said, who didn't go blond in the '30s—bleached her hair to play Phyllis Dietrichson. Her name an ironic allusion to the simple lovelorn shepherdesses of Arcadia, Phyllis is the far-from-comic, sexualized version of the gold digger of the '20s. She studies the economics of death—lusting after the money she'll receive on a "double indemnity" insurance policy for the ac-cidental death of her husband. Cold steel, she admits to killing her husband's first wife and to using her lover, the insurance salesman, to help her kill her husband and collect on the policy (figure 28).

John Huston's *The Maltese Falcon* of 1941, the screen version of Dashiell Hammett's 1929 novel, had seen the light as a film twice before—in 1931 as *Dangerous Female* (with Ricardo Cortez and dark-haired Bebe Daniels) and in a comic remake of 1936, *Satan Met a Lady,* starring not one, but two blondes: Bette Davis as Valerie Purvis, the attractive murderess, and Marie Wilson, the apparently dizzy but surprisingly clever secretary of a detective agency (her smarts must be genetic; her uncle is a college professor). One of the char-acters sagely remarks: "Blondes been the death of many a man." But that's because, as Valerie Purvis says to detective Ted Shayne/Warren William, as she's handcuffed and led off by the police: "Now you've found a woman *can* be as smart as you are. Someday you'll find one who'll be smarter. She'll marry you!" (And that's exactly what Marie Wilson's Miss Murgatroyd is likely to do.) The matriarchy clearly needed to be toppled. It might have fallen sooner

Fig. 28. Phyllis Dietrichson/Barbara Stanwyck and Walter Neff/Fred MacMurray inspect their handiwork in *Double Indemnity* (1944). (Courtesy of Photofest)

except for the political and military crisis building in Europe.

Cain's thriller *The Postman Always Rings Twice* (1934) was also scripted for Hollywood in 1946. His novels and their screen adaptations are both entries in the "high misogyny" category; *Postman . . .* , is not merely a study in antifeminism but is twinned with racism, its frequent partner-in-crime. In the novel, dark-haired Cora Papadakis, who helps the drifter Frank Chambers kill her husband, confronts Frank when they first meet:

> "You think I'm Mex."
> "Nothing like it."
> "Yes, you do. You're not the first one. Well, get this. I'm just as white as you are, see? I may have dark hair and look a little that way, but I'm just as white as you are. You want to get along good around here, you won't forget that." (6)

But blond Lana Turner starred as Cora. The viciously cold-blooded blonde—

dark roots now visible—was, by this time, de rigueur in film noir (as was her death by film's end). She was also the usual fare in noir detective fiction of the late '40s and early '50s—*Double Indemnity* of 1936 being a precocious example of the genre. As the crime-fiction writer Ed McBain (the nom de plume of Evan Hunter, screenwriter of Alfred Hitchcock's *The Birds*) explains: "I always started a P.I. [private eye] story with a blonde wearing a tight shiny dress. When she crossed her legs, you saw rib-topped stockings and garters taut against milky white flesh, boy. . . . Usually the P.I. fell in love with her by the end of the story, but he had to be careful because you couldn't trust girls who crossed their legs to show their garters." There was also another variation on this genre: the "Woman in Jeopardy" story. She was usually innocent, but "in some of the stories she wasn't all that innocent. In some of the stories she once did something sinful but not too terribly sinful. . . . It was also good to give her any color hair but blond. There were no innocent blondes in crime fiction."[37] "Whither [had] fled the visionary gleam" of blond (higher) innocence—that is, the experienced blonde who'd been around the block once or twice but could wind up reading children's animal stories to her convalescing lover?

The war divided an old from new world, almost in the middle of the century. While it definitively ended the Depression, it also interrupted the move to gender equality, which had briefly gained momentum in the 1930s. Films of the '40s both reflected and told that story. But they were only part of the "pop" cultural campaign to diminish women's authority and respect.

Alberto Vargas's airbrushed, mostly blond "pinups," collectively known as the "Varga Girls," appeared monthly in *Esquire*, making soldiers pant and young women despair of their own imperfect bodies. These, even before film noir blondes, reintroduced retrograde images of women.[38] Vargas's "portraits" of near-naked, immobilized girls, erect nipples clearly outlined under tight sweaters, or actually visible under sheer veils (figure 29), were pinned, even before soldiers pinned them up in barracks, to the (specimen) drawing board. While subjectivity had defined the enterprising women of '30s films, these paintings objectified their smiling "subjects," often in contortionist poses only a sadist could have dreamed up.

The powerful studio system, which had retained actors and actresses under contract to production/distribution companies, had had, at least, the virtue of promoting female stars by keeping them before the public in film after film. Something of the economic strength of these women was doubled in the won-

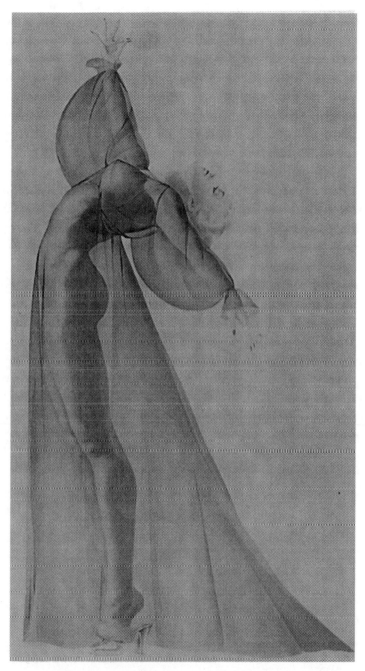

Fig. 29. The Varga Girl of September 1941. (Courtesy of the Hearst Corporation)

derfully energetic and interesting characters they played. But in the late '40s to early '50s, the system was breaking up; its demise meant a loss to actresses of their recognizable star power and professional clout. Good roles for women began to disappear. From stars they dwindled into leading ladies, playing "good" women or aggressive creatures—scheming, treacherous, and money hungry. A window of opportunity closed for both blondes and brunettes. Images of well-adjusted women were mostly limited to those of happy wives or mothers. The domestic suburbs had arrived.

Nor would blondes fare much better in the 1950s. The sexy forthrightness of Harlow or the energetic, breathless truth-telling of Lombard or Miriam Hopkins was far more interesting than Doris Day's studies of virginal repression in her career-girl/past-mistress-of-the-sexual-tease roles.[39] The only blondly sunny spots in the early '50s were Marilyn Monroe's hilariously comedic gold-digger performances in *Gentlemen Prefer Blondes* and *How to Marry a Millionaire* (both 1953). These films, as well as *The Seven Year Itch* (1955) and *Some Like It Hot* (1959), gave the blonde permission to be zanily (and physically) funny in an update of screwball. While film noir survived into the '50s with antifeminist movies like *Niagara* and *Vertigo*—Alfred Hitchcock perfected a cinematic version of the blond ice-queen when he wasn't immediately icing her (as he would Janet Leigh in *Psycho*)—Monroe's comedies offered moments of bright good humor to ordinary women and men who left their homes for a night out at the movies. Although Marilyn has been analyzed in (and to) death as a troubled and enigmatic offscreen personality, her brilliant representation of the innocent and dizzy but clever blonde restored energy and interest to female roles and positively reconnected women's sexuality and intelligence.

Five

Monroe at the Gates

"A blond plumber?"
—Billy Wilder, *The Seven Year Itch*

On October 23, 1945, Jackie Robinson signed a contract with the Brooklyn Dodgers that effectively integrated baseball. On July 26, 1948, President Harry S. Truman signed the executive order that integrated the Armed Forces. And on May 17, 1954, the Supreme Court issued its decision *Brown v. Board of Education of Topeka, Kansas,* declaring segregated public schools "inherently unequal." These three documents represented important moments in the long-overdue dismantling of racially segregated institutions in America. To note that they followed shortly after World War II only begins to speak to the tremendous changes the war made in Americans' lives.

Truman could not have avoided the terrible paradox that black soldiers had just helped to liberate three continents from the appalling deployment of a supremacist ideology but came home to a nation tolerating and abetting deep inequalities among its citizens. His order to integrate came only nine days after a group of southern Democrats, the "secessionist" Dixiecrats, or "States' Rights Party," nominated J. Strom Thurmond, then governor of South Carolina, and Mississippi governor J. Fielding Wright as candidates for president and vice president. The party made the preservation of segregation its raison d'être.[1]

Proof of how much work must be done after documents are signed, to make substantial social change, was the bloody civil rights struggle, from the '50s through the '60s, to integrate schools and public transportation and facilities. The violent response to school integration, to lunch counter sit-ins, bus boycotts, and "Freedom Summer"—the campaign organized by black and white student activists to register black Americans to vote in Mississippi and other states of the Deep South—was a continuation not only of the savagery that made national news (the lynchings and burnings) but also of the lower-level daily abuse inflicted on blacks since slavery and the rising of the Klans. In 1964, the year of Freedom Summer, Robert Lowell published *For the Union Dead*. A hundred years after the Civil War, in the title poem of the collection, he writes of the St. Gaudens bas relief commemorating the first U.S. regiment of black soldiers from Massachusetts, led by the white Col. Robert Gould Shaw. Now, "propped by a plank splint," and awaiting eventual replacement in Boston Common, it serves as the occasion for a public conversation. Conflating past and present, the poem, in turn, commemorates a succession of deaths: the death, two months after the regiment left Boston, of half the men; the "death" of the Aquarium in South Boston; the "death" of Boston Common, dug up to build a subterranean parking garage. But Lowell also commemorates a hope embodied in the black children, themselves brave soldiers on the line to integrate the schools of the South.

> When I crouch to my television set,
> the drained faces of Negro school-children rise like balloons.

> Colonel Shaw
> is riding on his bubble,
> he waits
> for the blessed break.

> The Aquarium is gone. Everywhere,
> giant finned cars nose forward like fish;
> a savage servility
> slides by on grease.   (72)

With economy, he captures the struggles of blacks in this country to achieve recognition amidst a national narrative mindlessly propelled by destruction and accumulation. The monument to the regiment, Lowell writes, "sticks like a fishbone / in the city's throat" (71).

Lowell forces us to look hard at that fishbone. The entertainment industry in the 1950s, responding to and shaping the values of the entire nation—on radio, in the movies, and now in the new medium of television—was at its silent work, keeping alive racist values deeply embedded in American society but also creating images that prolonged, for women, thralldom to a myth of personal satisfaction and happiness, in line with midcentury aspirations to middle-class normalcy—for "whites only."

The white American GIs who had been dreaming of Alberto Vargas's blond pinups and Betty Grable during the war returned and, of course, married women with hair of every tint. But as Graham McCann comments in *Marilyn Monroe*, "Fifties movie moguls demanded the stereotype of a blonde, the dream (so they said) of returning soldiers and of *Men Only*, something Michelangelo might have carved out of candy" (20). Blondes were, QED, the whitest, most desirable of whites. And so the bleach that had been all the rage in the '30s was applied liberally to many heads—not only those in Hollywood—now readily accessible to middle-class women through the new "Miss Clairol" products. Bristol-Myers Ltd., parent company of "Miss Clairol," assisted in editing ethnicities other than Anglo-Saxon and Nordic—if only until the next application of its products. Malcolm Gladwell, in his 1999 *New Yorker* article "True Colors: Hair Dye, and the Hidden History of Postwar America," wrote: "In writing the history of women in the postwar era, did we forget something important? Did we leave out hair?" (72).

Editing, in the form of deletion, occurred in the media, as well. On television, Ethel Waters as Beulah (1950) and the black actors of the 1951 sitcom *Amos 'n' Andy*—among them, Alvin Childress and Spencer Williams Jr.[2]— were still very much the exception. In film, a stuttering black bartender like the one in *Blonde Venus* (1932), or the economic and racial contrast of black maids waiting on wealthy blond women, might no longer be politically acceptable. But Hollywood's inelegant fix, until the end of the decade, was to omit blacks almost entirely from the narrative of American life.

Yet while the silver screen was a virtual blank when it came to the national drama of race relations,[3] blondes—Betty Grable, Doris Day, Sandra Dee, Grace Kelly, Barbara Bel Geddes, Eva-Marie Saint, Tippi Hedren, Janet Leigh, Kim Novak, and, at the end of the decade, Brigitte Bardot—were everywhere. Represented as virginal and "good" (mostly in comedies) or experienced and disastrous (in film noir), their characters corresponded to ancient archetypes: "white"/innocent; "red"/knowing and sexual. Screenwriters and directors showed little interest in suggesting the complexity of real women; it simply didn't translate into box-office receipts.

It was the greatest good fortune of that blondest of blondes, Marilyn Monroe, that she could be synonymous with both types. Her film career, a few years longer than the decade of the '50s, originally included roles at both ends of the sexual spectrum but settled, by 1953, on the comedic and the *mainly* innocent; that combination was her unique gift.[4] In at least seven of her comedies, this platinum blonde, whether briefly or for the duration, inhabited the American cityscape, a pastoral refuge of fantastical childlike or naive sexuality—always a feature of the "Greenwood" from Eden, to Arcady, to the Forest of Arden. My purposely ambiguous referent for "refuge" makes the point that "the City"—New York City—and the blonde had merged and emerged in '50s films from the dark shades of film noir into the brightly sunny and intoxicating days of perpetual American hopefulness and prosperity. "New York, New York / You high and mighty / Bright and Shiny / Fabulous place, New York!" goes Alfred Newman's extended musical tribute at the beginning of *How to Marry a Millionaire*. "New York, New York, / Where millionaires and Cinderellas / Rendez-vous at the Stork." The lively City and the beautiful blonde, coupled as in romantic comedies of the 1930s (so many opening with street scenes or the skyline of New York), were offered as the rich entitlements of a society that, with great effort, pain, and loss had triumphed over despair and evil. Marilyn was the "parfait," the *perfectly* delicious but guilt-free confection that could be consumed again and again, for just the price of a ticket, with no fear of weight gain or extra baggage. Norman Mailer, describing the collective male response, similarly compared the sexual promise of her smile to delectable edibles: "ice cream"; "sweet peach bursting"; "a chocolate box for Valentine's day"; "honey from the horn" (15–17). But wives and girlfriends couldn't mind very much.

Although there's no venomous snake in her comedic paradise, comedy's tickling worm still reminds the viewer of other possibilities. Consciousness, Monroe's and ours, of the precariousness of pastoral pleasurably threatens to destroy innocence—an instability that defined the 1950s. The adorably dapper and cheerful cartoon snake, looking more like a worm than a snake, who wiggled his way across the opening credits of Preston Sturges's *The Lady Eve* in 1941, had become, by 1953, an element of the mise-en-scène of *Gentlemen*

Prefer Blondes, when the knowing but innocent "little girl from Little Rock" suggestively shook her shoulders and breasts as she sang "Diamonds Are a Girl's Best Friend." Lorelei Lee's earnest explanation to her pal Dorothy, that the diamond mine owner "Piggy"/Charles Coburn was embracing her only to demonstrate how an African python squeezes a goat, is the story of "original" sin. But it's not about knowledge or sex. The real "fall" is caused by the alluring perfume of the material world beyond the First Garden's gates—the scent of money and (despite their inertness) of diamonds. Who could look at Charles Coburn and think otherwise?

Monroe, in her comic roles, anticipated by her performance as the aspiring "dumb-blonde" starlet Claudia Caswell in *All About Eve* (1950), represents an ingenuousness that accorded with her audience's belief in an uncomplicated past but, simultaneously, the wish for a pleasantly fallen world of abundance and an increasingly overt, but still safe, sexuality. In her earlier films, her pastoral held steady, but there's delight in peering beyond the gates into experience as long as the return to innocence, by movie's end, is assured. Yet in the inimitable words of Osgood Fielding/Joe E. Brown, at the end of *Some Like It Hot* (1959), nothing and "Well, nobody's perfect." And thank goodness! Her performances, which fissure the smooth surface of cinematic narrative, teach us both about the extraordinariness of Monroe and of the culture of which she was a product.

In her early noir films, *The Asphalt Jungle* (1950) and *Don't Bother to Knock* (1952), she inhabited a world made dangerous by desire. In *Niagara* (1953), Rose Loomis, a truly disastrous wife, is an iconically simplified figure of feminine evil, a throwback to Dracula's wives and the deadly Theda Bara. There is no compelling reason that explains why Rose should want to kill her husband George/Joseph Cotten rather than simply leave him. But sex, the drive that causes a woman to cheat on her husband, probably has something to do with it. The visual proof is that Polly Cuttler/Jean Peters, the "normal," happily married, dark-haired foil to Rose, doesn't know how to make herself sexy, for which, of course, even domesticated men wish. Her husband, Ray (in a cinematically contrived moment), trying to snap her picture, has to coach her to sit in profile and stick out her chest; Polly and the erotic are not even distantly related. Rose, by contrast, dresses provocatively and lowers her eyes in a narcissistic embrace of her own shoulders and breasts. She makes sultry love, with her expressively open mouth, to every man she meets. The narrative intimates that a woman, *because* she's sexual, desires to murder her man.

But remembering an innocent America and celebrating a safe feminine desirability rather than desire were especially important in the 1950s, so shortly after the war. Alfred Kinsey's *Sexual Behavior in the Human Female* (1953), which proved statistically that women, like men, were physiologically and anatomically capable of sexual responsiveness, made a dent in Hollywood's representation of women only later in the decade. Films of the period, like the romantic comedies of the 1930s, primarily focused on healing the wounds created by six years of bloodshed and the Great Depression before it.

The representation of sexualized innocence began, as I've said, in World War II with Betty Grable's legs and those blond Varga girls, whose remarkably ripe bodies were cheery reminders to soldiers of the potential pleasures of the peace they were fighting for. Although "Li'l Abner," Al Capp's wildly popular and widely syndicated comic hero was "born" in 1934, he finally married Daisy Mae, the delectably buxom blonde who had vigorously pursued him, only in 1952. After their marriage, Capp showed that her sexiness was matched by her domestic excellence; she was a paragon of patience and loyalty. TV family sitcoms like *Father Knows Best* demonstrated the benefits of domesticity and recaptured an innocence that existed merely by virtue of the distorting prism of historical distance. However, the overwhelming social imperative to bring order out of chaos, to curb eccentricity, both political (the House Un-American Activities Committee hearings) and social (the regularizing and disciplining efforts of family entertainment) had, even in the '50s, its equal and opposite reaction: the subversion of order and conformity. When Larry Gelbart, creator of *M*A*S*H*, was asked, with reference to comedy, "What happened after the '50s?" he answered: "The '60s." And we know what happened then.

That Monroe should have starred in *Niagara*, *Gentlemen Prefer Blondes*, and *How to Marry a Millionaire*, all in 1953, typifies the cleavage[5] in the American psyche that believed in the destruction of paradise by Woman at the same moment that it tried so vigorously to reinvent that garden with her as its naturalized deity. Yet either way, the woman had to be blond. The divergent roles assigned to Monroe (and what aspiring starlet could turn them down?—especially as she was under contract to Fox Pictures)—became an important illustration of the double vision of woman. She is a fascinating embodiment of American culture at that moment in our nation's history. And yet she was something more than merely the pawn of 20th Century Fox and the incarnation of a society's dreams or nightmares. The something more—one cannot watch her without recognizing the surplus value of her performance—is that she was a great actress who complicated and subverted the films and the unidimensional roles she was assigned—roles meant to reveal women's true designs on men, whether of a marrying or murderous kind, and that put them in their domestic place or punished them for their deadly transgressions. As the decade and Monroe's career progressed, the comic mode alone revealed the rage for order but also for congenial chaos and carnival, leading to a freer definition of sexuality and sexual relations. She expressed American culture's ambivalent attitudes toward women as no actress of the '50s did, whether blond (Doris Day; Grace Kelly; Sandra Dee) or brunette (Elizabeth Taylor; Audrey Hepburn).

In 1942, when Carole Lombard died as she was returning to Los Angeles from her war bonds tour, President Franklin D. Roosevelt, extraordinarily, issued a tribute to the star, emphasizing her inestimable value to friends and ordinary Americans: "She brought great joy to all who knew her and to millions who knew her only as a great artist. She gave unselfishly of time and talent to serve her government in peace and war. She loved her country. She is and always will be a star, one we shall never forget, nor cease to be grateful to" (quoted in Ott 187). Twenty years later, President John F. Kennedy had not only been saluted by Monroe when she sang "Happy Birthday, Mr. President" at his glitzy birthday bash in Madison Square Garden but, most probably, had been her lover. Although there is a long history of liaisons between political figures and actresses, the sexual intimacy of Monroe and Kennedy, made semipublic at that moment, signaled a seismic shift in American politics, really "a new social contract between politics and popular culture" (McCann 27), marking the beginning of the "star system" of American statecraft, particularly prominent in the Clinton presidency and such that Senator John McCain more recently could quip that Washington, D.C., is "the Hollywood of the ugly."

Monroe's importance to the cultural landscape of America, by the time of her premature death and beyond, cannot be underestimated. The persistence of fascination with her beauty and life up to the present is proof of her significance,[6] as Paige Baty is at pains to demonstrate in *American Monroe: The Making of a Body Politic*. Many trees have been felled to manufacture paper for articles and books detailing the minutiae of Monroe's life and speculating about her tragic death at thirty-six on August 4, 1962. While undeniably her star power was, perhaps more than for any other, a synergistic meeting of her life offscreen with her image on-, my discussion is limited to the representation of the blonde in films, through which Monroe first and preeminently came to the attention of her fans and the American public.

Lombard and Monroe . . . both were bleached blondes; Lombard was married to Clark Gable when she died in 1942; Monroe and Gable costarred in *The Misfits* (1961), the last film either of them would complete before their deaths—his, three weeks after the movie was finished, hers several months later. Was it pure coincidence that Monroe's first studio name was Carole Lind?[7] However, there is a far more important similarity between the two stars—one that enlists Monroe in a cinematic tradition begun by blond actresses in the 1930s but suspended during the war years. Like Lombard, West, Harlow, and Hopkins, Marilyn Monroe was a comic genius. It's not merely a coy adaptation of her character's own assessment in *The Seven Year Itch*—"I have lots of other things, but I have no imagination"—to say that she could do others things magnificently, but she was particularly gifted as a comedienne, performing slapstick and comedy with inspired talent. Graham McCann asserts that "Foolishly, the studios kept underpaying her and casting her as the dumb blonde; Monroe came to satirise sex while still embodying it" (26). He sees their strategy as a lost opportunity, and, of course, Monroe herself begged Fox for more nuanced roles. But his view overlooks the point that her comic performances were exactly what distinguished her from the general run of '50s blond "sex goddesses." He also ignores the satiric element of the narratives of *Gentlemen Prefer Blondes* and *How to Marry a Millionaire*—critiques, if blithe, of the conventions that govern relations between the sexes. While it may be true that "Sexuality, as Foucault (1982) has stressed, is indicative of the process by which power relations are arranged and enforced" (McCann 19), to be able to make others laugh is an equally powerful "arrangement" between actor and audience—particularly female actor and audience—and "nothing to be sneezed at." Monroe understood the power of laughter. Not only did she "consent to be photographed as a fairly comic figure" (McCann 70), but she was also willing to compromise her great beauty in hilarious episodes that only added to her star power. Julia Louis-Dreyfus, commenting on television's great female comics, defined how a woman must act to be really funny: "You can't be afraid to look ugly. You have to give into it completely. Then you'll get your laugh. The laugh will wait for you on the other side. . . . For a woman, it's divine." Marilyn Monroe never went as far as Lucille Ball in giving "into it completely," but she came much closer than any other "goddess" of the early '50s. Despite the conventions of the times and the constraints of the roles she was offered by Fox, she did, on more than one occasion, achieve comic "divinity," ignoring the limitations of being merely a beautiful object for the camera's lens to caress.

But the business of the camera's lens, as it helps to create a star, instead of merely recording a performance, must be considered before approaching Monroe's comedic talents. Without it, those talents would never have been realized. She appeared in nineteen films from 1947 through 1952, mostly comedies, although her own roles—many of them only walk-ons—weren't particularly funny. At first too insignificant even to have a name, she was then Peggy Martin, the young love interest in *Ladies of the Chorus* (1949), and the dumb blond starlet Claudia Caswell in *All About Eve* (1950). She played minor roles as the sexually attractive, yet unavailable secretary Iris Martin in *Home Town Story* (1951) or the "other" woman in *Love Nest* (1951), *Monkey Business* (1951), *As Young as You Feel* (1951), and *Let's Make It Legal* (1951). But she was never meant to be a real threat to wives. Her more significant though still minor or supporting roles were in noir films: Angela Phinlay, the naive mistress of Alonzo Emmerich, the crooked, two-timing lawyer in *The Asphalt Jungle*, and, in *Clash by Night* (1952), Peggy, the loving but immature girlfriend of Joe. As the "natural" woman in that movie, she was meant to contrast with the hard-hearted Mae/Barbara Stanwyck, the experienced and adulterous older sister of Peggy's boyfriend. In most of these films, nothing special distinguished her from any other pretty starlet.

D. W. Griffith was the first director to popularize the close-up shot (McCann 14), a privileged examination of an actor's face, which stands in for the viewer's intimacy with the subject. The camera's presence also creates the possibility of psychological revelation. Griffith said that with the close-up he was trying to "photograph thought" (McCann 14). It has become such a familiar camera shot that we ignore its complete unreality.

In life we get close to another's face on few occasions: with our lovers; our children; those whose infirmities require that we tend them; or in the exercise of domination. With the exception of the "lovers" category, the other instances are all about unequal power. The slang metaphor "in your face" is used to describe the behavior of a person who violates the decorum of social relations by not respecting the physical space ordinarily kept between people as they converse. Yet in the created, artificial world of cinema, an actor's face can fill the screen, allowing us to see the subtle play of emotion as muscles alter facial contours.

By convention, the artful close-up is no trespass. In fact, the actor/subject, aware of its economic implications, welcomes the camera's intimacy because it helps to make an actor a star both by bringing her to special notice in the public's consciousness and by keeping her there. Along with publicity stills, photo shoots for magazines, gossip columnists' stories, and newspaper accounts of her love life, whereabouts, and public appearances, the close-up IDs the actor, helping the audience remember her from film to film. Conversely, the close-up is often the signal to the audience that the subject *is* a star, important enough for special visual interrogation.

With the exception of *The Asphalt Jungle,* the camera in Monroe's early movies almost uniformly ignores the medium shots and close-ups of her face that become, in later films, the signature of her career. Strikingly, Monroe, in her early pictures, without these images, is not interesting to the viewer, either as a character or actor. Her great beauty, sex appeal, and comedic talent are not yet attention-riveting as they are in later films; in fact, she hardly gets a second look. We focus, for example, far more on the devious Eve/Anne Baxter than on Monroe in those few scenes in which they appear together in *All About Eve.* But then Baxter, central to the drama, is the subject of close-ups and commands our psychic attention; we're interested in her machinations while Claudia Caswell's artlessness[8] is merely amusing and forgettable.

Of course, by 1950 Fox Studio had decided to make Monroe a star. But perhaps the reason that she came to reviewers' notice in *The Asphalt Jungle* (directed by John Huston), despite her minor role, is that the camera was permitted to fall in love with her, and she with it. Although she appears in only two scenes with Emmerich/Louis Calhern, Huston makes the most of her screen time, focusing far more on her than on Calhern. The camera pans in for a close-up, documenting her every change in position as she sensually wakes from sleep, and lingers on her figure as she leaves the set. In both scenes she's the sole woman, which immediately rouses interest (from a narrative point of view, her sexual "isolation" also says something about her relations with men). The camera relentlessly focuses on her, monitoring her reactions, no matter who is speaking. Her vulnerability, often noted as her great attraction, is quite real here, built into the storyline when the police force her to confess that she's lied to create an alibi for Emmerich. Her youth and guilelessness are accentuated by her lover "Uncle Lon" when he repeats: "Some sweet kid!" The ingenue and genuine innocent, who gets breathlessly excited when Emmerich suggests a trip, and who punctuates her sentences with the juvenile "yipe!" appealed to both young and older men, who appreciated the generous and naive sexuality of this startlingly beautiful and seemingly available young woman (she was only twenty-four). She may have closed the door of her room against the camera, but that last shot of her, as she lingers in the jamb, firmly associated her with bedrooms.

Two years and ten movies later, she was featured in *Don't Bother to Knock,* a noir film in which her scenes as Nell Forbes were shot almost entirely in one hotel room—a visual emblem of the young woman's mind-trapping psychosis. Monroe's sensitive portrayal of the unbalanced girl, on the verge of killing the child for whom she babysits, was captured by the camera's close-ups of the subtle changes in her emotions—from vacant to conniving to desperate to triumphant to vacant to terrified. Her performance revealed a truly talented actress, but the role allowed the audience neither to sympathize with the character nor to love the actor for whom this role was not quite a star turn.

Rose Loomis in *Niagara* represented a more advanced degree of degeneracy but was generally cut from the same psychotic bolt of cloth. The character of Rose was the midcentury update of the vamp; her husband, George, admits to Polly Cuttler, a happily married visitor to Niagara Falls, that he's unable to free himself from her spell. But unlike Theda Bara's vamp, Rose tries to murder her husband without taking anything from him—neither blood nor money. The charged close-ups of Monroe's face exploit the cliché of autoeroticism, arousing but, at the same time, a sign of a woman's inaccessibility and, therefore, danger; Japanese blowfish would be the gastronomical equivalent. The demonizing of this blonde and sexuality—Kim Novak's Judy in *Vertigo* is another example[9]—is one of the most negative portraits of women in popular culture of this period.

But close-ups of Rose, aware of her sexual power as she stands sinisterly shadowed by the eaves of the cabin at Niagara Falls (figure 30), created a dissonance for the viewer that couldn't be reconciled except by casting Monroe in a very different kind of role. For the very quality that men and women, too, found exciting—her physical but, even more, her emotional, accessibility—was in tension with the self-love of the femme fatale. That is, the permission granted by the nearness of the camera is denied by the character's dangerous impenetrability. The conflict was resolved by allowing Monroe to invite intimacy through an unthreatening comic performance. The "ever so" blatant

Fig. 30. Rose Loomis/Marilyn Monroe, posing as the femme fatale, in a publicity still for *Niagara* (1953). (Courtesy of Photofest)

gold digger of a girl "like she," frankly (and charmingly) scheming, preferring her man alive to dead (because alive he keeps on giving), was the move into comedy that settled the question of Monroe's screen persona.

Richard Dyer in *Heavenly Bodies* writes that "Monroe may have been a wit, a subtle and profound actress, an intelligent and serious woman; I've no desire to dispute this and it is important to recognise and recover those qualities against the grain of her image. But my purpose is to understand the grain itself, and there can be no question that this is overwhelmingly and relentlessly constructed in terms of sexuality" (20). While it would be absurd to deny the potency of Monroe's sexuality and its effect on midcentury American culture—no matter that Dyer parses its difference from that of other stars as a question of its innovative "naturalness" (like her hair?)—it cannot, by itself, explain her impact. She was much, much more than a twentieth-century fox. Without her comic gifts, she would have been a Brigitte Bardot—sexy and beautiful, but without the *quoi* that naturalness alone doesn't explain. Molly Haskell's comment, in fact, about Bardot's own sexual naturalness diminishes the importance of that quality: "Bardot's appeal, and the unfortunate evanescence of that appeal, lies in her purely sexual nature. She is a waif and a nymphet, a woman of the world and a child of nature. By being frankly and freely sexual, she is no longer a sex object, that is, she cannot be bought or bartered. . . . [She] express[es] a kind of sexual knowledge and spiritual innocence that defies the sexual and romantic categories constructed by men" (297). But today Bardot, as Haskell adds, is "a magnetic dot in the universe" (297), remembered only as an image in a snapshot, her beautiful breasts barely covered by her bikini bra, a perfect woman/child's body—nothing more. Dyer, Mailer, and others make too much of Monroe's "naturalness," unless they mean by it merely the opposite of embarrassment or discomfort. Before the camera, it was a practiced behavior, a characteristic of her artfulness, as was her other exceptional quality—her comic ability—which she mined, like a diamond, in her next film, *Gentleman Prefer Blondes.*

The project, directed by Howard Hawks, was based on the 1926 play by Anita Loos and the 1949 musical version by Jule Styne and Leo Robin, starring Carol Channing (both based on Loos's 1925 novel of the same name).[10] Although Jane Russell got top billing and was paid far more than her costar, it was a perfect vehicle for Monroe, who stole the show. We remember it today as her film, not Russell's. It opens as Marilyn's flamboyantly blond Lorelei Lee and Jane Russell's dark-haired and forthright Dorothy Shaw, dressed in black sequined gowns, sing "A Little Girl from Little Rock" on the stage of a New York nightclub. The song supplies their history—where they're from ("we lived on the wrong side of the tracks") and the reason they're in New York (their broken hearts)—but also Lorelei's economic motivation for being a gold digger and, with amusing innuendo, what it's taken to succeed ("And I worked at it all around the clock"). Because "someone broke [her] heart in

Little Rock," and "men are the same way everywhere," Lorelei understands that the sexual calculus works out to a girl's having to invest her energy in the acquisition of "hard" assets, before her "charms" are lost "in the end." Monroe's hands, gesturing to various parts of her body, make the pun visual, indicating, in this song and later in "Diamonds Are a Girl's Best Friend," that "square cut or pear-shaped" "rocks" "don't lose their shape," as eventually do bosom and bottom—hostage, like everything else in this world, to time.

The funniest scenes in the movie, to which description can't do justice, are those in which Lorelei attempts to recover the reputation-damaging role of film taken of her in the arms of Piggy, by P.I. Ernie Malone. Having searched unsuccessfully for it in Malone's stateroom, Lorelei finds herself locked in, able to escape only through the porthole. But despite her (amusing) preparatory estimate (figure 31) of the widest parts of her anatomy, she gets stuck; the camera plays on her wriggling hindquarters. Then, shot from deck-side, Lorelei's struggling head and upper torso are framed by the porthole, when Mr. Spofford, a seven year old, happens by. She asks in desperation for his help, to which he agrees, because, as he logically points out in his deadpan voice, no one would put anyone as young as he in prison for abetting a thief, and, besides, Lorelei has lots of "animal magnetism" (canned humor, but we hardly care). The crisis worsens as Piggy walks toward them. Thinking quickly, Mr. Spofford orders Lorelei to put a deck-chair blanket around her neck, under which he hides. Monroe is transformed into a giant. Her head, with the blanket falling from just below her chin, towers above the perplexed Piggy, who asks: "I say, whatever are you doing up there?" When she declines his offer to go for a sherry, saying she isn't well, he asks to feel her pulse. Mr. Spofford again comes to the rescue, extending his own hand from under the blanket. Piggy, amazed at its small size, calls it "such a little flowery hand" (figure 32). The moment is pure vaudeville. "Mr. Spofford," in his surprising basso profundo, orders Piggy: "Stop that!" Lorelei resourcefully feigns laryngitis to account for the suddenly low timbre of her voice.

When she reports that she hasn't found the film, Dorothy invites Malone to her stateroom, the better to search his pockets. Lorelei has improved the time by mixing a knockout of a cocktail. Although Dorothy worries that the drink is too potent, Lorelei, in demonic-scientist mode, directs Dorothy: "Be quiet! When a thing's worth doing, it's worth doing well!" Dorothy's compliment to Lorelei on the quality of her intellect—"You know, sometimes your brain amazes me!"—is entirely sincere.

Fig. 31. Lorelei Lee/Marilyn Monroe making her preparatory estimate—will she fit through the porthole?—in *Gentlemen Prefer Blondes* (1953). (Courtesy of Photofest)

Malone's reaction to the drink, downed in a gulp, and to the chaser of straight vodka is, understandably, extreme. The girls make him more "comfortable" by removing his jacket (and searching its pockets). Dorothy then spills water on his trousers, which, amid fervent apologies for their clumsiness, the two pull off, for another search (figure 33). At this moment, Pierre, of the ship's staff, appears in the open stateroom door. Seeing the trouser-less Malone, he exclaims "Ooh, la la!" Lorelei helps Ernie into a frilly peignoir as Pierre escorts the unmanned and very sleepy private eye back to his own stateroom.

Lorelei's persona in these slapstick episodes is one of many she inhabits

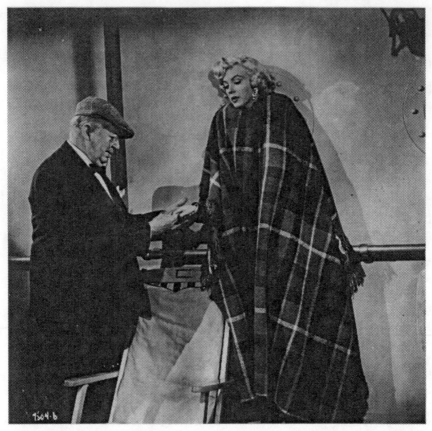

Fig. 32. "Piggy"/Charles Coburn, diamond mine owner, examining Lorelei's "little flowery hand." (Courtesy of Photofest)

throughout the film. In addition to the clever, scheming woman, there's the untutored, grammatically inventive dame. "A girl like I" asks: "Excuse me, sir. Is this the way to Europe, France?" Then there's the faux-innocent with the baby voice, and the entirely sexualized and self-conscious cabaret performer. If the movie had depended on the unity of her character, it should have failed miserably. However, her fractured persona and its disjunctive effect on the narrative draw attention to Monroe's extraordinary range of performance. Although she plays these very different roles serially, we are so completely aware of the shifts in her personal kaleidoscope that they not only expose the tensions in women's positions but, as well, point to their origins (the expectations and behavior of men). Which of these characters is the real Lorelei?

The oscillations from one to another, which prevent the audience from really knowing, become a subversive challenge to those who think women are mere objects and also provide the basis for the audience's multiple identifications. In an era in which sexual mores seem only inches beyond Victorian values, women expressed anger (and jealousy) that Monroe, in her many roles always played up to men (from publicity about her, they assumed she did in life, too), but they could take pleasure in Lorelei's inventive stratagems.

Lorelei also gets almost the last word in the film, showing genuine command of her unique "dialectical materialism." When Gus (whom Lorelei calls "Daddy") tells his father, newly arrived in Paris, that he loves and wants to marry her, Mr. Esmond, the real "Daddy," and Lorelei duke it out with words. Lorelei deploys syllogistic logic to great effect:

MR. ESMOND: You admit that all you're after is his money.

LORELEI: No I don't. I love him. I want to marry him for *your* money. Aren't

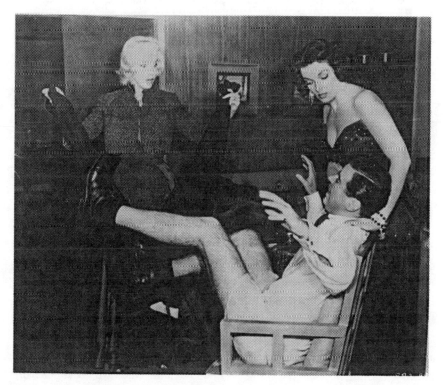

Fig. 33. Off with his pants! insist Lorelei and Dorothy. (Courtesy of Photofest)

you funny! Don't you know that a man being rich is like a girl being pretty? You might not marry a girl just because she's pretty. But it wouldn't hurt. And if you had a daughter, wouldn't you want her to have the most wonderful things in the world and to be very happy? Then why is it wrong for me to want those things?

MR. ESMOND: Say, they told me you were stupid! You don't sound stupid to me.

LORELEI: I can be smart when it's important, but most men don't like it, except Gus. He loves me for my brains.

MR. ESMOND: No he doesn't. He's not that stupid!

Advantage Lorelei until Mr. Esmond trumps her impeccable argument with innuendo that transforms her, once more, into the extraordinary physical being our own eyes confirm. But we've enjoyed her momentary triumph. Besides, the next scene onboard the ocean liner, played to Mendelssohn's "Wedding March," is the real moment of "Lorelei *victrix*" as she and Dorothy make their grand entrance. The movie ends on a freeze frame as they approach their husbands-to-be. The two "redeemed" women, in identical white wedding dresses, complete a narrative circle that began with their cabaret performance in those sexy black gowns.

Hawks's sympathetic portrait of the gold digger is enhanced by another distinctive feature of *Gentlemen Prefer Blondes*. It's a female "buddy" movie—hardly a staple of Hollywood fare in 1953 or any other time. Two attractive women, friends of the same age, one blonde, the other dark, are portrayed not as rivals but as sidekicks. Female friendship or at least economic necessity, although lacking in the warmth and loyalty that characterize the Lorelei-Dorothy bond, is the plot engine for Monroe's next film, *How to Marry a Millionaire*, in which beautiful but hard-up fashion models Schatze Page/Lauren Bacall, Pola Debevoise/Monroe, and Loco Dempsey/Betty Grable club together on a sublet of a fashionable Sutton Place apartment, which they mean to use as base camp for their husband hunting.

The limited ambitions of women in '50s popular culture define this movie. Does Schatze Page, newly arrived from a Reno divorce, want to tie the knot again? "Of course, I want to get married again," she says. "Who doesn't? It's the biggest thing you can do in life!" The movie has none of the racy charm of *Gentlemen*, but the fault doesn't lie with Monroe's performance. As the ex-

Fig. 34. Pola Debevoise/Marilyn Monroe checks her appearance before leaving the ladies' lounge. Publicity still for *How to Marry a Millionaire* (1953). (Courtesy of Photofest)

tremely nearsighted Pola, who refuses to wear her glasses in public (men don't make passes at girls, etc.), she has one very funny scene that almost saves the movie.

In the ladies' lounge of a New York nightclub, she expertly checks her appearance, front and aft, in a many-paneled mirror (figure 34). Then, removing her glasses before returning to the club, she walks quickly toward the exit, smacking the wall inches away from the door—like a windup toy set in motion and unable to change direction. She ably demonstrates a Bergsonian principle of the comic: "What life and society require of each of us is a constant alert attention that discerns the outlines of the present situation, together with a certain elasticity of mind and body to enable us to adapt ourselves in consequence"; "The attitudes, gestures and movements of the human body are laughable in exact proportion as the body reminds us of a mere machine" (Bergson 72, 79).

While one might make the case that this scene is nothing but a regressive portrayal of feminine imbecility, Monroe's deft comic timing momentarily induces the viewer to slip out of the narrative stream to marvel at her skills as a mime. For despite the gendered put-down the narrative implies (reducing the woman to a thing driven by the forces of contemporary social custom and costume), her comic ability—the actual elasticity of her mind and body that makes the moment possible—elevates the real woman. Oddly, Bergson's theory of laughter omits the particular qualities of the actor that make him or her especially funny when another performer is not. Kathleen Rowe's study of the carnivalesque in *The Unruly Woman* (8), like Bergson's, focuses on narrative form to the exclusion of the comedic potential of the actor. But it seems obvious that laughter is a response to their blessed union.

Screenwriter Nunnally Johnson's running (and thin) gag—that women are too vain to wear glasses—is trumped by a larger narrative joke, which intentionally undermines the women's rich-husband hunting. Schatze Page comes closer than the others to putting love aside for some Texas gushers owned by the invariably considerate and autumnal William Powell. The wedding never does come off because Schatze admits she's in love with someone else, Tom Bookman, who she believes is at the retail end of the oil business—a poor "gas pump jockey." The movie's conclusion, meant to restore our faith in the gold diggers' underlying decency, is that despite their original ambitions, all three marry for love (Loco, a forest ranger from Maine, and Pola, the penniless, tax-evading owner of the Sutton Place apartment the girls are subletting). But Schatze Page's virtue in turning down the wealthy oilman is rewarded by discovering that her "gas pump jockey" is really a millionaire, too. The frog prince, it seems, inhabits the big City, reminding us that the jungle of skyscrapers is the new forest of Arden.

In this film, we can admire Monroe's acting talents while dismissing the limited character she portrays—an assertion that applies more or less to all of her roles except perhaps for Roslyn Taber in *The Misfits*, whose character approaches the conventions of complexity that prevail in the most nuanced of contemporary films. Yet while or because the disparity between the intelligence of the actor and simplicity of the character enforces a kind of double vision, we can very much enjoy her performances that, no matter her totally feminine appearance and movements, share something with Mae West's "female impersonations." Like West's stereotypical interpretations of sexuality, Monroe's are purposely over-the-top; they function as satiric commentary on the entire heterosexual enterprise. Yet unlike West's stagy, "drag" performances, they remain sexy. In fact, Monroe's sexual "masquerade"—in the broadest sense of that word, making us aware of the ambitions of the living soul but also of the rigid social customs (here, the clichéd movements and gestures) in which the soul apparels itself to gain its ends—might well serve as another instance of Bergson's explication of the comic: "Any image, then, suggestive of the notion of a society disguising itself, or of a social masquerade, so to speak, will be laughable. Now, such a notion is formed when we perceive anything inert or stereotyped, or simply ready-made, on the surface of living society. There we have rigidity over again, clashing with the inner suppleness of life" (89). McCann's negative view that "Monroe came to satirise sex while still embodying it" doesn't begin to explain the power developed by this doubled position at a moment in which the Production Code Administration's grip on the film industry was beginning to loosen (Rosen 286). More than any other star of the period, Monroe helped to blur the distinction between the virgin and whore, conferring on women, through the artifice of her performance, a complexity that merged sexuality and desire with innocence, and making them acceptable and accepted.[11] Richard Dyer in *Stars* cites Monroe's "combination of sexiness and innocence, as effecting a magical synthesis of these opposites" (30). But a more nuanced reading of her powers would reveal that where others either played the virgin or "vamped," Monroe, whose performance was nothing if not a social masquerade, audaciously and deliciously "camped." And audiences loved her for it.

The divide between performer and character also called attention to traditional feminine behavior, which, in the 1950s, was beginning to alter. Marriage might still be billed as "the biggest thing you can do in life," but the very hyperbole cast doubt on the claim. Nowhere is this more the case than in *The Seven Year Itch* (1955) and *Some Like It Hot* (1959), both directed by Billy Wilder.

The male perspective appears to dominate in these films. Nevertheless, a demiurge is at work, subverting it and complicating Laura Mulvey's "controlling male gaze" so that the blonde becomes an active (and very funny) subject and agent of change. The plots—which bend, if not completely violate, gender boundaries—but also Monroe's comic genius destabilize Hollywood's usual take on heterosexual relations. *Some Like It Hot* is the later of the two films, but I'll discuss it first because Monroe's role in it isn't iconoclastic. However, she's just as brilliant as she is in *The Seven Year Itch*.

The premise supporting the riotously funny moments in the movie—so hilarious it was voted funniest comedy of the twentieth century when lists of the "best" and the "most" were published just before the millennium—is that, of the two choices, being dead and being a woman, being a woman is preferable. This isn't saying much for having two "X" chromosomes, but that's screen-writers Billy Wilder and I. A. L. Diamond's point.

In *Some Like It Hot*, two impoverished jazz musicians, Jerry/Daphne (Jack Lemmon), a bass player, and Joe/Josephine (Tony Curtis), a tenor saxophon-ist, are down on their luck in Chicago in 1929. Out of work, hocking even their overcoats for another of Joe's bad tips at the track, they desperately make the rounds of the booking agents. But the only job available for a bassist and a saxophonist is off-limits to them. Sig Poliakoff tells them they don't fit the bill: "Ya gotta be under twenty-five" [they can pass, they say]; "Ya gotta be blond" [they can manage that]; "And ya gotta be girls" [no, they can't, they say at first]. However, after they witness a Mob "rubout" on St. Valentine's Day, to avoid being killed (Mob rule number 1: the only good witness is a dead witness), they create their own witness protection program, creatively cross-dressing and signing on with "Sweet Sue's Society Syncopators"—an all-girls, all-blondes band headed for a three-week engagement at a fancy Flor-ida retreat for septuagenarian millionaires. The two men's instant attraction to Sugar Kane/Monroe—formerly Sugar Kowalczyk, the band's ukulele player and vocalist (figure 35)—and the millionaire Osgood ("Zowie!") Fielding's "hots" for Daphne create the intense hilarity that only the delicious tension of sexual masquerade doubled by double entendre can produce.

Because expressing their sexual interest in Sugar could lead to discovery and worse, Joe/Josephine sternly reminds Jerry/Daphne: "You're a girl!"—a lesson Daphne aims to internalize by repeating "I'm a girl! I'm a girl!" and, with deep regret (for having to pass on Sugar), "*I'm* a girl!" Their walk to the train to join the band, inexpertly managed on high heels, brings admiration for Sugar. "Look at that! Look how she moves! It's just like jello on springs!" says Jerry, as the camera, after tracking the men's awkward gait, tracks Sugar's from the rear. But Jerry's admiration is only partly sexual; the rest follows from an understanding of what women endure. "I tell ya," he adds, "It's a whole different sex!"

A depressed Sugar's heart-to-heart with Josephine in the ladies' room ("All the girls drink; it's just that I'm the one who gets caught") is the one moment in the movie in which the female character accounts for the dilemmas women face (figure 36). "What's the matter with you, anyway?" asks Josephine. Sugar explains she's got a thing for tenor saxophone players. "I don't know what it

Fig. 35. Joe/Josephine/Tony Curtis, Jerry/Daphne/Jack Lemmon, and Sugar Kane/Marilyn Monroe in the all-girls band "Sweet Sue's Society Syncopators" in *Some Like It Hot* (1959). (Courtesy of Photofest)

is. They just curdle me. All they have to do is play eight bars of 'Come to Me, My Melancholy Baby,' and my spine turns to custard, I get goose-pimply all over, and I come to 'em," she explains. But then, she says, they start borrowing money from you, and you find out they're betting on the horses and spending your money on other women. "Then one morning, you wake up, the guy's gone, the saxophone's gone. All that's left behind is a pair of old socks and a tube of toothpaste—all squeezed out."

Although Sugar explains her recidivism as an individual disability, we know she's far from unique. From Dido to Dorothy and Lorelei, some man has always broken some woman's heart, leaving her in the lurch—although the squeezed-out toothpaste is a new twist on an old affliction. Instead of a man "with money like Rockefeller and shoulders like Johnny Weissmuller," Sugar tells Josephine, "I want mine to wear glasses" (as in her life, Monroe had divorced the muscle man Joe DiMaggio and married the intellectual Arthur Miller) because "Men who wear glasses are so much more gentle and sweet and helpless." Wilder is continuing a conversation, begun four years earlier in *The Seven Year Itch,* which reconfigures the "ideal husband." But he doesn't play it entirely straight here, as he did in the earlier movie, unable to resist a gold-digger joke with a zinger. Such men, Sugar explains, "get those weak eyes from reading [so far, so good] . . . you know [she comically mimes myopia], those long, tiny little columns in *The Wall Street Journal?*"

Yet while the question of how men ought to act with women is still important, the focus in *Some Like It Hot* is on what it feels like *to be* a woman. When Daphne gets pinched in the elevator by Osgood, s/he comes rushing back to Joe, burning with indignation. "Humph! Dirty old man! I just got pinched in the elevator!" adding, "I'm not even pretty!" "Now you know how the other half lives," answers Joe. And Joe/Josephine ends the exchange: "They don't care, just so long as you're wearing a skirt. It's like waving a red flag in front of a bull." The personal pronouns tell an interesting story of gender transformation. Jerry's "I'm" (as in "not even pretty") shows he's jumped the gender "gap." Joe is doing the same, regarding men as "they"—the adversary and the beast—while the ordinarily genderless "you," with which he addresses Daphne, carries the freight of a feminine pronoun. In the comic register, this film takes its place alongside others in a subgenre of the "passing" story—actually, "reverse passing." The white man "becomes": the Jew in *Gentlemen's Agreement,* the 1947 adaptation of Laura Hobson's novel about anti-Semitism; the black in *Silver Streak* of 1976, with Gene Wilder and Richard Pryor; and, notoriously, the woman—and, most apt for comparison with *Some Like It Hot*—in *Tootsie* (1982) with Dustin Hoffman. In all of these films, the protagonist absorbs deep truths about the life of the "Other" that mere sympathizing can never achieve. The lesson in *Some Like It Hot* is learned through an assault on the rigidities of gender; but the assault itself acquires the properties of a

Fig. 36. Sugar Kane has a heart-to-heart with Josephine; tenor saxophonists "just curdle" her. (Courtesy of Photofest)

catalytic reaction. Engaging in the process, Billy Wilder suggests, confirms the pleasure inherent in the relaxation of some of the distinctions.

The movie—because it's played as outrageous camp—more easily raises questions about the fixity of gender through the story of Jerry and Osgood than through that of Joe and Sugar. However, an exception is the wonderfully inverted seduction scene aboard Osgood's yacht, "borrowed" by Joe. Impersonating the figure of the frigid "homosexual" heir to the Shell Oil fortune, he at first pretends to be impervious to Sugar's kisses. Kathleen Rowe argues that Joe's disguise is reminiscent of Cary Grant's characters as Joe manipulates Sugar into "seducing" him "by playing the role of the 'gentle and sweet and helpless' professor-hero": "Her efforts to get him to take off his glasses echo Susan's in *Bringing Up Baby*" (Rowe 190). But the homosexual impersonation (because we know it to be impersonation)—unlike Grant's straight persona in the 1937 movie—is more likely the natural extension of Wilder's own creation, Richard Sherman, in *The Seven Year Itch*, from only four years earlier.

The scene is remarkable because of the interaction of narrative and Monroe's consummate performance—much funnier than Curtis's, though his lines are wonderful, too. She plays the naive for all the part's worth as Sugar makes her best efforts to turn "Shell Oil" on. She's awed by everything about "his" yacht (owning one was on Sugar's list of a millionaire's desirable "qualities"), asking, for example, the name of the (big game) fish mounted on the wall. When he tells her that it's a sardine, she beautifully mimes puzzlement over how "they get them into those tiny cans." Her comic timing is perfect.

Wilder let his imagination range in *Some Like It Hot* beyond the alteration of sexual relations in his earlier comedy; Jerry thinks and feels like a women. Joe's successful seduction of Sugar makes him want to "do the right thing" for once, which means giving Sugar the flowers and diamond bracelet that Osgood had presented to Daphne/Jerry. Both have been feminized by their experiences—to their advantage.

Joe's heartfelt change is obvious when Sugar sings "I Wanna Be Loved by You." It's an earnest registration of the same "girl" questions raised in the brilliantly comedic moment when Jerry, "blissed out" and wielding his maracas on his hotel bed, thinks back to his evening of tangoing with Osgood—alone on the dance floor, the blindfolded band playing just for them. "I'm engaged," says Jerry. "Congratulations! Who's the lucky girl?" Joe wants to know. "I am!" he returns. "But you're not a girl—you're a guy!" "And why would a guy want to marry a guy?" asks Joe. "Security!" answers Jerry. Men like Joe have been leaving girls like Sugar forever. Why wouldn't a girl, who has given all—her love, her money, and her toothpaste—want (and deserve) security in exchange?

Well, nothing is perfect—not even this nearly perfect script—at least from the perspective of feminists like Rowe, who would prefer the Monroe character to be smarter and more assertive than she is. (At the end of the film she does tell Joe to shut up before she changes her mind about following him.) This is a movie about which it doesn't bear to ask: "What happens after the last freeze frame?" Just forget the desire for neat resolution and settle for the deliciously precarious pleasure of the final moments in the motor launch, as Jerry enumerates the reasons he can't marry Osgood (among them, that "she" isn't a "natural blonde"). Osgood's responses change the landscape of sexual relations by suggesting the benefits of a more fluid definition of gender and more empathic understanding and treatment of women by men. Sugar may be in the back of the launch, forgotten by us as Osgood offers his memorable response,[12] but the male-centered comedy is propelled by those revelations Sugar makes to Joe about "guys'" treatment of girls.

The Seven Year Itch offers the blonde a more active role despite the apparent objectification of "The Girl" in the famous skirt-blowing/subway grate scene—the filming of which contributed to the unraveling of Monroe and jealous "Joltin' Joe" DiMaggio's marriage.

The movie seems to tell a simple story of sexual temptation if examined casually—that is, from a traditional, male point of view. Richard Sherman, a book editor who sends his wife, Helen, and son, Ricky, to Maine while he toils in the sweltering heat of a Manhattan summer, is tempted to take advantage of his temporarily single state with the very attractive blonde who has sublet the upstairs apartment in his townhouse. The movie, however, shouldn't have been called *The Seven Year Itch*. The title comes from a chapter in a Freudian tome by Dr. Brubaker, which Richard's firm will publish—*Of Man and the Unconscious*—about the married man's adulterous potential. A more appropriate title would have been "Some *Don't* Like It Hot," or "Some Like It Cool," because its real subject is more subtle—a recalibration, at a lower temperature, of the relations between women and men. Richard Sherman has air-conditioning in every room of his apartment—a matter of pride, but also a mechanism, in both senses of the word, that drives the plot. One way of regarding air-conditioning, a rarity in 1955, is to see it as proof of Sherman's excellence as "homo economicus."

The extreme heat of a Manhattan summer becomes, from the opening scene, a metaphor for sexual desire. The voice-over describes the middle-class ritual of sending wives and children away for the summer to avoid the heat and humidity. The scene, with Alfred Newman's clichéd, tom-tom thumping rendition of "Indian" music as the accompaniment, focuses on Manhattan Island's "original" inhabitants' (only the men were "original"!) sending their wives and children off to the highlands (the Catskills?) or, "if they could afford it," the seashore while they "remain behind on the steaming island to attend to business—setting traps, fishing, and hunting." The "business," especially the hunting, soon means something else. As the squaws and children paddle away, the braves troop after a seductive single female who just happens to stroll by.

Cut to the waiting room of Grand Central Station, five hundred years later, as husbands, who have just sent off wives and children so they can "remain behind in the steaming city to attend to business—setting traps, fishing, and hunting"—salaciously pursue a modern "squaw" with a feather in her hat. How much *hasn't* changed! Her walk across the terminal, exactly like the Indian maiden's on the riverbank, is similarly tracked by the camera. But Richard Sherman, who has mindlessly followed the crowd, pulls himself up short. Talking aloud, as he'll do throughout the film, he says: "Aw no, not me, *not me!* And I'm not going to smoke, either. (directing his gaze to the other men) Look at them! Isn't it awful? Train isn't even out of the station yet!" He's promising himself he'll be different from the other husbands. He won't give in to the "itch" (the urge) or the thumb twitch (its symptom)—"The Repressed Urge in the Middle-Aged Male: Its Roots and Its Consequences" (another chapter in *Of Man and the Unconscious*). These first two scenes are merely the norm against which Sherman's exception will be measured; the movie will redefine the interaction of the sexes.

The most telling deviation from traditional gender norms is Richard's extraordinary imagination. His wife, Helen, remarks (naturally, in a scene he imagines) that he's begun to imagine "in CinemaScope with stereophonic sound"—which we can verify as many of the scenes of the movie are "projections" of his imagination. But the first mention of Sherman's imagination is actually by the voice-over, in connection with Brady and Company, the twenty-five-cent pocketbook publisher Richard works for (the voice-over points out that Sherman is the real economic engine of the firm). Miss Morris, the secretary, asks Sherman to approve a cover design for a new edition of Louisa May Alcott's *Little Women*. With an eye for what will sell, Sherman takes his marker and strikes lines through the bodices of the four sisters' dresses, creating for each a deeper décolletage. "You can sell anything," says the voice-over. "It's all a question of imagination. And Mr. Sherman has a *lot* of imagination!"

The linking of imagination and masculine economic advantage is significant as it undercuts the stereotype of hypermasculine "homo economicus," a nineteenth-century invention personified by the men at Grand Central who stay behind to attend to "business." J. G. A. Pocock traces the connection of imagination and economic advantage further back, to the eighteenth century: "Economic man as masculine conquering hero is a fantasy of nineteenth-century industrialisation. . . . His eighteenth-century predecessor was seen as on the whole feminised, even an effeminate being, still wrestling with his own passions and hysterias and with interior and exterior forces let loose by his fantasies and appetites, and symbolised by such archetypically female goddesses of disorder as Fortune, Luxury, and most recently Credit herself" (114). The film is exactly about Richard's "wrestling with his own passions and hysterias and with interior and exterior forces let loose by his fantasies and appetites." Tommy Ewell's comic interpretation of Richard's character is a study in the avoidance of stereotypical male gesture and movement. Showing triumph, for example, not by swaggering but by adding a jaunty, comical bounce to his walk, Richard, without being fey, is far from the typical "stud" or "masculine conquering hero." Ewell is literally redefining masculinity as he walks.

Equally surprising, considering the association of women with imagination (frequently, code for irrationality, as Pocock points out), is the Monroe character's insistence that she has none. Late in the movie, Richard, although completely innocent, is overwhelmed with guilt because The Girl from upstairs has slept in his apartment to beat the heat of her flat. He suffers a powerful fantasy, imagining that his wife has returned from Maine on the early morning train. She enters the apartment, accuses him of infidelity (The Girl is showering in his bathroom), and shoots him. "Wounded," Sherman tumbles dramatically to the bottom of the "staircase to nowhere" (The Girl's name for it), which connects his apartment with hers. In extremis, he calls out: "Helen, I'm going fast!—give me a cigarette." "A cigarette," she rebuts. "You know what Dr. Murphy told you about smoking!"[13]

As the figure of Helen fades from view, The Girl emerges from the bathroom to find Sherman, prostrate on the couch, in the grip of his imagination, "dying" of his bullet wounds. When she tells him he's merely dreaming, he returns to reality:

SHERMAN: It's just my imagination. Some people have flat feet, some people have dandruff. I have this appalling imagination!

GIRL: I think it's just *elegant* to have an imagination! I just have no imagination at all! I have lots of other things, but I have *no* imagination!

She's no Pandora. Sherman and The Girl have traded places, claiming and dis-avowing a faculty that, literally, in myth and story over centuries, has defined female nature. In addition to this feminine character trait, Richard's sexual fantasies, which he shares with his wife (of course, in imagination) about his attractiveness to women, put him in the supine (that is, "feminine") position. He is irresistible, he tells Helen's ghostly presence. "I arouse something in them, I bother them," he explains. "It's a kind of animal thing I've got." In each of three erotic "memories," with his secretary, a nurse, and Helen's best friend, he's pinned down by the insatiable woman. Always "on the bottom," he's overwhelmed by a female "creature from the black lagoon" (the movie that, later in the story, he and The Girl will see). The last of the women—in a conscious quotation of another famous beach scene—repeats Sherman's own words: "What is this strange animal thing you have? It bothers me. And it'll bother me always . . . from here to eternity!" But even his imagined storytell-ing ends in comic self-deflation. Helen laughs ironically: "The only extraordi-nary thing about you is your imagination."

The single instance in which fantasy transforms him into a Lothario allows Richard to experience seduction from the woman's point of view, as Joe does in *Some Like It Hot*. Wearing a satin dressing gown, his hair graying suavely at the temples, he plays Rachmaninoff on the piano as The Girl, wearing a tiger-striped strapless gown, decorously descends the stairs of the townhouse and floats through his temporarily translucent door. Her platinum hair, no longer innocently fluffed, is styled in a sophisticated pageboy. She leans languorously against the piano, confessing, in the words Sugar Kane will use: "It shakes me! It quakes me! It makes me feel goose-pimply all over!" But as he's about to kiss her, Mr. Krahulick, the janitor, on his mundane mission to save the rugs from the moths, breaks into Richard's romantic reverie.

Reality thwarts Richard at every turn. When The Girl really joins him for champagne, she responds naively to his recording of Rachmaninoff: "This is what they call classical music, isn't it? I can tell because there's no vocal." Sherman is not off to a good start. And it's "Chopsticks," not Rachmaninoff, that they play on the piano. Sherman's attempt at a romantic kiss turns into disaster as the two fall off the piano bench (figure 37). "What happened?" asks The Girl. "I kinda lost track." Sherman is tremendously contrite: "I don't know! This is terrible! There's nothing that I can say—except that I'm terribly sorry." The unromantic demise is literally of the "fallen world." Hardly Don Juan, he asks her to go, which, reluctantly, she does—but not before she says,

Fig. 37. "The Girl"/Marilyn Monroe and Richard Sherman/Tom Ewell "kinda lose track" in *The Seven Year Itch* (1955). (Courtesy of Photofest)

"I think you're very nice!" John Keats's promise of "a finer tone" "here after" for those who live a "life of sensations" has become, in Richard's "earthly" case, an illustration of Bergson's principles of "repetition."[14]

This platinum blonde is the "Dazzledent Toothpaste" girl. Dressed in a sexy strapless outfit (in one of Sherman's fantasies), she tells her audience (much larger, she points out, than Sarah Bernhardt's ever was!) in her fourteen-second commercial on "The Dazzledent Toothpaste Hour," every other week: "I had onions at lunch; I had garlic dressing at dinner. But he'll never know because I stay kissing-sweet, the new Dazzledent way!" With logic uniquely her own, she explains to Richard that she "wouldn't be lying on the floor in the middle of the night in some man's apartment if he wasn't married" because "with a married man, it's all so simple—I mean, it can't possibly ever get drastic." "Drastic," according to her idiosyncratic definition, has nothing to do with sex but with offers of marriage. Men ask her to marry them all the time, she explains, adding:

"All I know is, I don't want to get married. Not yet, anyway. Getting married! That'd be worse than living at the club [a single women's residence]! Then I'd have to start getting in at one o'clock again!" Here she is, just two years and a 180-degree turn from marriage as "the biggest thing you can do in life!" The Girl has come to New York City from Denver not to hunt for a husband but to start a career. Monroe's "Girl" and her "Elsie Marina," the "showgirl" in *The Prince and the Showgirl* (1957) both refute Marjorie Rosen's assertion that in films "throughout the fifties the female artist-actress consistently chose, or was forced to reconsider, marriage over theatrical ambitions" (266).

Furthermore, she's the one who invades Sherman's space, literally "pushing his button" to get into the townhouse; asking him to buzz it again because her "fan's caught in the door"—emphasized by a punning shot of her curvaceous bottom (figure 38); dropping her tomato plant onto his garden chair (and then, when she arrives at his door for a drink, making a pun, unintentionally, by reminding him of who she is: "The tomato from upstair!"). Later, she pries the nails out of the square of flooring—a secret "trap door" that now covers the former stairwell in her apartment—and descends the "stairway to nowhere" into Sherman's flat. She happily points out that they'll be able to "do this all summer." She's the one who, literally, goes "inwardly, downwardly" (Sherman's parody of the florid, sexualized prose of his imagined rival, Tom MacKenzie), assuming the prerogative of the mid-twentieth-century "masculine conquering hero." It will require the "violence" of Richard's final hallucination, featuring his gun-slinging wife, to reset the "controls" of desire and so redefine gender norms.

Imagining what Helen would actually do were she to discover "the strange blonde in the shower," he tells The Girl that his wife would probably think she were a plumber. "A blond plumber?" asks The Girl, doubtfully. But, yes, Richard insists, his wife isn't jealous at all. Why, last year, when he came home from the office Christmas party with lipstick on his collar, Helen asked if he'd gotten cranberry sauce on his shirt! A pretty girl doesn't want him, he imagines. She wants Gregory Peck. But The Girl is defiant.

> You and your imagination! You think every girl's a dope. You think a girl goes to a party and there's some guy—a great big lunk in a fancy striped vest, strutting around like a tiger, giving you that "I'm-so-handsome-you-can't-resist-me" look. And from this she's supposed to fall flat on her face! Well, she doesn't fall on her face. But there's another guy in the room—way over

Fig. 38. The Girl's "fan's caught in the door." (Courtesy of Photofest)

in the corner. Maybe he's kind of nervous and shy and perspiring a little. First you look past him, but then you sort of sense he's gentle and kind and worried—and he'll be tender with you—nice and sweet. That's what's *really* exciting! If I were your wife, I'd be very jealous of you—I'd be very, very jealous! (kisses him) I think you're just elegant!

She's done more than invade Sherman's physical space. This unsophisticated, yet not "dumb," blonde has become the wise tutor of his imagination, recalibrating for him and us the temperature of sexual attraction—a role she would also play with the aggressive cowboy Bo in the comedy *Bus Stop* (1956) and (seriously) with the wild mustang "rustler" Gay in her last completed movie, *The Misfits*. She even empowers Richard to face off with Tom MacKenzie, who arrives to pick up Ricky's paddle. Believing he's been found out, Sherman tells a bewildered Tom that he can explain everything: the stairs, the cinnamon toast, the blonde in the kitchen. "Now wait a minute, Dicky boy," says Tom. Now let's just take it easy. What blonde in the kitchen?" "Wouldn't you like to know!" responds Sherman. "Maybe it's Marilyn Monroe!" As in Harlow's *Bombshell*, here's another example of self-referentiality long before its postmodernist invention.

The paddle, which Helen had left behind in her rush for the train at Grand Central, has figured as a none-too-subtle phallic substitute throughout the scarce two days of Sherman's "bachelorhood." "Forgotten" by his wife, it poses a danger to Sherman—that is, he might "use" it (Sherman has become a convert to Dr. Brubaker's Freudian interpretations of behavior as, of course, had many in the urban middle class by the 1950s). To prevent such a possibility, he had spent the entire night, while The Girl was sleeping in his bed, "wrapping" it to send to Maine in the morning (encumbering it by safely sheathing it but, more practically, staying out of the bedroom!). Now he declares that *he* will take the paddle to Helen himself. He grabs it, giving The Girl permission to sleep in his air-conditioned apartment for the entire time he's away. But The Girl has the last words: "Just one more thing. I've got a message for your wife. (kisses him again) Don't wipe it off. If she thinks it's cranberry sauce, tell her she's got cherry pits in her head!" Sherman dashes madly and shoelessly from the flat. Once again, The Girl comes to his rescue, throwing his loafers to him from the window—perhaps the second-most famous sequence from the film. She waves good-bye as he salutes her with the paddle (from a safe distance!), dashing off to catch the train. Domestic reality will replace the imaginative idyll.

This girl has become a force for change. Speaking sweetly but with real authority, she knows much better than Sherman what women really like in a man. It took a Billy Wilder—an emigré writer and director—in the land of John Ford and John Wayne to rewrite the script of sexual relations and to restore the blonde to something like the complicated figure of comic sexuality, but also of subjective statehood and power, that she had begun to be in Depression-era films. However, he couldn't have done it without Monroe, about whom he said: "She was an absolute genius as a comic actress, with an extraordinary sense for comic dialogue. It was a God-given gift. Believe me, in the last fifteen years there were ten projects that came to me, and I'd start working on them and I'd think, 'It's not going to work, it needs Marilyn Monroe'. Nobody else is in that orbit; everyone else is earthbound by comparison" (quoted in McCann 111).

Monroe's detractors, among them Marjorie Rosen in *Popcorn Venus* and Jo-anna Pitman in *On Blondes,* have done as much to deflate her importance and destroy a nuanced portrait of her as they would claim the Hollywood moguls did, motivated by greed and "mammary madness" (Rosen 282). Pitman argues that it was the studio bosses' "job . . . to anticipate and reflect the social (male) desires of the day . . . by creating a film star [Monroe] in a completely new mould whose job was subconsciously to subvert [a] growing female independence" (226). She also suggests an unpleasant narcissism, quoting Wilder, without citation, about *Some Like It Hot:* "It was Monroe's luminescent hair that generated the extraordinarily powerful erotic charge of her sexual persona. Billy Wilder recalls that she was entirely aware of this. 'She knew it. There was another girl in the band who had blonde hair. And she said to me: "No other blonde. I'm the only blonde"'" (226). Such stories have a whiff of the apocryphal about them. If Pitman faithfully cites him, Wilder's memory of his own film was faulty. Whether or not any other blonde had Monroe's erotic charge, there wasn't *one* other blonde in the band; all of Sweet Sue's "Society Syncopators" were blond, as anyone would know who has watched *Some Like It Hot* and remembers Sig Poliakoff's words—"Ya gotta be blond" (perhaps his name is meant as a sly reference to Shirley Polykoff, creator of Clairol's "Does She or Doesn't She?" ad campaign, also of 1955).[15] But Monroe's luminosity was not merely owing to her hair and her breasts, though she wouldn't have been Monroe without these. There have been many other blondes with similar accouterments—Anita Ekberg, Jayne Mansfield, Brigitte Bardot. But there has been only one Monroe and not because her hair was more dazzling or her proportions more pleasing and sensational than the other stars'. Like Cleopatra, she was a woman of "infinite variety." Her appeal was the result of a happy combination of physical and intellectual gifts—her body and beauty, certainly, but also her wit and comic timing, the embracing warmth of her extraordinary smile, her ability to put over a song, and her magical reconciliation of cultural incompatibilities. But most of all, she fully inhabited every role she played.[16] Whether or not she was a narcissist, whether, in her deepening depression and as her marriage to Arthur Miller fell apart, she developed physical illnesses and became an unreliable worker—showing up late, forgetting her lines—before the camera she forgot *herself*, becoming the character, acting, as the saying goes, in the moment. There is no comparison between her abilities and those of the others blondes. Wilder put them in economic terms but with sense that reverberates far beyond dollars and cents: "I have an aunt in Vienna, also an actress. Her name, I think, is Mildred Lachenfarber. She always comes to the set on time. She knows her lines perfectly. She never gives anyone the slightest trouble. At the box office she is worth fourteen cents. Do you get my point?" (quoted in McCann 105).

She was a supernova—not merely a "star." The intense light of her image has lingered beyond her explosive screen appearances. She has become a cultural phenomenon that still has power to grip and intrigue more than forty years after her death. She achieved the compelling complexity that distinguished Kate Chopin's fin-de-siècle portrait of Calixta, whose wit, archness, *and* desire sadly grace only two short stories. Monroe was, indeed, the last truly original blonde.

I've taken up Richard Dyer's challenge to recover Marilyn Monroe as "a wit, a subtle and profound actress, an intelligent and serious woman," not only "against the grain of her image" but also against the views of many contemporary film and cultural critics. The stereotypical picture of the innocent, needy, malleable, dependent, and neurotic "sexpot" hardly explains the extraordinary interest she continues to excite. Her best films, worth a close reexamination, and certainly more than the few sentences often given to each in studies like Molly Haskell's *From Reverence to Rape,* reveal an interest, narrative complexity, and great talent unfortunately overshadowed by speculations about her mysterious death. (While Haskell does accord Monroe some of the reverence due her, her tribute is merely that she gave "more warmth" to her roles than they deserved.) Monroe's best work was done in a historical moment of social and cultural tension and transition, just as women were beginning to aspire to something beyond "shit and string beans"—Marilyn French's shorthand in *The Women's Room* for their lives in the new suburbs of America. In 1953, *The Kinsey Report* testified to their sexual desire. Sputnik, launched by the Russians in 1957, energized America to create an intellectually competitive population. Women and men of my generation would benefit from the changes in attitude and opportunities these events authored.

Except for Monroe, the blonde in the '50s, whether depraved, sexual, or innocent, was monodimensional. A variety of social, cultural, and economic conditions, encouraging more complexity of cinematic characters, would remove her from the screen in the changing film industry of the 1960s. But Monroe's contribution remains a signal moment. It was, perhaps, the last in which the blonde—as was her devout wish for herself—wasn't made a joke.

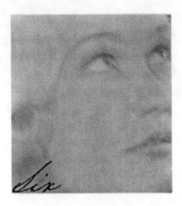

Six

Even Darker Shades

"Do you think there is a difference between blondes and brunettes?" asked Bertlef, visibly skeptical about Dr. Skreta's experience with women.

"You bet!" said Dr. Skreta. "Blonde hair and black hair are the two poles of human nature. Black hair signifies virility, courage, frankness, activity, while blonde hair symbolizes femininity, tenderness, weakness, passivity. Therefore a blonde is in fact doubly a woman. A princess can only be blonde. . . . A blonde unconsciously adapts herself to her hair. Especially if the blonde is a brunette who dyes her hair yellow. She tries to be faithful to her hair color and behaves like a fragile creature, a shallow doll, she demands tenderness and service, courtesy and alimony. She's incapable of doing anything for herself, all refinement on the outside and coarseness on the inside. If black hair became a universal fashion, life in this world would clearly be better. It would be the most useful social reform ever achieved."

—Milan Kundera, *Farewell Waltz*

There really was nowhere new to go after Marilyn Monroe. *Gidget* (1959), San-dra Dee's beach movie, was a sterilized version of blond sexual innocence of the late 1950s, meant to appeal to a much younger audience than Monroe's films. The portmanteau of "girl" and "gadget" is the affectionate but patron-izing sobriquet bequeathed by college-age beach bums to Francine Lawrence, a flat-chested and otherwise undeveloped (that is, not yet interested in boys) but sweet high school girl. The entire plot is devoted to her spending the sum-mer on a southern California beach, learning to surf the waves and like boys. Along the way, she almost sacrifices her virginity to Cliff Robertson, the "Big Kahoona," to make her real crush, "Moondoggie," jealous. But sex as a subject, along with Gidget, was consciously trying to grow up. It was treated overtly and ponderously by Delmar Daves, also in 1959, in the really terrible movie *A Summer Place*, in which Dee plays another high school innocent, until she "goes all the way" and gets pregnant, while her father has an affair with and then (because this was 1950s Hollywood) marries his first and unrequited love, the mother of the Dee character's boyfriend (Troy Donoghue). The byzantine complexity of these familial relations only begins to give some idea of the tediousness of this interminable film, larded with obvious, wooden dialogue. The single surprise, if it can be called one, is the censorious words the girl's father (Richard Egan) speaks to his first wife, an exceptionally nasty social climber, whose sole purpose in the film is to serve as the ideological straw woman. He turns Victorian values out of the house before leaving himself. "So," he says to his wife, "you insist on de-sexing her [their daughter]—as if sex were synonymous with dirt!" And later: "Must you persist in making sex it-self a filthy word?" The serpent of the First Garden was in big trouble. While the movie, based on the 1958 novel, was meant to be an enlightened treatment of the "problem" of sex, it had, unfortunately, none of the charm of *Some Like It Hot* of the same year—the latter film proving that by indirection, direction might be found out far more elegantly.

By 1968, in *Where Were You When the Lights Went Out?*, the bedroom comedy based on the November 1965 Northeast blackout that darkened the East Coast from Ontario, Canada, to New York City, Doris Day, as a star in a Broadway run, giving an interview to a women's magazine reporter, explains: "I was hoping that Broadway would maybe give me a change of image. . . . So what happens? I'm still the constant virgin." She is, of course, wryly look-ing back on her own film history—another version of blondness—in which she perfected the "good girl" career woman: attractive but barely interested in bedrooms unless her talent as an interior decorator were needed. In this movie, in which her husband's real, if brief, and her apparent, but nonexistent, sexual indiscretion provide the thin comedy of this counterfeit Feydeau farce, Day's character, true to its cinematic predecessors, rejects infidelity: "Call it my *corn-tasseled*, Yankee-Doodle, middle-class morality. But that's the kind of *hairpin* I am [my emphasis]." Her words consciously link her blond hair and the mythos of the "virgin land" of America—white, Anglo-Saxon, and middle class—which leaves much and many out of our nation's history and contemporary life. To characterize her personal virtues, we might consider the warning, still apt, of Thomas Wyatt's sixteenth-century sonnet: "Noli me tangere, for Caesar's I am, / And wild for to hold, though I seem tame."[1]

Day's explanation of her "hairpin" and "corn-tasseled" nature begins a story that shows that her particular embodiment of blondness is no longer current and serviceable. Times had altered; girls had to change with them. Her eventual reconciliation with her repentant husband (he has a brief fling with the magazine reporter)—signaled by a mad rush to the labor ward of a New York City hospital, nine months later—proves that a woman must be interested in sex to keep her husband's interest.

Screenplays of the late '40s and early '50s, in which blondness was clearly an attribute with various (and contrary) meanings—vice or mere naughtiness, or innocence, and their physiological variants, sexiness and frigidity—were for the most part not self-commenting, anthropological readings of the phenomenon. The blondes in them were simply made to play out various stories featuring a feminine knack for evil or good. Audiences were left to draw their own conclusions. But by 1959, as Doris Day and Rock Hudson sparred in *Pillow Talk*, trading charges of "bedroom problems" and suspicions of "impotence," and on into 1960s, sex was becoming a topic in the national conversation, especially after the arrival of "the Pill" and the "youth culture," which encouraged the fluid mix of antiwar protest, sex, drugs, and ever heavier, more metallic rock. The blonde was drawn into an overt discussion of feminine sexuality, no longer simply an expression of her individual character.

But despite Monroe's blond complexity, Bardot's taloned sex kitten, Day's traditional blondness (a contemporary update of the folk- and fairy-tale heroine, whose Prince Charming needed some education, himself), the coolly refined victim-blondes of grace and breeding (Grace Kelly, Eva-Marie Saint), or neovamps like Kim Novak in *Vertigo*, the blonde in the 1960s was beginning to recede from her position of prominence in American film. The refreshing sexuality and naturalness associated with her in the '30s and Monroe's sexuality, if not naturalness, in the 1950s suffered a cultural eclipse.

The blonde's disappearance was also, in part, caused by a slowing of the Hollywood juggernaut and the end of the Production Code Administration's hammerlock on the film industry. European and Asian films, featuring darker, more natural or "real" female stars, more representation of actual sex, and greater realism of character and narrative, which formerly would have been seen only by the small percentage of the public that frequented "art" houses in large cities, now enjoyed a wider audience, thanks to the demise of the studio system and the economically successful competition of independent distributors. Perhaps, as well, dark-haired heroines were an accommodation to the civil rights struggle as beautiful and glamorous black women like Lena Horne or Dorothy Dandridge were still unplaceable in "white" narratives.[2] But also importantly behind the interest in European films was increasing access to higher education through "Higher Education Opportunity Programs," which created a more sophisticated moviegoing audience. The liberalization of sexual attitudes and a greater diversity in personal aesthetics of the rebellious under-thirty cohort, and an increase in international travel, also explain their growing popularity.

Malcolm Gladwell has written that in the period between the 1950s and 1970s, we had "a strange moment in American history when hair dye somehow got tangled up in the politics of assimilation and feminism and self-esteem" (77). I would qualify his statement by shortening the span of years for which it was true. In the 1950s, Clairol marketed a hair dye that could be applied by women at home, just by shampooing. It turned them into blondes with little cost, trouble, and no expertise. Shirley Polykoff of Foote, Cone, and Belding, the Madison Avenue ad agency that handled the Clairol account, created the brilliant "Does she . . . or doesn't she?" campaign and several others that followed.[3] She made irreproachable for middle-class women what had formerly been racy or outré. The attention-getting, inflaming innuendo of her question was safely doused by the "answer" that followed: "Hair color so natural only her hairdresser knows for sure." A woman from 1955 on certainly could say "for sure" that it was time for her to live her one life as a blonde. But although Bristol-Myers's profits on sales of Clairol continued to rise,[4] as did the population, in the later '60s, the young women of the "Woodstock generation," profoundly influenced by the civil rights movement and later by the

Vietnam War, the counterculture, and second-wave feminism's consciousness-raising, rejected blondness, in fact rejected "artificial" grooming—the careful coiffures, dyes, hair sprays, sanitizing deodorants, perfumes, lotions, makeup (sometimes even baths and showers)—on which their mothers in the cities and suburbs were spending millions. The only dyeing that captivated them was tie-dyeing. They didn't pack Max Factor of Hollywood among their possessions as they trekked west to "the Haight." In a geographical lexicon, San Francisco figured as the antonym of Los Angeles, only four hundred miles down the Pacific Coast Highway to the south. Young women, less interested than girls of the 1950s in early marriage, and protected by reliable contraception, were enjoying sex and freedom and rejecting the uptight values of their parents (actually, of anyone older than thirty), that were responsible, they believed, for the Vietnam War, racism, sexism, poverty, and all other social ills. Whites, along with blacks, were transformed by the "Black is Beautiful" catchphrase of the Black Nationalist movement. Afros and dashikis gained cachet. In ten years, American youth had exchanged Dick Clark and *American Bandstand* for Jimi Hendrix and the Fillmore, both East and West.

Perhaps as Clairol leveled the playing field by making blondness possible for all women, the color lost its originality and zing. Or in this sexually relaxed climate, the fantasy sexpot blondes of the '50s were becoming de trop. Who needed them if they had real sex between real sheets or inside sleeping bags? Of course, there were blondes on the silver screen who were interesting, sophisticated, disaffected (like their young audiences)—most of them European: Monica Vitti in *L'Avventura* (1959), *La Notte* (1960), *L'Eclisse* (1962), and *Red Desert* (1964); Jeanne Moreau in *Jules et Jim* (1962); Julie Christie, who won an Oscar in 1965 for her terrific portrayal of a narcissistic, amoral cover girl in *Darling;* Catherine Deneuve in *Repulsion* (1965) and *Belle de Jour* (1967). These women were more complicated than their American counterparts, the films in which they appeared more engrossing than the usual Hollywood fare, and the sex far more graphic. Foreign films gave the phrase "bedroom scene" new meaning. Antonioni's 1966 *Blowup,* for example, provided a rather daring representation (for a mainstream movie) of voyeuristic penetration when photographer Thomas/David Hemmings walks in on his ex-girlfriend and her mate (nobody locks doors in this film); she gestures to him helplessly from underneath her partner as he grunts with pleasure in the act of lovemaking. Marjorie Rosen notes in *Popcorn Venus* that of the 798 pictures licensed for showing in New York houses in 1962, 582 were from abroad (372).

The '6os and '7os, as Molly Haskell writes, were decades, unlike the '3os, in which "the ideal white woman . . . was not a woman at all, but a girl, an inge-nue, a mail-order cover girl: regular featured, generally a brunette, whose 'real person' credentials were proved by her inability to convey emotion beyond shock or embarrassment and an inarticulateness that was meant to prove her 'sincerity'" (329–30). The blonde was reduced to a frigid, that is, dangerous woman in *Belle de Jour*, in which, from the perspective of the most obvious reading, she's indirectly responsible for her husband's being shot by a too-attentive client of her prostituted afternoons; to a demented somnambule in *Repulsion*; or to a chilled personality in Eric Rohmer's *My Night at Maud's* (1970).

Yet there is a difficulty in cataloging the films of this period, as both Rosen and Haskell do, fairly ungenerously, as merely a nadir for female actors. What was signally impressive about the 1930s movies is that from the moment "talk-ies" arrived, women spoke to the American public, as well as moved, with verve, gusto, moxie, and wit. The nearly ubiquitous blonde stood in for all women who were moving in the direction of emotional and social equality with their mates. The screenplays were well-made and engaging if not believ-able treatments of the many problems of Depression America. European mov-ies of the '6os were—from the viewpoint of craft, political commentary, and general interest—incomparably more sophisticated than the American prod-uct, but images of women in them (unlike those of the '3os) might be beside the point to verging on the disastrous. Yet to reverse the elements of the maxim, a critical throwing out of the babe has the unfortunate effect of also pitching out the bath water.

Take, for example, *Darling*—a thoughtful and compelling movie. The opening of the film, with the credits running, shows a brush-wielding hand papering over a London hoarding with a new ad. The copy reads: "'Mystery . . .' beginning today in IDEAL WOMAN." The enlarged image of blond Diana Scott is "erasing" the faces of black children in the "World Hunger" advertisement underneath. Throughout the movie, Diana's selfish, narcissistic blondness is not merely linked to, but is the epitome of, superficial, striving, materialist "mod" London. She is the auctioneer at a charity event (figure 39), organized by cosmetics giant Glass of "the Glass Group" (a stereotypical fig-ure, he's a cigar-chewing, Jewish business man, the name of whose big corpo-rate headquarters, "Glass House," is itself the stone the scriptwriters mean to hurl in the direction of such interests). A humorless MP makes a constipated, cliché-ridden speech, thanking the bored and fashionably wan, or bloated, be-jeweled women and their slack and paunchy consorts for their "private generosity": "I'm sure I have no need to bring to your attention (pained pause) the plight of our brothers (pause) of every creed, race, color (pause) in every far-flung corner of the earth (pause) who at this very moment are suffering the humiliation, degradation, shame, of the agonies of malnutrition." The camera cuts to three young black boys, dressed in powdered wigs and eighteenth-century livery, standing, like statues, against the wall. The world hasn't changed so much that Dickens's point in *Bleak House* has become obsolete. His satire on Mrs. Jellyby's "telescopic philanthropy"—her "African project" (29), with its scheme for helping "natives" by settling white coffee growers in Borrioboola-Gha (29)—a reminder that charity begins at home, is unfortunately still apropos. In the film, one of the guests, Lord Grout (the names are wonderfully suggestive—one might even say, Dickensian), remarks: "I like your black boys, John. I suppose I can't wrap one up and take him home?" To which the overreaching Miles (another expressive name)/Laurence Harvey cynically replies: "They're all numbered, Alex, and I wouldn't try changing your luck, if I were you." The Western blonde, the narrative implies, may give a little back, but her existence depends not only on such men but also on her "brothers" of darker races and colors, "in every far-flung [only, of course, from the perspective of the center of empire] corner of the earth."

Blond Diana Scott, first Miss "Honeyglow," "hereinafter known as 'the Happiness Girl,'" bears the opprobrium of the decadence. Sleeping her way to the top, she ends up trapped in a castle, a *principessa* by marriage to the Italian *principe* she has met while shooting a "medieval"-themed commercial for chocolates. When her husband leaves for a business trip, she despondently wanders the castle, miserable and bored (figure 40). Fed up, and having determined to leave her opulent prison, she flies back to London, where she's met by her first adulterer-in-arms, and the only man she has probably ever loved, Robert Gold, a television interviewer of some serious intellectual vision. But after a one-night stand, "for old times' sake," as he cynically tells her, Robert, much against Diana's will, books a return flight for her. She's bartered pure Gold for dross. Early on, she had refused to learn Italian when planning a holiday to Italy. Now she'd do well to learn the language. Otherwise, she'll lead an arid existence in the barren rooms of the castle, emptied of occupation and interest. The fairy tale is over . . . or maybe it's just beginning.

Fig. 39. Diana Scott/Julie Christie at a charity event in *Darling* (1965). (Courtesy of Photofest)

It's difficult now for an actor or even a private citizen to be a blonde without quotation marks. Once innovative and arresting, the blonde has become a cultural cliché, promoted by the film and cosmetics industries to make women believe that gentlemen really do prefer them—despite the truth that they also marry brunettes.[5] With few exceptions, veins of golden ore appear to have been culturally mined to depletion as women's desire for originality and self-definition, if these, indeed, are still desires, have found other means of expression. As "streaking" and "highlighting"—contemporary feints in the direction of "natural" blondness—or a palette of shades of the color have grown more and more common (platinum is out), blondness has dwindled to citation of older meanings: Diana Scott/Julie Christie quoted the gold diggers of the late '20s and early '30s; Madonna has very specifically reprised Monroe in an aggressively sexual, dissonant register; Sharon Stone's lesbian-vampire in *Basic Instinct* (1990) quoted Dracula's brides. Blonding their hair for "twenty-some-

Fig. 40. A bored *principessa* roams an empty castle. (Courtesy of Photofest)

thing" actors like Renée Zellweger and Reese Witherspoon and their television counterparts is simply part of the business, as clones of stories-past (*Chicago* as a remake of *Roxie Hart*) appear on screens across America year after year. In Witherspoon's *Legally Blonde* cinematic fluff, the "dumb blond" former sorority sister majoring in fashion design has been uncloseted as a genius and "animal rights" advocate with a near-perfect LSAT score.

But blondness is no longer a permanent feature, which is to say that there are no more stars, in the old sense of that word: actors with identities that trail after their appearances from film to film, like the afterglow of spent fireworks floating slowly earthward. As hair coloring has become common (the redesignation of the "dyeing" process neutralizes negative associations), an actor like Madonna may trade shades or go from dark to blond to dark with impunity. And what's true for actors is equally true for Jane Doe. Copy for a 1997 "Clairol Ultress" ad reads: "Linda Evangelista is wearing Ultress No. Z5" (figure 41). The verb implies that tomorrow she may well "dress" her hair in another shade. But there's a price to pay for such manipulation. Renée Zellweger, blaming the industry, has commented on how hard it is on hair. Repeated

Fig. 41. "Feel the Power of Color." (Courtesy of Photofest)

use of double-volume peroxide, less damaging than double-process, still turns hair brittle. Spiritual costs are another matter.

The 1997 Ultress ad displays, in bold italics, the words: "Feel the Power of Color." The peculiar *power* of "power" is its migration from the noun "color" to the (understood) pronoun "you"—the woman who uses it. Blondness is no longer promoted as a matter of what the world (more specifically, men) will notice, or of a woman's self-esteem (for example, Ilon Specht's 1970s L'Oréal "Preference" copy: "Because I'm Worth It"). Rather, it's about a woman's power—either her own—in the case of, say, Senator Hillary Clinton or Barbara Walters—or derivative, as with wealthy, less public women, such as the wives, some of them "trophy," of investment bankers, corporate lawyers, and CEOs on New York's Upper East Side and in exclusive enclaves across America. Week after week, photos of female guests at charity events in the "SundayStyles" section of the *New York Times* show their preference for a uniform shade of light blond. Power in our culture is synonymous with youth. Why not, then, choose blond over gray? If they begin coloring early and make other alterations as necessary, the moment when these women reach "a certain age" will be less certain. The comfort, as Shirley Polykoff divined long ago, is that only their hairdressers (and plastic surgeons) will know for sure. However, there may be a waste of spirit in writing oneself into the oppressive narrative of eternal blond youthfulness.

The recent association of women, especially blond women, and power—the barely hidden motive for the land-office business in snide blonde jokes—is the contemporary reinterpretation of the marriage plot. Like the hero of Woody Allen's *The Purple Rose of Cairo,* emerging into the darkened auditorium and from there into the real world, the action has moved offscreen. The power of blondness, as I'd begun to argue, no longer simply projects from films, where it has lost its freshness, but is found in the audience, among women who think they have made it work for them. To their blonded hair and cosmetic surgery, they have added the less radical but still strong medicines of Botox, dermabrasion, and skin peels—new weapons in the armamentarium for defying the aging process. Should we count these as advances, or should we read the poison of Botox as a caution sign? To what lengths are we willing to go to be "Beautiful for Ever"? The choice of so many who can afford to do so to stave off the inevitable by such means becomes, literally, the "operative" answer to these questions. However, they might be answered differently.

A positive exception to the exhaustion of blond meaning is the in-your-face, brazen theater performed by young women and men of all races by going freakishly blond. Blond roots under dark hair are a declaration of rebellion, a political critique of racist assumptions. We can also think of the flamboyant, bleached hair of former Chicago Bull Dennis Rodman or the blond wig of RuPaul. Their styles are as radical as Mae West's marcelled, platinum "do" of seventy-plus years ago. They serve a democratic purpose: to challenge the position of the fair-complected people of the world. Self-esteem need no longer be the monopoly of the blond and blue-eyed, as Toni Morrison's victimized Pecola in *The Bluest Eye* believed. "If black hair became a universal fashion, life in this world would clearly be better. It would be the most useful social reform ever achieved," says Dr. Skreta.

It hasn't been my purpose merely to echo Dr. Skreta's prescription. Rather, I have tried to de-naturalize blondness, to show the evolution of its representation in our culture—a doppelgänger, variously, of both successes and failures in the fight against sexism and racism. However, as I have read and watched, I have begun to wonder whether women haven't squandered the legacy of the more subversive and enlightened meanings willed to us by nineteenth-century women novelists and early twentieth-century actors. We seem, once again, to be circumscribing or exchanging these meanings for something approaching their traditional fairy-tale significance. The one notable difference is that now the blonde's hoped-for prize may not always be Prince Charming. Sometimes it's the corner office.

And sometimes it's time to move on, to find new images and metaphors for what we most care about. We can no longer seriously invoke the Romantics' vision of high peaks to express our sublimities or their "corresponding breeze" to suggest a belief in a hoped-for congruency with nature. Each generation of imaginative writers and artists—painters with words, with brushes, with bodies—makes us see the world in new ways. Cinderella's "glass slipper" long ago ceased to be an image for our serious reflections. "Glass ceiling,"[6] on the other hand, when it was first used in 1987, was a fresh image that caught our attention because it named and identified an obstruction that had negatively influenced the lives of some women—those who had moved from the castle or the house into the corporate structures of the global economy. It may now be on the way to becoming one of George Orwell's "dying metaphors"—expressions that "have lost all evocative power and are merely used because they save people the trouble of inventing phrases for themselves" (371). However, before we retire it, it might help us to see something that was not meant by its coiner—that in our desire for power or even power sharing, we have lost sight of what most matters for most women, men, and children.

As the world changes and populations shift, new figures must and will be invented to model our aspirations. We can, in fact, already see this happening. "Generation E.A.: Ethnically Ambiguous," a lead article in the *New York Times* "SundayStyles" section, confirms the existence of a trend I've noticed in film and advertising:

> Among art directors, magazine editors and casting agents, there is a growing sense that the demand is weakening for P&G (Proctor & Gamble), industry code for blond-haired, blue-eyed models.
>
> "People think blond-haired, blue eyed [*sic*] kids are getting all the work, but these days they are working the least," said Elise Koseff, vice president of J. Mitchell Management . . . which represents children and teenagers for ads and television. Instead, Ms. Koseff said, actors like Miles Thompson, 13, who is Jamaican and Eastern European, are in demand. (Laferla)

The fashion industry is taking its lead from Hollywood as ethnic ambiguity has gained vogue with stars like Selma Hayuk, Jennifer Lopez, and Christina Aguilera, who have "deliberately tweaked their looks, borrowing from diverse cultures and ethnic backgrounds" (Laferla) to increase their sex appeal. "Their willful masquerade reflects a current fascination with the racial hybrid, according to Linda Wells, *Allure*'s editor in chief, a fascination the magazine does not hesitate to exploit. 'Five years ago, about 80 percent of our covers featured fair-haired blue-eyed women, even though they represent a minority,' Ms. Wells said. Today such covers are a rarity. 'Uniformity just isn't appealing anymore,' she said" (Laferla).

This trend in popular culture and advertising also reflects the academic consensus that the concept of race is a fiction, "invented to categorize the perceived biological, social and cultural differences between human groups."[7] Gene pools aren't distinct and haven't been for thousands of years, a truth reflected by ordinary people—not merely those appearing before Hollywood's cameras and in the pages of glossy magazines. The focus on racial blending in advertising "reflects a societal trend, not a marketing trend."[8] Notice of the trend may have resulted from a recent acceleration of the phenomenon; acceptance of it is an even more hopeful sign.

Despite new reproductive technologies, women continue to do the lioness's share of the work of conceiving and nurturing of new generations. The world has, quite literally, depended on us for its future. Conception, however, in its other meaning, is understanding and making and seeking. We are, as ever, in need of new models, new pictures, to help us see and to create a better life for all. The most famous of blondes, Marilyn Monroe, expressed an earnest wish in 1962, shortly before her death: "What I really want to say: that what the world really needs is a real feeling of kinship. Everybody: stars, laborers, Negroes, Jews, Arabs. We are all brothers. Please don't make me a joke. End the interview with what I believe."[9] Her heartfelt desire tragically goes unanswered to this day but is no less admirable because of the continued failure of our imaginations and political will to transform vision into reality.

I, too, want to end with what I believe. When I think of the avoidable suffering of so many all over the world—bred of fear and hatred of difference—the fresh appeal of the new "Generation E.A.," as small a sign as it is, encourages me to hope that other ways of thinking and, then, being may not be illusory. Representation influences what we see and how we feel. If not our daughters, then I must dream that the daughters and sons of our daughters will be the ones to paint their words and so reflect faithfully the world's exquisite array of colors.

Introduction

1. "Harvard Gazette Archives," *Harvard University Gazette* (20 May 2002). http:// www.news.harvard.edu/gazette/2002/05.16/99-gould.html.

2. See Marina Warner, *From the Beast to the Blonde*, for the racial implications of blondness: "For fairness was a guarantee of quality. It was the imaginary opposite of 'foul', it connoted all that was pure, good, clean. Blondness is less a descriptive term about hair pigmentation than a blazon in code, a piece of a value system that it is urgent to confront and analyse because its implications, in moral and social terms, are so dire and are still so unthinkingly embedded in the most ordinary, popular materials of the imagination" (364).

3. W. R. Greg, "The Foreign Policy of the English Government and the English Nation," 470.

4. Anne Knight, in a letter to the Grimké sisters, American feminists. Quoted in Anderson and Zinsser, 358. Sororal support was a trans-Atlantic conversation.

5. See Martha Vicinus, *Suffer and Be Still*.

6. *Eliza Cook's Journal* (1849) was edited by Eliza Cook; the *English Woman's Journal* was first published in 1858 and edited by Bessie Parkes and Mathilda Hays. This latter magazine was actually printed in a building in Langham Place in London that was purchased by the women who published the *Journal*. Their cooperative venture was the first of its kind, putting into action the very principles of women's rights and claims to independence that they promulgated in the pages of their magazine and fought for in the political campaigns in which they engaged.

7. See Nancy Armstrong, *Desire and Domestic Fiction*, 97–98. Although the domestic novel, whether written by men or women, was a "feminized" genre, expressing the dominant cultural position of women in the nineteenth century, there are significant differences between the Romance and the realist novel as written by male and female authors, respectively, specifically in the representation of female characters.

8. See, for example, Alexander Pope, "The Rape of the Lock," *Norton Anthology of English Literature* 1:2233–52. Unruly Belinda is compared to "swarthy Moors" and "Afric's sable sons."

9. His method depended on a new chemical, paraphenylenediamine. His company's name, the "French Harmless Hair Dye Company," was changed a year later (showing marketing savvy) to "L'Oréal." Hydrogen peroxide and ammonia are the main ingredients.

10. Maria DiBattista's designation in *Fast-Talking Dames*.

11. See Anonymous, *Un siècle de modes féminines: 1794–1984*, and Jean Starobinski et al., *Revolution in Fashion: European Clothing, 1715–1815*. For the "cage crinoline" petticoat, see Penelope Byrde, *Nineteenth-Century Fashion*, 54.

12. For example, Delphine Seyrig herself: "By the mid–1970s, Seyrig had become an active feminist working with directors Marguerite Duras in 'India Song' (1975), Chantal Akerman in 'Jeanne Dielman, 23 Quai du Commerce, 1080 Bruxelles' (1975) and Ulrike Ottinger in 'Freak Orlando' (1981)." http://www.hollywood.com/celebs/detail/celeb/191992.

One. Thackeray's Blondes

1. For example, an article in the *Englishwoman's Review* (1 [October 1866]: 35) begins with the vocative: "WIVES AND MOTHERS."

2. The arrogant, racist treatment of Indians in the British Raj leaves little doubt that Anglo-Indians were not merely innocent victims. See Frances M. Mannsaker, "East and West: Anglo-Indian Racial Attitudes as Reflected in Popular Fiction, 1890–1914." Especially after the Rebellion, distinction in Anglo-Indian novels between light and dark functioned as a barometer, suggesting both the ineptitude and turpitude of Eurasians and Indians as, for example, in E. W. Savi's *The Daughter-in-Law* (London: Hurst and Blackett, 1913): "Self-indulgence and indolence [are] expressed in every line of his over-fed countenance, and sensuality breathe[s] from his coarsened lips" (24).

3. W. R. Greg, "Principles of Indian Government," 2.

4. These are the words of "some unknown correspondent" (106) about Amelia; they are even more fitting for blond Lady Crawley.

5. The novel's subtitle, which appeared on the wrapper of the monthly numbers in 1847, was "Pen and Pencil Sketches of English Society" (*Vanity Fair* xxvii).

6. Leonard Wolf, ed., *The Essential "Dracula,"* by Bram Stoker, 277 n. 11: "Eric Partridge's *A Dictionary of Slang and Unconventional English* cites 'clear grit.' Both 'grit' and 'sand' used about someone's character imply courage, stamina, or spirit."

7. Graves's description of the Goddess's "deathly pale" skin, lips "red as rowanberries," and "fair" hair, and her association with "Night Mare"—"one of the cruellest aspects of the White Goddess" (26)—suggest Coleridge's Life-in-Death.

8. On the split in the representation of the blonde in Victorian culture, see Elisabeth G. Gitter, "The Power of Women's Hair in the Victorian Imagination." "When the powerful woman of the Victorian imagination was an angel, her shining hair was her aureole or bower; when she was demonic, it became a glittering, snare, web, or noose" (936); "Well-read in such fairy tales ["Rapunzel," "The Goose Girl," etc.] and steeped in a culture that insisted on the preciousness of hair, Victorian writers inevitably focused

their general interest in women's hair on golden hair in particular. And because it links wealth and female sexuality, the image of golden hair enabled them not only to mine the fairy-tale tradition but also to express most fully their own shifting and ambivalent attitudes toward the power and value of both money and women" (942). I differ from Gitter in focusing on the social underpinnings of the racial obsession with golden hair as adjunct to the rising national myth of a superior and purely Saxon history. I also see a division between the male poets and male novelists, on the one hand, and female fiction writers of the period (Thackeray being the great exception), on the other. The male poets largely demonized females by insisting on the frightening totemic properties of golden hair; the male novelists reduced the blonde to dysfunctionality, insignificance, or even elimination through death. Women, by comparison, demythologized or "naturalized" the blonde. By reducing her cultural and genetic value, they, paradoxically, enhanced the worth of all women.

9. Mario Praz, *The Romantic Agony.* See chapter 4, "La Belle Dame Sans Merci," 199–300, esp. 201, 215, 216, 231. Praz importantly defined the type of the "femme fatale," which takes an interesting turn in the twentieth century, with her resurrection in the cinema (see chapter 4 of this volume).

10. See my discussion of Mae West in chapter 4.

11. See Jennifer DeVere Brody, *Impossible Purities* (113). Thackeray's contemporary Charles Reade, who wrote a story of a cross-dressing woman, "Androgynism: or, Woman Playing at Man," "was aware of the power of appearances and of women's particular penchant for female impersonation, implicit in idealized performances of femininity." Perhaps Reade was thinking of that consummate actress Becky Sharp.

12. John Ruskin, "Traffic," in *The Crown of Wild Olives,* vol. 18, *Works,* ed. E. T. Cook and Alexander Wedderburn (London: George Allen, 1905), 448. Ruskin also points out: "For, observe, while to one family this deity is indeed the Goddess of Getting-on, to a thousand families she is the Goddess of *not* Getting-on" (453).

13. *The New Columbia Encyclopedia,* 1745. For another reading, see Maria DiBattista, "The Triumph of Clytemnestra: The Charades in *Vanity Fair,*" 189.

14. Nathaniel Hawthorne, "Young Goodman Brown," in *Norton Anthology of Short Fiction,* ed. R. V. Cassill (New York: W. W. Norton, 1989), 407. I am indebted to my colleague Herbert Perluck for this insightful reading of Hawthorne's story.

15. Thackeray uses almost the same figure to implicate both male and female in a sexual dance in *The Virginians: A Tale of the Last Century:* "Two fish-pools irradiated by a pair of stars would not kindle to greater warmth than did those elderly orbs into which Harry poured his gaze. Nevertheless, he plunged into their blue depths, and fancied he saw heaven in their calm brightness. . . . Ah! What a heap of wreck lie [*sic*] beneath some of those quiet surfaces!" (1:223–24).

Two. Brontë and Eliot

1. Jin-Ok Lee, in her Ph.D. dissertation, "Female Desire and Community in Charlotte Brontë's Works" cites the following: Lillian Faderman, *Surpassing the Love of*

Men: Romantic Friendship and Love between Women from the Renaissance to the Present (New York: William Morrow, 1981); Barbara Gates, "Down Garden Paths: Charlotte Brontë's Haunts of Self and Other," *Victorian Newsletter* 83 (1993); Linda C. Hunt, "Sustenance and Balm: The Question of Female Friendship in Shirley and Villette," *Tulsa Studies in Women's Literature* 1 (1982).

2. John Donne, "Elegy XIX," "Loves Progress" (ll. 33–36): "Although we see Celestial bodies move / Above the earth, the earth we Till and love: / So we her ayres contemplate, words and heart, / And virtues; but we love the Centrique part." *The Complete Poetry and Selected Prose of John Donne*, ed. Charles M. Coffin (New York: Modern Library, 1952), 81. In this edition, the poem is numbered "Elegie XVIII."

3. George Eliot would be even more cutting about the meaning of female identity. In *The Mill on the Floss*, Mr. Wakem says to his son, Philip: "We don't ask what a woman does—we ask whom she belongs to" (345).

4. *The New Columbia Encyclopedia*, 2344.

5. See Linda K. Robertson, "From Reality to Fiction: Benefits and Hazards in Continental Education," and Linda K. Robertson, *The Power of Knowledge: George Eliot and Education*.

6. George Eliot, "Silly Novels by Lady Novelists," *Westminster Review* 66 (October 1856): 442–66, reprinted in *Essays of George Eliot*, ed. Thomas Pinney (New York: Columbia University Press, 1963), 317. Quoted in Auerbach, *Woman and the Demon*, 54.

7. For an opposing view, see Barbro Almqvist Norbelie, in *"Oppressive Narrowness,"* 142–43, who doesn't believe Eliot's "female communities" bear witness to "nurturing and supportive female relationships." Neither does she admit that friendships or moments of accord between women of dissimilar temperaments function as evidence of a future toward which women might strive in a world made more perfect by so striving.

8. *Our Bodies, Ourselves* may have been in print in the early '70s, but even Eve Ensler would likely not have been able to mount her performance of *Monologues* in a large, public theater, just off Broadway, thirty, or even twenty, years ago.

9. Josephine Butler in 1869 organized the Ladies' Association for the Repeal of the Contagious Diseases Acts, which granted police "the right to arrest and examine any woman suspected of being a prostitute in any of eleven port cities and garrison towns." Butler believed that prostitution was economic, "caused neither by female depravity or male licentiousness, but simply by underpaying, undervaluing and overworking women so shamelessly that the poorest of them are forced to resort to prostitution to keep body and soul together" (Anderson and Zinsser 2:182–83).

Three. Dyeing the Blonde a Darker Shade

1. See, for example, Elaine Showalter, "Desperate Remedies: Sensation Novels of the 1860s"; Elaine Showalter, *A Literature of Their Own*; Patrick Brantlinger, "What Is 'Sensational' about the 'Sensation Novel'?"; Lyn Pykett, *The "Improper" Feminine: The Women's Sensation Novel and the New Woman Writing*; Randa Helfield, "Poisonous Plots: Women Sensation Novelists and Murderesses of the Victorian Period."

2. Jenny Bourne Taylor with Russell Crofts, introduction to *Lady Audley's Secret*, by Mary Elizabeth Braddon, xiv.

3. See M. M. Bakhtin, "Discourse in the Novel," in *The Dialogic Imagination*, 259–422, esp. 261–63.

4. Taylor, introduction to *Lady Audley's Secret*, xxii.

5. Ibid., xxiv.

6. Madame Rachel Leverson "had opened a shop in New Bond Street, selling cosmetics and beauty treatments at outrageous prices. The slogan over the door, 'Beautiful for Ever', and the prominent position of the shop, acknowledged openly for the first time that ordinary women who were neither prostitutes nor actresses used cosmetics. But Rachel Leverson carried on other more criminal activities in the Bond Street premises (which, like the building which houses Mrs Oldershaw's shop in *Armadale* [Wilkie Collins], had two entrances), as was proven at her trial for blackmail in 1867, after the publication of *Armadale*" (Catherine Peters, introduction to *Armadale*, xiv). She was first convicted of conspiracy on 25 September 1868, and then, on 10 and 11 April 1878, of a misdemeanor for obtaining money and jewels from a Mrs. Pearce, for "beautifying," and was sentenced to five years penal servitude. The use of cosmetics by "ordinary" women had not yet erased their moral ambiguity, as Peters's note suggests.

7. Showalter writes in "Desperate Remedies": "Braddon means to show that the dangerous woman is not the rebel or the intellectual, but the pretty little girl whose indoctrination in the feminine role has taught her deceitfulness almost as a secondary sex characteristic" (3). But she doesn't go the further step of suggesting that Braddon implicates the culture for harmfully indoctrinating its female children.

8. The Spirit's words and sentiment echo the reviewer's in the *Westminster Review* in 1866: "[Just so does] Sensational Mania in Literature burst out only in times of mental poverty. . . . From an epidemic, however, it has lately changed into an endemic. Its virus is spreading in all directions, from the penny journal to the shilling magazine, and from the shilling magazine to the thirty shillings volume. Bigamy is just now its typical form. Miss Braddon first brought the type into fashion. No novel can now possibly succeed without it." *Westminster Review* 25 (July 1866): 269–70. Quoted in P. D. Edwards, *Some Mid-Victorian Thrillers*, 5–6; 30 n. 12.

9. Stoker describes the noses of the dark-haired vampires as aquiline. His omission of the blonde's hooked nose is probably owing to the racialized aesthetic judgment of the English, who rejected "oriental" features.

10. See Bram Dijkstra's *Evil Sisters* for a critique of the Jungian archetypes as false science and spreaders of the infection of misogyny also spawned by Stoker's novel.

11. Leonard Wolf proposes another interpretation: "Lucy's name can be interpreted symbolically as 'Light of the West' or, conversely, 'Lucifer.' In '*Dracula;* The Gnostic Quest and Victorian Wasteland' [*Dracula; The Vampire and the Critics* (Ann Arbor: UMI Research Press, 1988), 88], Mark H. Hennelly, Jr. suggests 'the principle of right light'" (71 n. 1).

12. Charles Berg, *The Unconscious Significance of Hair* (Washington, D.C.: Guild Press, 1951); Phyllis A. Roth, "Suddenly Sexual Women in *Dracula*."

13. See Barbara Green, *Spectacular Confessions*.

14. http://www.utilitarianism.com/felicalc.htm.

15. The title of Michael Pollan's book (New York: Random House, 2001).

16. Thomas Doherty, *Pre-Code Hollywood*, 17.

Four. Double-Peroxide, Moving Parts, and Mobile Mouths

1. Meredith, incidentally, thought very well of *Emma* from the viewpoint of the exercise of the comic spirit. He wrote: "There is Miss Austen, whose Emma and Mr. Elton might walk straight into a comedy, were the plot arranged for them" (41).

2. From the Margaret Sanger Papers Project, Department of History, New York University:

> The Birth Control Clinical Research Bureau (BCCRB) began in 1923 as the Clinical Research Bureau (CRB), the first legal birth control clinic in the country. . . . It quickly emerged as the nation's primary facility for the testing and study of contraceptive methods and devices. . . . The BCCRB served as an autonomous clinic and research facility from 1928 to 1939. . . . The BCCRB, which continued to function as the largest contraceptive clinic in the country, changed its name to the Margaret Sanger Research Bureau (MSRB) in 1940 in honor of its founder.
>
> The BCCRB served well over 10,000 patients each year by the 1930s. It provided contraceptive instruction for married women and couples, a range of gynecological services, and training for physicians and students. The BCCRB also established a nationwide network of affiliated clinics and supervised numerous field projects in the rural south. http://www.nyu.edu/projects/sanger/birth_control_clinical_research_bureau.htm.

3. Dijkstra, *Evil Sisters*, 47. Born Theodosia Goodman, Theda Bara, whose screen name might have been an anagram for "Arab Death," was a Jewish woman from Ohio.

4. Thomas Dixon, *The Clansman: An Historical Romance of the Ku Klux Klan* (New York: Doubleday, Page, 1905) and *The Leopard's Spots: A Romance of the White Man's Burden, 1865–1900* (New York: Doubleday, Page, 1902).

5. The source for my discussion of the music for *Birth of a Nation* is Martin Miller Marks, *Music and the Silent Film*. The film opened in New York City at the Liberty with Breil conducting the orchestra (137, 141).

6. The 1916 Chapell collection score, selectively reproduced by Marks, has phrases like "Mulatto aroused" (115); "Sumner orders hat" (116); "Lydia picks up hat" (117); and "Lydia puts hand to mouth" (118) hand-penned either above or under bars of music and meant to time orchestral themes to the film's action.

7. Used as early as 1912 but no longer necessary when panchromatic film became the standard stock in 1926. Exhibition, American Museum of the Moving Image, Astoria, New York.

8. The tag is itself a comical anachronism. This figure is many removes from the physical labor implied by it.

9. "Siren of the River Rhine" (Rule 70). Anita Loos chose her heroine's name carefully, as she did that of her down-to-earth sidekick Dorothy, which means "gift of God."

10. There seems to have been a silent movie from 1928 that is presumed lost. www.silentera.com/PSFL/data/G/GentlemenPreferBlondes1928.html.

11. Marie's words (visible in the intertitle) are "heard" by Babe Winsor. But the "insider's" joke, meant for the entire cinemagoing audience, is that they overtly link her character to Theda Bara's vamp in *A Fool There Was* (1915), demonstrating the already significant cultural penetration of the film industry in its brief history.

12. Although already apparent in popular culture by 1915, when *A Fool There Was* and *Birth of a Nation* were released, the crescendoing in the '20s of white supremacist sociological and medical "proof" of the inferiority of dark-skinned people and the growing political fortunes of the National Socialist Party in Germany in the latter years of the decade did not implicate the new-style vamp, the blond gold digger, in the sexist/racist linking of the predatory woman with non-Europeans. See Bram Dijkstra, *Evil Sisters*, especially chapters 7–10.

13. See Walter Benjamin, "The Work of Art in the Age of Mechanical Reproduction," 217–51.

14. In *Goodness* (107–8), West writes that there was a class of saloons on the Bowery known as the Raines Law Hotels. Their owners had "attached bedrooms to their taverns in order to be able to sell liquor on Sundays. According to the Raines Law, only a licensed hotel, having at least ten bedrooms, could do so. The Raines Law Hotels were really disorderly houses."

15. Although the story is set just before the turn of the century, it can't be unintentional that the Russians are the bad-guy masterminds of a white slavery ring, ultimately exposed by the undercover agent Captain Cummings/Cary Grant, alias "The Hawk," who works at the nearby Rescue Mission. For this was 1933, the depths of the Great Depression. It didn't hurt to tarnish the Russians, whose competing political and economic system was attracting American workers fed up with failing capitalism. Just months before, in March 1932, for example, angry workers had stormed the Ford Motor Company's River Rouge plant in Dearborn, Michigan, demanding the "immediate establishment of Soviet America" (Smith, *The Shattered Dream* 96).

16. http://www.pitt.edu/~amerimus/ofah.htm. http://www.pdmusic.org/foster/scf60i.txt.

17. John Tuska, in *The Films of Mae West* (90), praises West's moral nature. Of *I'm No Angel*, he says:

In her very personal relationship with the people around her—to Benny Pinkowitz [her Jewish lawyer], to Big Bill, to her colored maids (and their honest regard for her) . . . Tira embraces all of life, and all of man, without hatred or pettiness, but with wit, tolerance, equality, and with personal capability, mastery of herself and her world, the world in which she lives and, by extension, the world in which all of us must live.

His judgments of West's personality and tolerance are validated by the ethos she expresses in her autobiography.

18. Although her reviewers made invidious comparisons, as did Robert Garland in his notice after the opening of *Diamond Lil* on 5 April 1928: "So regal is Miss West's manner, so assured is her artistry, so devastating are her charms in the eyes of all red-blooded men, so blond, so beautiful and so buxom is she that she makes Miss Ethel Barrymore look like the late lamented Mr. Bert Savoy" (quoted in West, *Goodness* 111).

19. Miguel Covarrubias, an artist of the 1930s, captured figures of the Harlem Renaissance in drawings and caricatures.

20. West's generous and joking relationship with her maid in real life could well have served as a model for her screen versions, as this story from her autobiography proves. Howard Merling, she writes,

> came backstage to my dressing room for a visit after a matinee performance. Bea Jackson, my colored maid, interrupted us.
>
> "You said, Miss West, I could leave early to go uptown to Harlem to see my aunt. I gotta be back in time for tonight's show."
>
> "Sure, Bea, run along. I hope your aunt wears a derby hat and dances well at the Savoy." (*Goodness* 140)

21. Laura Mulvey's 1975 thesis in "Visual Pleasure and Narrative Cinema"—that Hollywood films are a reflection of "the controlling male gaze at the highly fetishised figure of a woman, thus confirming the traditional active male/passive female dichotomy" (discussed in Pam Cook, "Border Crossings: Woman and Film in Context," in *Women and Film* xviii)—is not supported by West and her films (in the production and screenplays of which, as well as her own dialogue and direction, she played a controlling role). The viewer is compelled by her dominance in any scene in which she acts.

22. But in *Boy Meets Girl* (1938), a silly film in which Cagney starred with Pat O'Brien and blond Marie Wilson, he was quite the dandy, both in manners and speech.

23. Phyllis Haver's blond temptress was there before Harlow's, but Harlow's career in "talkies" took off as Haver's never did.

24. Throughout the film, Vantine calls Dennis "Fred" while he calls her "Lily." These names represent the moral potential of each character, as revealed in their final actions, which, in turn, resolve the sexual conflicts of the plot. "Lily" is associated with the Madonna and purity; "Frederick," from the Old German, means "peaceful ruler," "a man not greedy or aggressive" (Rule 69, 140).

25. See H. Rider Haggard, *She*. The Englishman Holly describes Ayesha: "I gazed . . . at her face, and—I do not exaggerate—shrank back blinded and amazed. I have heard of the beauty of celestial beings, now I saw it; only this beauty, with all its awful loveliness and purity, was evil—at least, at the time, it struck me as evil" (155). As played by Ursula Andress in the 1965 remake of the original 1935 movie (starring Helen Gahagan), Ayesha, or "She," was blond. Andress/Ayesha refers to herself as "She Who Waits"—something of a comedown for the powerful sex goddess!

26. The racist portrayal and treatment of the Indochinese plantation workers and the "houseboy" Hoi, who talks in the stereotypically broken English ascribed to Asians in films of the 1930s through '50s, is embarrassing to a contemporary audience.

27. The term "screwball" was itself of very recent origin, dating from the 1928 invention of a baseball pitch. During the flight from pitcher's mound to home plate, the ball would unexpectedly change direction, fooling the batter.

28. See Frederick W. Ott, *The Films of Carole Lombard,* for the story of the first day of Lombard's rehearsal for *Twentieth Century,* as Howard Hawks recalled it in his autobiography. It was a disaster, just like Lily Garland's. Hawks said to her:

> we're going back in and make this scene and you kick him, and you do any damn thing that comes into your mind that's natural, and quit acting. If you don't quit, I'm going to fire you this afternoon. You just be natural. . . . And we made about an eight page scene and she made a kick at [Barrymore] and he jumped back, and he started reacting and they went right through the scene. He made his exit, and I said cut and print it. And he came back in and he said to Lombard, that was marvelous, what've you been doing, kidding me? And she started to cry and ran off the stage. And he said, what happened? I said you've just seen a girl that's probably going to be a big star, and if we can just keep her from acting, we'll have a hell of a picture. And she became a star after the picture. (26–27)

The premium that Hawks placed on acting naturally—his proto-"method-acting" lesson—complemented the cultural imprimatur on naturalness for women in the 1930s.

29. Thomas Carlyle, "The Everlasting Yea," in *Sartor Resartus: The World Out of Clothes,* in *The Victorian Age: Prose, Poetry, and Drama,* ed. John Wilson Bowyer and John Lee Brooks, 2nd ed. (New York: Appleton-Century-Crofts, 1954), 169.

30. In *Vanity Fair,* Thackeray examines a corollary of this fear—that the role will infect the person playing it: "At the little Paris theatres, on the other hand, you will not only hear the people yelling out *'Ah gredin! Ah monstre!'* and cursing the tyrant of the play from the boxes; but the actors themselves positively refuse to play the wicked parts, such as those of *infâmes Anglais,* brutal Cossacks, and what not, and prefer to appear at a smaller salary, in their real characters as loyal Frenchmen" (78).

31. The Black Bottom was introduced to white America by Perry Bradford in Nashville, Tennessee, in 1919 when he wrote the song "The Black Bottom Dance." "The stage play 'Dinah' in 1924 introduced the Black Bottom to the public and almost overnight [it] became as popular as the Charleston." http://www.streetswing.com /histmain/z3blkbtm.htm.

32. Dickens used the symbolic freight of "straying" curls in his portrait of wayward Em'ly in *David Copperfield;* Braddon describes Lady Audley's "snaky" locks. Roxie's change in hair style is an acknowledgment of hair's symbolic power, as was Ginger Roger's decision to dye her hair red for this movie.

33. Greenberg's translation of Shakespeare's words from *The Merchant of Venice* (3.1.55–75) broadens the category of victims from Jews to all Poles. Although his de-

liberate rhetorical inclusiveness has been criticized, I see it as a morally evolved contribution by Lubitsch. Virulent Polish anti-Semitism didn't save Poland from the Nazis.

34. Julio Cortàzar, *Hopscotch*, trans. Gregory Rabassa (New York: Pantheon, 1966), 32.

35. Manny Farber in the *New Republic* (23 February 1942) wrote: "There is a lot of maneuvering of people and scenes to get laughs which sound more like titter. Such manipulation leads to the kind of laugh that comes from a gagline and not from something inherently funny in the situation." Edgar Anstey, in the *Spectator* (London), 8 May 1942, wrote: "Amongst our more solemn citizens, *To Be Or Not To Be* will become a touchstone of good taste: if you disapprove of it you will gain credit for a sense of the serious character of the war and of the sufferings of the Nazi-occupied countries; if you find it the funniest comedy of the year, then you are very likely to be damned as politically irresponsible." But the film critic of *Life* was most in tune with the judgment of posterity: "In years to come the fact that Hollywood could convert part of a world crisis into such a cops and robbers charade will certainly be regarded as a remarkable phenomena [*sic*]." All reviews quoted in Frederick W. Ott, *The Films of Carole Lombard*, 184–85.

36. See Parker Tyler, "The Somnambules," in *The Hollywood Hallucination*, 74–99. Tyler argues that "the somnambule's myth essentially signifies the 'ritual' readying of woman for sex by depriving her of her conscious powers through hypnotism" (74).

37. Ed McBain, "She Was Blond. She Was Trouble. And She Paid 3 Cents a Word," *New York Times*, "The Arts" section, 29 March 1999.

38. For a selection of wartime "Varga Girls," see Tom Robotham, *Varga*.

39. See Maria DiBattista, *Fast-Talking Dames* (336–37) for a positive reading of Day's characters.

Five. Monroe at the Gates

1. http://www.alabamamoments.state.al.us/sec54.html.

2. The NAACP protested the black sitcom's racial stereotypes of "the shiftless, conniving, not-too bright blacks," but *Amos 'n' Andy* was very popular in the early 1950s and enjoyed an afterlife of reruns into the 1960s. The roles of Amos and Andy were originated by white actors, Freeman Gosden and Charles Correl, in the radio version of the 1940s. http://www.geocities.com/Hollywood/2587/history.htm.

3. Dorothy Dandridge and Lena Horne, the latter having made no movies in the 1950s (although, in 1957, Horne was in the ensemble cast of *The Heart of Show Business*, a "short subject" on that subject), were great exceptions. *The Defiant Ones*, starring Tony Curtis and Sidney Poitier, a feint in the direction of the possibility for cross-race friendship, was released in 1958.

4. *The River of No Return* (1954), in which she played a morally complex woman, was a box-office flop. Audiences liked their Monroe innocent but knowing, available, sexy, and funny.

5. The "Madonna/whore" divide, which has characterized male reaction to women over the centuries, began to moderate in the 1950s as attitudes toward sex became more liberal. It was permissible for Marilyn Monroe to be "sexy" (an object) but not "sexual" (a subject), an important distinction, which depends on the woman's not having desires of her own.

6. As recently as March 2003, Bloomingdale's ran an add in the *New York Times* for a clutch bag with multiple images of Andy Warhol's iconic portrait of Monroe emblazoned on its side.

7. http://www.crimelibrary.com/notorious_murders/celebrity/marilyn_monroe/2.html?sect=26.

8. When Bette Davis haughtily says to Claudia/Monroe, "I believe I don't know you," Miss Caswell artlessly responds, "That's because we've never met." Her indisputable logic comically trumps the Davis character's frigid slight.

9. Midge/Barbara Bel Geddes, a "natural" blonde, is Scottie Ferguson/James Stewart's "pal"—a nonthreatening woman who hasn't "covered up" or erased her dark hair and darker motives with bleach. However, she does own a brassiere with "revolutionary uplift . . . [which] works on the principle of the cantilever bridge," designed by an "aircraft engineer down the peninsula" (Alec Coppel and Samuel Taylor, *Alfred Hitchcock's Vertigo* 7). This would have been the kind of bra that Howard Hawks had specially designed for Jane Russell for *Gentlemen Prefer Blondes*. The weirdly conical appearance it gave to breasts lost out to the natural, rounded look favored in the 1960s.

10. A 1928 silent version of *Gentlemen Prefer Blondes*, produced by Paramount Famous Lasky Corporation and distributed by Paramount Pictures, is "presumed lost."

11. Rosen cites the Kinsey study's claim that "one-half of all married young women had premarital sexual experiences" (303). Films actually lagged behind life in depicting women's sexuality.

12. Rowe asserts that "Sugar cannot free herself from a restrictive femininity" and that as "half of the storybook couple—[she] remains confined to a narrow and pitiful role in the back seat of the boat" (189).

13. This scene perfectly illustrates Bergson's comic principle: "From the idea of travesty . . . we must go back to the original idea, that of a mechanism superimposed upon life. . . . Twenty years ago, a large steamer was wrecked off the coast at Dieppe. With considerable difficulty some of the passengers were rescued in a boat. A few custom-house officers, who had courageously rushed to their assistance, began by asking them 'if they had anything to declare'" (90).

14. When a group of characters is brought together "to reproduce, under ever fresh circumstances, one and the same series of incidents or accidents more or less symmetrically identical," the second scene is reproduced "in another key," "the rendering . . . naturally less refined" (Bergson 119, 120).

15. http://www.ciadvertising.org/studies/student/99_fall/theory/maddux/polykoff/polyintro.htm.

16. Her desire to perfect her performance of Sugar Kane, demanding retake after retake, drove others in the cast and crew of *Some Like It Hot* crazy.

Six. Even Darker Shades

1. The silly scene at the end of *Pillow Talk,* in which Rock Hudson, Hollywood caveman, carries a kicking and struggling Day through the streets of New York City to his apartment, suggests the congruity of Wyatt's sonnet.

2. I owe this insight to my colleague David Corey.

3. Robert McG. Thomas Jr., "Shirley Polykoff, 90, Ad Writer Whose Query Colored a Nation." The answer to her first question was: "Hair color so natural only her hairdresser knows for sure." Her later copy included: "Is It True Blondes Have More Fun?"; "If I've Only One Life to Live, Let Me Live It as a Blonde." Her obituarist says that Polykoff, named the "1967 Advertising Woman of the Year," disconcerted feminists, who saw her as a terrific role-model for professional woman but recognized that her success was built on helping to turn women into vain sex objects for the delectation of men.

4. According to the Polykoff obituary, sales rose from $25 million in 1956 to $200 million a decade later, as "nearly half of all American women were regularly coloring their hair." Hair coloring was not, however, favored by the "flower children" of the new "Youth Culture."

5. *But They Marry Brunettes* is Loos's sequel to *Gentlemen Prefer Blondes.*

6. "Invisible barrier to women or minorities in corporate promotions. This image of an unexpected see-through obstruction was coined in the mid–1980s. Alice Sargent, a Fortune 500 consultant and author of 'The Androgynous Manager,' told the 'Washington Post' in 1987 that 'women in corporate America are 'bumping their heads on the glass ceiling. Women are looking up at the top and not making it into the board room or the executive suites.'" (William Safire, *Safire's New Political Dictionary* [New York: Random House, 1993]). http://phrases.shu.ac.uk/bulletin_board/5/messages/295. html.

7. Professor Evelyn Hammond (quoted in "Generation E.A."). See also Michael J. Bamshad and Steve E. Olson, "Does Race Exist?": "If races are defined as genetically discrete groups, no. But researchers can use some genetic information to group individuals into clusters with medical relevance" (80).

8. Laferla, "Generation E.A." Laferla quotes John Parilla, CEO of Brand Buzz: "'For once,' Mr. Parilla added, 'it's about art imitating life.'" He follows Oscar Wilde: art, no longer a sui generis world of "Proctor & Gamble" blond beauty, reflects life.

9. Quoted in McCann 219. Richard Meryman, to whom Monroe gave her last interview ("Fame may go by and—so long, I've had you" [*Life* 53, no. 5 (3 August 1962): 31–36]), didn't honor her request to include this statement in the article. http://www.angelfire.com/va/spresly/marylin.htm.

Bibliography

Alcott, Louisa May. *Behind a Mask: The Unknown Thrillers of Louisa May Alcott*. Introduction by Madeleine Stern. New York: Quill, 1984.

Anderson, Bonnie S., and Judith P. Zinsser. *A History of Her Own: Women in Europe from Prehistory to the Present*. 2 vols. New York: Harper and Row, 1988.

Anonymous. "La Rose D'Amour: Or the Adventures of a Gentleman in Search of Pleasure." In *Venus Disposes: An Amorous Admixture of Victorian Writings*. New York: Carroll and Graf, 1988.

——. *Should Woman Obey? A Protest against improper matrimonial and prenatal conditions, showing causes, prevention and remedy of needless inharmonies and unhappiness, etc.* Edited by Ernest Loomis. Chicago: Ernest Loomis, 1900.

——. *Un siècle de modes féminines: 1794–1984*. Paris: Charpentier et E. Fasquelle, 1894.

Armstrong, Nancy. *Desire and Domestic Fiction: A Political History of the Novel*. New York: Oxford University Press, 1987.

Auerbach, Nina. *Woman and the Demon: The Life of a Victorian Myth*. Cambridge: Harvard University Press, 1982.

Austen, Jane. *Mansfield Park*. Introduction by Mark Schorer. New York: Dell, 1961.

——. *Northanger Abbey*. Introduction by Mark Schorer. New York: Dell, 1962.

——. *Pride and Prejudice*. Edited by Mark Schorer. Cambridge, Mass.: Houghton Mifflin, 1956.

Bach, Steven. *Marlene Dietrich: Life and Legend*. New York: Morrow, 1992.

Baker, Roger. *Drag: A History of Female Impersonation in the Performing Arts*. New York: New York University Press, 1994.

Bakhtin, M. M. *The Dialogic Imagination: Four Essays*. Edited by Michael Holquist. Translated by Caryl Emerson and Michael Holquist. Austin: University of Texas Press, 1981.

Bamshad, Michael J., and Steve E. Olson. "Does Race Exist?" *Scientific American* 289, no. 6 (December 2003): 78–85.

Banner, Lois W. *American Beauty*. New York: Alfred Knopf, 1982.

Banta, Martha. *Imaging American Women: Idea and Ideals in Cultural History.* New York: Columbia University Press, 1987.

Barfoot, C. C. "Beyond *Pug's Tour:* Stereotyping Our Fellow-Creatures." In *Beyond Pug's Tour: National and Ethnic Stereotyping in Theory and Literary Practice.* Amsterdam and Atlanta: Rodopi, 1997.

Bassinger, Jeanine. *A Woman's View: How Hollywood Spoke to Woman, 1930–1960.* Hanover, N.H.: Wesleyan University Press, 1993.

Baty, S. Paige. *American Monroe: The Making of a Body Politic.* Berkeley and Los Angeles: University of California Press, 1995.

Bayley, John. "Art, Life and Love: Seeing Iris in 'Iris.'" *New York Times,* "Arts and Leisure" section, 9 December 2001.

Beetham, Margaret. *A Magazine of Her Own? Domesticity and Desire in the Woman's Magazine, 1800–1914.* London: Routledge, 1996.

La Belle Assemblée or, Bell's Court and Fashionable Magazine (February 1806); (July 1812); n.s., 18 (1 July–31 December 1818).

Benjamin, Jessica. "A Desire of One's Own: Psychoanalytic Feminism and Intersubjective Space." In *Feminist Studies/Critical Studies,* edited by Teresa de Lauritis, 78–101. Bloomington: Indiana University Press, 1986.

Benjamin, Walter. *Illuminations.* Edited by Hannah Arendt. Translated by Harry Zohn. New York: Schocken Books, 1969.

Berger, John. *Ways of Seeing.* London and New York: Penguin Books, 1977.

Bergson, Henri. "Laughter." In *Comedy,* edited by Wylie Sypher. Baltimore: Johns Hopkins University Press, 1980.

Bermingham, Ann. *Landscape and Ideology: The English Rustic Tradition, 1740–1860.* Berkeley and Los Angeles: University of California Press, 1989.

Bernstein, Susan David. "Dirty Reading: Sensation Fiction, Women, and Primitivism." *Criticism* 36, no. 2 (1994): 213–41.

B.H. *"Married Off":* A Satirical Poem. With eight illustrations by Florence Claxton. London: Ward and Lock, 1860.

Bloch, Konrad. *Blondes in Venetian Paintings, the Nine-Banded Armadillo, and Other Essays in Biochemistry.* New Haven: Yale University Press, 1994.

Bordwell, David, Janet Staiger, and Kristin Thompson. *The Classical Hollywood Cinema: Film Style and Mode of Production to 1960.* New York: Columbia University Press, 1985.

Braddon, Mary Elizabeth. *Lady Audley's Secret.* Introduction by Norman Donaldson. New York: Dover, 1974.

Brantlinger, Patrick. "What Is 'Sensational' about the 'Sensation Novel'?" *Nineteenth-Century Fiction* 37, no. 1 (1982): 1–28.

Briggs, Asa. "Trollope the Traveller" and "Saxons, Normans, and Victorians." In *The Collected Essays of Asa Briggs: Volume Two,* 89–115; 215–35. Urbana: University of Illinois Press, 1985.

Brody, Jennifer DeVere. *Impossible Purities: Blackness, Femininity, and Victorian Culture.* Durham: Duke University Press, 1998.

Brontë, Charlotte. *Jane Eyre*. Edited by Q. D. Leavis. London: Penguin, 1978.

————. *Shirley.* 1849. Edited by Andrew and Judith Hook. Harmondsworth, Middlesex, England: Penguin, 1979.

————. *Villette.* 1853. Edited by Mark Lilly. Harmondsworth, Middlesex, England: Penguin, 1979.

Brontë, Emily. *Wuthering Heights*. Edited by William M. Sale Jr. New York: W. W. Norton, 1972.

Brown, Laura. *Alexander Pope*. Oxford: Basil Blackwell, 1985.

————. *Ends of Empire: Women and Ideology in Early Eighteenth-Century English Literature*. Ithaca: Cornell University Press, 1993.

————. *English Dramatic Form, 1660–1760: An Essay in Generic History*. New Haven: Yale University Press, 1981.

Brownstein, Rachel M. *Becoming a Heroine: Reading about Women in Novels*. New York: Penguin, 1984.

Buckley, Jerome Hamilton. *The Victorian Temper: A Study in Literary Criticism*. New York: Vintage, 1964.

Bullfinch, Thomas. *Bullfinch's Mythology*. New York: Crown, 1979.

Burns, Sir Alan. *History of the West Indies*. 1954. London: George Allen and Unwin, 1965.

Butler, Marilyn. *Romantics, Rebels, and Reactionaries*. New York: Oxford University Press, 1982.

Byrde, Penelope. *Nineteenth-Century Fashion*. London: B. T. Batsford, 1992.

Cagidemetrio, Alide. "A Plea for Fictional Histories and Old-Time 'Jewesses.'" In *The Invention of Ethnicity*, edited by Werner Sollors, 14–43. Oxford: Oxford University Press, 1981.

Cain, James M. *Double Indemnity*. New York: Vintage, 1992.

————. *The Postman Always Rings Twice*. New York: Vintage, 1992.

Cavell, Stanley. *Contesting Tears: The Hollywood Melodrama of the Unknown Woman*. Chicago: University of Chicago Press, 1996.

————. *Pursuits of Happiness: The Hollywood Comedy of Remarriage*. Cambridge: Harvard University Press, 1981.

————. *The World Viewed: Reflections on the Ontology of Film*. New York: Viking, 1971.

Chandler, Raymond. *The Raymond Chandler Omnibus*. Random House, 1980.

Chopin, Kate. *The Awakening and Selected Stories*. Edited by Sandra Gilbert. New York: Penguin, 1986.

————. *Kate Chopin's Private Papers*. Edited by Emily Toth and Per Seyersted. Bloomington and Indianapolis: Indiana University Press, 1998.

Christie, William. "'To Advantage Drest': Poetics and Cosmetics in *The Rape of the Lock*." In *Imperfect Apprehensions: Essays in English Literature in Honour of G. A. Wilkes*, edited by Geoffrey Little, 133–47. Sydney: Challis Press, 1996.

Claxton, Florence. *The Adventures of a Woman in Search of Her Rights*. London: Graphotyping Company, 1871.

Cohen, Michael. "Reform, Rescue, and the Sisterhoods of *Middlemarch.*" *Victorian Literature and Culture* 21, edited by John Maynard and Adrienne Munich, 89–109. New York: AMS, 1993.

Coleridge, Samuel Taylor. "Christabel"; "Kubla Khan"; *The Rime of the Ancient Mariner.* In *Romanticism: An Anthology,* 2nd ed., edited by Duncan Wu. Oxford: Blackwell, 1998.

Colley, Linda. *Britons: Forging the Nation, 1707–1837.* New Haven: Yale University Press, 1992.

Collins, Wilkie. *Armadale.* Edited by Catherine Peters. New York: Oxford University Press, 1991.

————. *Basil.* Edited by Dorothy Goldman. New York: Oxford University Press, 1992.

————. *Man and Wife.* Edited by Norman Page. New York: Oxford University Press, 1995.

————. *The Moonstone.* New York: Bantam Books, 1982.

————. *No Name.* Edited by Virginia Blain. New York: Oxford University Press, 1986.

————. *The Woman in White.* Edited by Julian Symons. Harmondsworth, Middlesex, England: Penguin, 1974.

Congreve, William. "The Way of the World." In *Restoration and Eighteenth-Century Comedy,* edited by Scott McMillin. New York: W. W. Norton, 1997.

Conrad, Barnaby, III. *The Blonde: A Celebration of the Golden Era from Harlow to Monroe.* San Francisco: Chronicle, 1999.

Cook, Pam, and Philip Dodd, eds. *Women and Film: A Sight and Sound Reader.* Philadelphia: Temple University Press, 1993.

Cooper, James Fenimore. *The Last of the Mohicans.* Introduction by Richard Slotkin. New York: Penguin, 1986.

Coppel, Alex, and Samuel Taylor. *Alfred Hitchcock's Vertigo.* 1957. Unpublished filmscript.

Cunningham, J. S. *Pope: "The Rape of the Lock."* London: Edward Arnold, 1961.

David, Deirdre. *Rule Britannia: Women, Empire, and Victorian Writing.* Ithaca: Cornell University Press, 1995.

Davis, Deanna Louise. "Household Sympathy and the Limits of Real Things: Dilemmas of a Feminine Morality in George Eliot and Elizabeth Gaskell." Ph.D. diss., University of California, Los Angeles, 1991.

DiBattista, Maria. *Fast-Talking Dames.* New Haven: Yale University Press, 2001.

————. "The Triumph of Clytemnestra: The Charades in *Vanity Fair.*" In *William Makepeace Thackeray's "Vanity Fair,"* edited by Harold Bloom, 83–100. New York: Chelsea House, 1987.

Dickens, Charles. *Bleak House.* Introduction by Morton Dauwen Zabel. Boston: Houghton Mifflin, 1956.

————. *David Copperfield.* Edited by Jerome Buckley. New York: W. W. Norton, 1990.

―――. *The Letters of Charles Dickens.* Volume 2, *1847–1857.* Edited by Walter Dexter. Bloomsbury: Nonesuch, 1938.

―――. *Little Dorrit.* Edited by John Holloway. Harmondsworth, Middlesex, England: Penguin, 1971.

―――. *Our Mutual Friend.* Edited by Stephen Gill. Harmondsworth, Middlesex, England: Penguin, 1971.

―――. *Selected Letters of Charles Dickens.* Edited by David Paroissien. Boston: Twayne, 1985.

―――. *A Tale of Two Cities.* Edited by Andrew Sanders. New York: Oxford University Press, 1998.

Dijkstra, Bram. *Evil Sisters: The Threat of Female Sexuality in Twentieth-Century Culture.* New York: Henry Holt, 1998.

―――. *Idols of Perversity: Fantasies of Feminine Evil in Fin-de-Siècle Culture.* New York and Oxford: Oxford University Press, 1986.

Doherty, Thomas. *Pre-Code Hollywood: Sex, Immorality, and Insurrection in American Cinema 1930–1934.* New York: Columbia University Press, 1999.

Douglas, Ann. *The Feminization of American Culture.* New York: Doubleday Anchor, 1998.

―――. *Terrible Honesty: Mongrel Manhattan in the 1920s.* New York: Farrar, Straus and Giroux, 1995.

du Maurier, George. *Trilby.* London and New York: Dutton, 1977.

Dyer, Richard. *Heavenly Bodies: Film Stars and Society.* New York: St. Martin's, 1986.

―――. *Stars.* London: British Film Institute, 1979.

―――. *White.* London and New York: Routledge, 1997.

Edelstein, T. J. "They Sang 'The Song of the Shirt': The Visual Iconology of the Seamstress." *Victorian Studies* 23, no. 2 (1980): 183–210.

Edgeworth, Maria. *Belinda.* Edited by Eiléan ní Chuilleanáin. London: J. M. Dent, 1993.

Edwards, Lee. "Women, Energy, and *Middlemarch.*" In *Middlemarch,* edited by Bert G. Hornback. New York: W. W. Norton, 1977.

Edwards, P. D. *Some Mid-Victorian Thrillers: The Sensation Novel, Its Friends and Its Foes.* St. Lucia: University of Queensland Press, 1971.

Eilberg-Schwartz, Howard, and Wendy Doniger, eds. *Off with Her Head!: The Denial of Women's Identity in Myth, Religion, and Culture.* Berkeley and Los Angeles: University of California Press, 1995.

Eliot, George. *Adam Bede.* Introduction by Robert Speaight. London: Dent, 1960.

―――. *Daniel Deronda.* Edited by Barbara Hardy. Harmondsworth, Middlesex, England: Penguin, 1986.

―――. *Middlemarch.* Edited by Gordon S. Haight. Boston: Houghton Mifflin, 1956.

―――. *The Mill on the Floss.* Edited by Carol T. Christ. New York: W. W. Norton, 1994.

Eliza Cook's Journal. Edited by Eliza Cook. London: Charles Cook, 1849–52.

The Englishwoman's Domestic Magazine. Edited by Samuel O. Beeton. Vols. 1–8 (1852–

60); 2nd ser., 1–7, (1860–63); n.s. 10, nos. 73–78; n.s. 11, nos. 79–84 (1871). London: Ward, Locke, and Tyler.

English Woman's Journal. Edited by Bessie Parkes and Mathilda Hays. 1, nos. 1–6 (March-August 1858); 3, nos. 15–16 (May-June 1854); 4, no. 21 (November 1859). London: The English Woman's Journal Company.

The Englishwoman's Review. Edited by Jessie Boucherett. 1 (October 1866); 3 (April 1867); 4 (July 1867); n.s., 10 (April 1872).

Ensler, Eve. *The Vagina Monologues.* Foreword by Gloria Steinem. New York: Villard, 1998.

Fahnestock, Jeanne. "Bigamy: The Rise and Fall of a Convention." *Nineteenth-Century Fiction* 36, no. 1 (1981): 47–71.

————. "The Heroine of Irregular Features: Physiognomy and Conventions of Heroine Description." *Victorian Studies* 24, no. 3 (1981): 325–50.

Ferber, Edna. *Show Boat.* 1926. New York: Penguin, 1994.

Ferris, Ina. *The Achievement of Literary Authority: Gender, History, and the Waverley Novels.* Ithaca: Cornell University Press, 1991.

Foucault, Michel. *The History of Sexuality: An Introduction.* Vol. 1. Translated by Robert Hurley. New York: Vintage, 1990.

————. *The Use of Pleasure: The History of Sexuality.* Vol. 2. Translated by Robert Hurley. New York: Vintage, 1990.

Fowler, O. S. *Creative and Sexual Science: or Manhood, Womanhood, and Their Mutual Interrelations.* 1870. Chicago, Follett Publishing Co., 1971.

The Freewoman: A Weekly Feminist Review. Edited by Dorothy Marsden and Mary Gawthorpe. 1, no. 1 (23 November 1911).

French, Marilyn. *The Women's Room.* New York: Summit, 1977.

Frith, Gill. "Playing with Shawls: George Eliot's Use of *Corinne* in *The Mill on the Floss.*" In *George Eliot and Europe,* edited by John Rignall, 225–39. Aldershot, Hants, England: Scolar Press, 1997.

Garcia, Hazel. "Of Punctilios among the Fair Sex: Colonial Magazines, 1741–1776." *Journalism History* 3, no. 2 (1976): 48–52.

Garnsey, Caroline John. "Ladies' Magazines to 1850: The Beginnings of an Industry." *Bulletin of the New York Public Library* 58, no. 2 (1954): 74–88.

Gaskell, Elizabeth. *The Life of Charlotte Brontë.* Edited by Alan Shelston. Harmondsworth, Middlesex, England: Penguin, 1985.

————. *North and South.* Edited by Dorothy Collin. Introduction by Martin Dodsworth. London: Penguin, 1972.

————. *Wives and Daughters.* Edited by Frank Glover Smith. London: Penguin, 1979.

Gelbart, Nina Rattner. "The Blonding of Charlotte Corday." *Eighteenth-Century Studies* 38, no. 1 (2004): 201–21.

Getty, Clive. "Physiognomy, Science and Romantic Visual Satire." In *Correspondences: Studies in Literature, History and the Arts in Nineteenth-Century France,* edited by Keith Busby. Amsterdam: Rodopi, 1992.

Gilbert, Sandra, and Susan Gubar. *The Mad Woman in the Attic: The Woman Writer and the Nineteenth-Century Literary Imagination*. New Haven: Yale University Press, 1979.

Gilbert, W. S. *Gilbert before Sullivan: Six Comic Plays*. Edited by Jane Stedman. Chicago: University of Chicago Press, 1969.

Gilman, Sander L. *Smart Jews: The Construction of the Image of Jewish Superior Intelligence*. Lincoln: University of Nebraska Press, 1996.

Gitter, Elisabeth G. "The Power of Women's Hair in the Victorian Imagination." *PMLA* 99, no. 5 (1984): 936–54.

Giusti, Ada. "The Politics of Location: Italian Narratives of Madame de Staël and George Sand." *Neohelicon* 22, no. 2 (1995): 205–19.

Gladwell, Malcolm. "Annals of Advertising: True Colors: Hair Dye and the Hidden History of Postwar America." *New Yorker*, 22 March 1999, 70–81.

Goldin, Eve. *Platinum Girl: The Life and Legends of Jean Harlow*. New York: Abbeville Press, 1991.

Gracombe, Sarah. "Converting Trilby: Du Maurier on Englishness, Jewishness, and Culture." *Nineteenth-Century Literature* 58, no. 1 (2003): 75–108.

Graves, Robert. *The White Goddess: A Historical Grammar of Poetic Myth*. New York: Farrar, Straus and Giroux, 1997.

Green, Barbara. *Spectacular Confessions: Autobiography, Performative Activism, and Sites of Suffrage, 1905–1938*. New York: St. Martin's, 1997.

Greg, W. R. "The Foreign Policy of the English Government and the English Nation." *National Review* 17 (October 1863): 465–92.

———. "Principles of Indian Government." *National Review* 6 (January 1858): 1–37.

———. "Why Are Women Redundant?" *National Review* 14 (April 1862): 434–60.

Gregory, Carl Louis, F.R.P.S. *Motion Picture Photography*. 2nd. ed. Edited by Herbert C. McKay, A.R.P.S. New York: Falk Publishing, 1927.

Grimm, Jacob, and Wilhelm Grimm. *Grimm's Complete Fairy Tales*. New York: Barnes and Noble, 1993.

Gross, David S. "'The Conqu'ring Force of Unresisted Steel': Pope and Power in *The Rape of the Lock*." *New Orleans Review* 15, no. 4 (1988): 23–30.

Gubar, Susan. *Racechanges: White Skin, Black Face in American Culture*. New York and Oxford: Oxford University Press, 1997.

Haggard, H. Rider. *She*. Edited by Daniel Karlin. Oxford and New York: Oxford University Press, 1998.

Haight, Gordon S. "The Heroine of *Middlemarch*." In *George Eliot's Originals and Contemporaries: Essays in Victorian Literary History and Biography*, edited by Hugh Witemeyer, 58–67. Houndmills, Basingstoke, Hampshire, London: Macmillan, 1992.

Hakluyt, Richard. *DIVERS voyages touching the discouerie of America, and the Ilands adiacent unto the same, made first of all by our Englishmen, and afterwards by the French-men and Britons*. London: Thomas Woodcocke, 1582.

Hall, Kim F. *Things of Darkness: Economies of Race and Gender in Early Modern England.* Ithaca: Cornell University Press, 1995.

Hamilton, Lady Emma. *The Memoirs of Lady Hamilton with Anecdotes of Her Friends and Contemporaries.* Edited by W. H. Long. London: W. W. Gibbings, 1891.

Hardy, Barbara. "Art and Nature." In *William Makepeace Thackeray's "Vanity Fair,"* edited by Harold Bloom, 19–35. New York: Chelsea House, 1987.

———. "The Miserable Marriages in *Middlemarch, Anna Karenina,* and *Effi Briest.*" In *George Eliot and Europe,* edited by John Rignall, 64–83. Aldershot, Hants, England: Scolar Press, 1997.

Harris, Nicola. "Hardy and Eliot: The Eye of Narcissus' Looking-Glass." *George Eliot Review* 28 (1997): 49–58.

Harris, Susan K. "'But Is It Any Good?': Evaluating Nineteenth-Century American Women's Fiction." *American Literature* 63, no. 1 (1991): 43–61.

Harvey, David. *The Condition of Postmodernity: An Enquiry into the Origins of Cultural Change.* Oxford: Basil Blackwell, 1990.

Haskell, Molly. *From Reverence to Rape: The Treatment of Women in the Movies.* Chicago: University of Chicago Press, 1987.

Helfield, Randa. "Poisonous Plots: Women Sensation Novelists and Murderesses of the Victorian Period." *Victorian Review* 21, no. 2 (1995): 161–88.

Hellerstein, Erna Olafson, et al., eds. *Victorian Women: A Documentary Account of Women's Lives in Nineteenth-Century England, France, and the United States.* Stanford: Stanford University Press, 1981.

Higbie, Robert. *Dickens and Imagination.* Gainesville: University Press of Florida, 1998.

Hill, Thomas E. *The Essential Handbook of Victorian Etiquette.* Edited by William P. Yenne. San Mateo, Calif.: Bluewood Books, 1994.

Holbrook, David. *Charles Dickens and the Image of Woman.* New York: New York University Press, 1993.

Holly, Grant I. "Prosopop(e)oeia." *New Orleans Review* 15, no. 4 (1988): 51–59.

Howitt's Journal of Literature and Popular Progress. Edited by William and Mary Howitt. London, 1847.

Hrdy, Sarah Blaffer. *Mother Nature: A History of Mothers, Infants, and Natural Selection.* New York: Pantheon Books, 1999.

Hyde, H. Montgomery. *Mr. and Mrs. Beeton.* Foreword by Sir Mayson Beeton K.B.E. London: George G. Harrap, 1931.

Ingham, Patricia. *Dickens, Women, and Language.* New York and London: Harvester Wheatsheaf, 1992.

Iser, Wolfgang. "The Reader in the Realistic Novel: Esthetic Effects in Thackeray's *Vanity Fair.*" In *William Makepeace Thackeray's "Vanity Fair,"* edited by Harold Bloom, 37–55. New York: Chelsea House, 1987.

Jameson, Fredric. *The Geopolitical Aesthetic: Cinema and Space in the World System.* Bloomington and Indianapolis: Indiana University Press, 1992.

———. *The Political Unconscious: Narrative as a Socially Symbolic Act.* Ithaca: Cornell University Press, 1981.

Jason, Heda, "The Fairy Tale of the Active Heroine: A Model for the Narrative Structure." *Israel Ethnographic Society Prepublication Series,* no. 11 (1982): 79–95.

Johnson, Edgar. *Charles Dickens: His Tragedy and Triumph.* New York: Simon and Schuster, 1952.

Kaplan, Fred. *Dickens: A Biography.* Baltimore: Johns Hopkins University Press, 1998.

Kaye, M. M. *The Ordinary Princess.* New York: Simon and Schuster, 1986.

Kenealy, Arabella. "New View of the Surplus of Women." *Westminster Review* 136 (November 1891): 465–67.

Kendall, Elizabeth. *Runaway Bride: Hollywood Romantic Comedies of the 1930s.* New York: Alfred A. Knopf, 1990.

Kestenberg, Judith S., and Joan Weinstein. "Transitional Objects and Body-Image Formation." In *Between Reality and Fantasy,* edited by Simon A. Grolnick, M.D., Leonard Barkin, M.D., and Werner Muensterberger, 75–95. New York: Jason Aronson, 1978.

Kettledrum, with which is united *Women's World, A Magazine of Arts, Literature, & Social Improvement* (Dux Foemina Facti). Pt. 1, n.s.; pt. 16 from Commencement (1869).

Kinsey, Alfred, et al. *Sexual Behavior in the Human Female.* Philadelphia: W. B. Saunders, 1953.

Kline, Salli J. *The Degeneration of Women: Bram Stoker's "Dracula" as Allegorical Criticism of the Fin de Siècle.* Rheinbach-Merzbach: CMZ-Verlag, 1992.

Knoepflmacher, U. C. "The Counterworld of Victorian Fiction." In *The Worlds of Victorian Fiction: Harvard English Studies 6,* edited by Jerome Buckley, 351–69. Cambridge: Harvard University Press, 1975.

Koppelman, Connie. "The Politics of Hair." *Frontiers: A Journal of Women Studies* 17, no. 2 (1996): 87–88.

Kozol, Wendy, and George Lipsitz. "Fifty Cents Worth of Looking: Spectacle and Desire in Dorothy Arzner's 'Dance, Girl, Dance.'" Unpublished manuscript, 1991.

The Ladies' Cabinet of Fashion. 1852–55.

The Ladies' Treasury for 1876, A Household Magazine. Edited by Mrs. Warren. London: Bemrose and Sons, 1876.

Laferla, Ruth. "Generation E.A.: Ethnically Ambiguous," *New York Times,* Sunday-Styles section, 28 December 2003.

Lambert, Ellen Zetzel. *The Face of Love: Feminism and the Beauty Question.* Boston: Beacon Press, 1995.

Langland, Elizabeth. "Inventing Reality: The Ideological Commitments of George Eliot's *Middlemarch.*" *Narrative* 2, no. 2 (1994): 87–111.

———. *Nobody's Angels: Middle-Class Women and Domestic Ideology in Victorian Culture.* Ithaca: Cornell University Press, 1995.

LaSalle, Mick. *Complicated Women: Sex and Power in Pre-Code Hollywood.* New York: St. Martin's, 2000.

Lawrence, Amy. *Echo and Narcissus: Women's Voices in Classical Hollywood Cinema.* Berkeley and Los Angeles: University of California Press, 1991.

Lawrence, D. H. *The Rainbow.* New York: Viking Press, 1961.

le Bourhis, Katell, ed. *The Age of Napoleon: Costume from Revolution to Empire 1789–1815.* New York: Metropolitan Museum of Art/Harry N. Abrams, 1989.

Lee, Jin-Ok. "Female Desire and Community in Charlotte Brontë's Works." Ph.D. diss., New York University, 1997.

Leng, Andrew. "Dorothea Brooke's 'Awakening Consciousness' and the Pre-Raphaelite Aesthetic in *Middlemarch.*" *AUMLA: Journal of the Australasian Universities Language and Literature Association* 75 (1991): 52–63.

Leo Africanus, Johannes. *Geographical Historie of Africa Written in Arabicke and Italian by Iohn Leo a More, borne in Granada, and brought up in Barbarie.* Translated and edited by John Pory. London: Georg. Bishop, 1600.

Levitt, Sarah. *Victorians Unbuttoned: Registered Designs for Clothing, Their Makers and Wearers, 1839–1900.* London: George Allen and Unwin, 1986.

Lonoff, Sue. *Wilkie Collins and His Victorian Readers.* New York: AMS Press, 1982.

Loos, Anita. *Fate Keeps On Happening: Adventures of Lorelei Lee and Other Writings.* Edited by Ray Pierre Corsini. New York: Dodd, Mead, 1984.

———. *"Gentlemen Prefer Blondes" and "But Gentlemen Marry Brunettes."* Introduction by Regina Barreca. New York: Penguin, 1998.

———. *Kiss Hollywood Good-by.* New York: Viking, 1974.

Lopes, José Manuel. *Foregrounded Description in Prose Fiction.* Toronto: University of Toronto Press, 1995.

Lougy, Robert E. "Vision and Satire: The Warped Looking Glass in *Vanity Fair.*" In *William Makepeace Thackeray's "Vanity Fair,"* edited by Harold Bloom, 57–82. New York: Chelsea House, 1987.

Lowell, Robert. *For the Union Dead.* New York: Farrar, Straus and Giroux, 1964.

Mack, Maynard. *Alexander Pope: A Life.* New Haven: Yale University Press in association with W. W. Norton, 1985.

Mailer, Norman. *Marilyn: A Biography.* New York: Warner Paperback Library, 1975.

Mannsaker, Frances M. "East and West: Anglo-Indian Racial Attitudes as Reflected in Popular Fiction, 1890–1914." *Victorian Studies* 24, no. 1 (1980): 33–51.

Marks, Martin Miller. *Music and the Silent Film: Contexts and Case Studies, 1895–1924.* New York: Oxford University Press, 1997.

Marlowe, Christopher. *The Tragicall History of the Life and Death of Doctor Faustus.* In *The Complete Plays of Christopher Marlowe,* edited by Irving Ribner. New York: Odyssey Press, 1963.

Maurat, Charlotte. *The Brontës' Secret.* Translated by Margaret Meldrum. New York: Barnes and Noble, 1969.

McBain, Ed. "She Was Blond. She Was Trouble. And She Paid 3 Cents a Word." *New York Times,* "The Arts" section, 29 March 1999.

McCann, Graham. *Marilyn Monroe.* New Brunswick, N.J.: Rutgers University Press, 1988.

McCracken, Grant. *Big Hair: A Journey into the Transformation of Self.* Woodstock, N.Y.: Overlook Press, 1995.

McGuire, Matthew J. *The Role of Women in the Novels of Charles Dickens.* Montreux and London: Minerva Press, 1995.

McLane, John R. Review of *The Great Mutiny: India 1857,* by Christopher Hibbert. *Victorian Studies* 24, no. 2 (1981): 237–38.

Mell, Donald C. *Pope, Swift, and Women Writers.* Newark: University of Delaware Press, 1996.

Melville, Herman. *Pierre or the Ambiguities.* New York: Grove, 1957.

———. *Typee: A Peep at Polynesian Life during a Four Months' Residence in the Valley of the Marquesas.* New York: New American Library, 1964.

Meredith, George. "An Essay on Comedy and Uses of the Comic Spirit." Published as "An Essay on Comedy" in *Comedy,* edited by Wylie Sypher. Baltimore: Johns Hopkins University Press, 1980.

Meryman, Richard. "Fame May Go By and—So Long, I've Had You." *Life,* 3 August 1962, 31–36.

———. "A Last Long Talk with a Lonely Girl." *Life,* 17 August 1962, 32–33.

———. "Behind the Myth the Face of Norma Jean." *Life,* 4 November 1966, 49–54.

Meyer, Susan. *Imperialism at Home: Race and Victorian Women's Fiction.* Ithaca: Cornell University Press, 1996.

Miller, D. A. *The Novel and the Police.* Berkeley and Los Angeles: University of California Press, 1988.

Miller, R. D. *A Study of Schiller's "Jungfrau von Orleans."* Harrogate, U.K.: Duchy Press, 1995.

Moers, Ellen. *Literary Women.* New York: Anchor, 1977.

———. "Performing Heroinism: The Myth of Corinne." In *The Worlds of Victorian Fiction: Harvard English Studies 6,* edited by Jerome Buckley, 319–50. Cambridge: Harvard University Press, 1975.

Moglen, Helene. *Charlotte Brontë: The Self Conceived.* New York: W. W. Norton, 1976.

Monroe, Marilyn. *My Story.* New York: Stein and Day, 1974.

Monsarrat, Ann. *An Uneasy Victorian: Thackeray the Man, 1811–1863.* New York: Dodd, Mead, 1980.

Mortimer, Armine Kotin. "Male and Female Plots in Staël's *Corinne.*" In *Correspondences: Studies in Literature, History, and the Arts in Nineteenth-Century France,* edited by Keith Busby. Amsterdam: Rodopi, 1992.

M.S.R. "The Domestic History of England." *Englishwoman's Domestic Magazine,* n.s., 1, nos. 1–5 (1860): 12–20; 59–66; 108–17; 156–62; 203; 252.

The New Columbia Encyclopedia. Edited by William H. Harris and Judith S. Levey. New York: Columbia University Press, 1975.

Nicholson, C. E. "A World of Artefacts: *The Rape of the Lock* as Social History." In *Alexander Pope's "The Rape of the Lock,"* edited by Harold Bloom, 67–79. New York: Chelsea House, 1988.

Norbelie, Barbro Almqvist. *"Oppressive Narrowness": A Study of the Female Community in George Eliot's Early Writings.* Uppsala: University of Uppsala Press, 1992.

Orwell, George. "Politics and the English Language." In *The Norton Reader: An An-*

thology of Expository Prose, 5th ed., edited by Arthur M. Eastman, 369–80. New York: W. W. Norton, 1980.

Ott, Frederick W. *The Films of Carole Lombard*. Secaucus, N.J.: Citadel Press, 1972.

Parker, Dorothy. *The Portable Dorothy Parker*. Introduction by Brendan Gill. New York: Penguin, 1976.

Paston, George. *Mr. Pope: His Life and Times*. London: Hutchinson, 1909.

The People and Howitt's Journal 1 (1846).

Phelps, Elizabeth Stuart. *The Story of Avis*. Edited by Carol Farley Kessler. New Brunswick, N.J.: Rutgers University Press, 1995.

Pitman, Joanna. *On Blondes*. New York and London: Bloomsbury, 2003.

Pocock, J. G. A. *Virtue, Commerce, and History: Essays on Political Thought and History, Chiefly in the Eighteenth Century*. Cambridge: Cambridge University Press, 1995.

Pollak, Ellen. *The Poetics of Sexual Myth: Gender and Ideology in the Verse of Swift and Pope*. Chicago: University of Chicago Press, 1985.

Pool, Daniel. *What Jane Austen Ate and What Charles Dickens Knew: From Fox Hunting to Whist—the Facts of Daily Life in Nineteenth-Century England*. New York: Touchstone, 1993.

Poovey, Mary. "Speaking of the Body: Mid-Victorian Constructions of Female Desire." In *Body/Politics: Women and the Discourses of Science*, edited by Mary Jacobus, Evelyn Fox Keller, and Sally Shuttleworth, 29–46. New York and London: Routledge, 1990.

———. *Uneven Developments: The Ideological Work of Gender in Mid-Victorian England*. Chicago: University of Chicago Press, 1988.

Pope, Alexander. "Epistle 2. To a Lady"; "Epistle to Miss Blount"; *The Rape of the Lock*. In *Norton Anthology of English Literature*, vol. 1., 6th ed., edited by M. H. Abrams. New York: W. W. Norton, 1993.

Praz, Mario. *The Romantic Agony*. Translated by Angus Davidson. Foreword by Frank Kermode. London: Oxford University Press, 1970.

Propp, V. *Morphology of the Folktale*. Edited by Louis A. Wagner. Translated by Laurence Scott. Introduction by Alan Dundes. Austin: University of Texas Press, 1990.

Pykett, Lyn. *The "Improper" Feminine: The Women's Sensation Novel and the New Woman Writing*. London and New York: Routledge, 1992.

Quinsey, K. M. "From Moving Toyshop to Cave of Spleen: The Depth of Satire in *The Rape of the Lock*." In *Alexander Pope's "The Rape of the Lock,"* edited by Harold Bloom, 81–97. New York: Chelsea House, 1988.

Ragussis, Michael. "Writing Nationalist History: England, the Conversion of the Jews, and *Ivanhoe*." *ELH* 60 (1993): 181–215.

Ray, Gordon N. *Thackeray: The Age of Wisdom*. New York: McGraw-Hill, 1958.

Redinger, Ruby V. *George Eliot: The Emergent Self*. New York: Alfred A. Knopf, 1975.

Rendall, Jane. "'A Moral Engine'? Feminism, Liberalism and the *English Woman's Journal*." In *Equal or Different: Women's Politics 1800–1914*, edited by Jane Rendall, 112–37. Oxford: Basil Blackwell, 1987.

258 ✦ *Bibliography*

Reynolds, Kimberley, and Nicola Humble. *Victorian Heroines: Representations of Femininity in Nineteenth-Century Literature and Art*. New York: New York University Press, 1993.

Riddell, N. N., Ph. D. *Human Nature Explained: A New Illustrated Treatise on Human Science for the People*. New York: New York Phrenological Institute, 1897.

Richardson, Angelique. "The Eugenization of Love: Sarah Grand and the Morality of Genealogy." *Victorian Studies* 42, no. 2 (1999–2000): 227–55.

Robertson, Linda K. "From Reality to Fiction: Benefits and Hazards in Continental Education." In *George Eliot and Europe*, edited by John Rignall, 156–65. Aldershot, Hants, England: Scolar Press, 1997.

———. *The Power of Knowledge: George Eliot and Education*. New York: Peter Lang, 1997.

Robotham, Tom. *Varga*. New York: Smithmark, 1995.

Roff, Sandra. "A Feminine Expression: Ladies' Periodicals in the New York Historical Society Collection." *Journalism History* 9, no. 3–4 (1982–83): 92–99.

Rosen, Marjorie. *Popcorn Venus*. New York: Avon, 1974.

Rossetti, Dante Gabriel. "The Blessed Damozel"; "The Orchard-Pit." In *Norton Anthology of English Literature*, vol. 2. 6th ed., edited by M. H. Abrams. New York: W. W. Norton, 1993.

Roth, Phyllis A. "Suddenly Sexual Women in Bram Stoker's *Dracula*." In *Dracula: The Vampire and the Critics*, edited by Margaret L. Carter, 57–67. Ann Arbor: UMI Research Press, 1988.

Rowe, Kathleen. *The Unruly Woman: Gender and the Genres of Laughter*. Austin: University of Texas Press, 1995.

Rule, Lareina. *Name Your Baby*. New York: Bantam Books, 1981.

Said, Edward. *Culture and Imperialism*. New York: Vintage Books, 1993.

Sarris, Andrew. *"You Ain't Heard Nothin' Yet": The American Talking Film, History and Memory, 1927–1949*. New York: Oxford University Press, 1998.

Schatz, Thomas. *Hollywood Genres: Formulas, Filmmaking, and the Studio System*. New York: Random House, 1981.

Schickel, Richard. *Matinee Idylls: Reflections on the Movies*. Chicago: Ivan R. Dee, 1999.

Schiller, Friedrich. *Wallenstein and Maria Stuart*. Edited by Walter Hinderer. Translated by Charles E. Passage. Introduction by Erika Swales. In *Critical Guides to German Texts*, edited by Martin Swales. New York: Continuum Publishing Company, 1991.

Schivelbusch, Wolfgang. *Tastes of Paradise: A Social History of Spices, Stimulants, and Intoxicants*. Translated by David Jacobson. New York: Vintage, 1993.

Schlissel, Lillian. Introduction to *Three Plays by Mae West: Sex; The Drag; The Pleasure Man*. New York: Routledge, 1957.

Schor, Naomi. "*Corinne:* The Third Woman." *L'Esprit Créatur* 34, no. 3 (1994): 99–106.

Scott, Sir Walter. *Essays on Chivalry, Romance, and the Drama*. Freeport, N.Y.: Books for Libraries Press, 1972.

————. *Ivanhoe*. Edited by Ian Duncan. New York: Oxford University Press, 1996.

————. *The Talisman*. In *The Betrothed, Chronicles of the Cannongate, The Highland Widow, The Talisman, Castle Dangerous*. New York: James Clarke, n.d.

Senf, Carol A., ed. *The Critical Response to Bram Stoker*. Westport, Conn.: Greenwood Press, 1983.

Shelley, Percy Bysshe. *The Cenci*. In *The Selected Poetry and Prose of Percy Bysshe Shelley*, edited by Carlos Baker. New York: Modern Library, 1951.

Showalter, Elaine. "Desperate Remedies: Sensation Novels of the 1860s." *Victorian Newsletter* 49 (spring 1976): 1–5.

————. *A Literature of Their Own: British Women Novelists from Brontë to Lessing*. Princeton: Princeton University Press, 1999.

Shuttleworth, Sally. *Charlotte Brontë and Victorian Psychology*. Cambridge: Cambridge University Press, 1996.

————. "Medical Discourse and Popular Advertising in the Mid-Victorian Era." In *Body/Politics: Women and the Discourses of Science*, edited by Mary Jacobus, Evelyn Fox Keller, and Sally Shuttleworth, 47–68. New York and London: Routledge, 1990.

Slater, Michael. *Dickens and Women*. London: J. M. Dent, 1983.

Slaughter, Frances Elizabeth. *The Sportswoman's Library*. Vol. 1. Westminster: Archibald Constable and Company, 1898.

Smith, Gene: *The Shattered Dream: Herbert Hoover and the Great Depression*. New York: William Morrow, 1970.

Smith-Rosenberg, Carroll. "Writing History: Language, Class, and Gender." In *Feminist Studies/Critical Studies*, edited by Teresa de Lauritis, 31–54. Bloomington: Indiana University Press, 1986.

Spain, Nancy. *Mrs. Beeton and Her Husband by Her Great Niece*. London: Collins, 1948.

Sperling, Diana. *Mrs. Hurst Dancing and Other Scenes from Regency Life: 1812–1823*. Watercolours by Diana Sperling. Text by Gordon Mingay. Foreword by Elizabeth Longford. London: Victor Gollancz, 1983.

Spurr, David. *The Rhetoric of Empire: Colonial Discourse in Journalism, Travel Writing, and Imperial Administration*. Durham: Duke University Press, 1997.

Staël, Germaine de. *Corinne, or Italy*. Translated by Avriel Goldberger. New Brunswick, N.J.: Rutgers University Press, 1987.

Staffel, Peter. "Recovering Thalestris: Intragender Conflict in *The Rape of the Lock*." In *Pope, Swift, and Women Writers*, edited by Donald C. Mell, 86–103. Newark: University of Delaware Press.

Stafford, Barbara Maria. *Body Criticism: Imaging the Unseen in Enlightenment Art and Medicine*. Cambridge: MIT Press, 1997.

Starobinski, Jean, Philippe Duboy, Akika Fukai, Jun I. Kanai, Torhio Horii, Janet Arnold, and Martin Kamer. *Revolution in Fashion: European Clothing, 1715–1815*. New York: Abbeville Press, 1989.

Steig, Michael. *Dickens and Phiz*. Bloomington: Indiana University Press, 1978.

Steinem, Gloria. *Marilyn: Norma Jeane*. Photographs by George Barris. New York: New American Library, 1988.

Stern, Madeleine B. *Heads and Headlines: The Phrenological Fowlers*. Norman: University of Oklahoma Press, 1971.

Stoker, Bram. *The Lair of the White Worm*. In *Bram Stoker's Dracula Omnibus*. Introduction by Fay Weldon. Edison, N.J.: Chartwell, 1992.

———. *The Essential "Dracula."* Edited by Leonard Wolf. New York: Plume, 1993.

Symonds, Sarah. "Blanche D'Aubigné." *Englishwoman's Domestic Magazine* 1, nos. 7–9 (1852): 202–7; 243–49; 260–67.

Taylor, Jenny Bourne, with Russell Crofts. Introduction to *Lady Audley's Secret*, by Mary Elizabeth Braddon. London: Penguin, 1998.

Tennyson, Alfred Lord. *The Poems of Tennyson*. Edited by Christopher Ricks. London: Longmans, 1969.

Thackeray, William Makepeace. *The Letters and Private Papers of William Makepeace Thackeray*. 2 vols. Edited by Gordon N. Ray. Cambridge: Harvard University Press, 1946.

———. *Rebecca and Rowena: A Romance upon Romance*. London: Rodale Press, 1954.

———. *Vanity Fair: A Novel without a Hero*. New York: Modern Library, 1950.

———. *The Virginians: A Tale of the Last Century*. Boston: Dana Ester, n.d.

Thomas, Robert McG., Jr. "Shirley Polykoff, 90, Ad Writer Whose Query Colored a Nation." *New York Times*, 8 June 1998.

Thompson, Nicola Diane. *Reviewing Sex: Gender and the Reception of Victorian Novels*. New York: New York University Press, 1996.

Tomalin, Claire. *The Invisible Woman: The Story of Nelly Ternan and Charles Dickens*. New York: Alfred A. Knopf, 1991.

Tozer, Jane, and Sarah Levitt. *Fabric of Society: A Century of People and their Clothes 1770–1870*. Carno, Powys, Wales: Laura Ashley, 1983.

Trollope, Anthony. *The Bertrams*. Edited by Geoffrey Harvey. Oxford: Oxford University Press, 1991.

Trumpener, Katie. "National Character, National Plots: National Tale and Historical Novel in the Age of *Waverley*, 1806–1830." *ELH* 60, no. 3 (1993): 685–731.

Tuska, John. *The Films of Mae West*. Introduction by Parker Tyler. Secaucus, N.J.: Citadel Press, 1973.

Tyler, Parker. *The Hollywood Hallucination*. Introduction by Richard Schickel. New York: Simon and Schuster, 1970.

———. *Sex in Films*. New York: Carol Publishing Group, 1994.

———. *Sex Psyche Etcetera in the Film*. London: Penguin, 1971.

Tytler, Graeme. *Physiognomy in the European Novel: Faces and Fortunes*. Princeton: Princeton University Press, 1934.

Vanden Bossche, Chris R. "Culture and Economy in *Ivanhoe*." *Nineteenth-Century Fiction* 42, no. 1 (June 1987): 46–72.

Van Ghent, Dorothy. "On *Vanity Fair*." In *William Makepeace Thackeray's "Vanity Fair,"* edited by Harold Bloom, 5–17. New York: Chelsea House, 1987.

Vicinus, Martha, ed. *Suffer and Be Still: Women in the Victorian Age*. Bloomington: Indiana University Press, 1972.

Victoria Magazine. Edited by Emily Faithfull. Vol. 26 (November-April 1875–76). London: Victoria Press.

Warner, Marina. *From the Beast to the Blonde: On Fairy Tales and Their Tellers.* New York: Farrar, Straus and Giroux, 1994.

Watt, Ian. *The Rise of the Novel.* Berkeley and Los Angeles: University of California Press, 1957.

Weissman, Judith. "Woman and Vampires: *Dracula* as a Victorian Novel." In *Dracula: The Vampire and the Critics,* edited by Margaret L. Carter, 69–77. Ann Arbor: UMI Press, 1988.

West, Mae. *Goodness Had Nothing to Do With It: The Autobiography of Mae West.* Englewood Cliffs, N.J.: Prentice-Hall, 1959.

———. *Three Plays by Mae West: Sex; The Drag; The Pleasure Man.* Edited by Lillian Schlissel. New York: Routledge, 1997.

Wiesenfarth, Joseph. "The Eliot Hypothesis." *Review* (Charlottesville, Va.) 16 (1994): 289–99.

Wilkes, Joanne, "When Gentlemen Preferred Blondes: Madame de Staël's *Corinne* and the Works of George Eliot." In *Imperfect Apprehensions: Essays in English Literature in Honour of G. A. Wilkes,* edited by Geoffrey Little, 248–59. Sydney: Challis Press, 1996.

Wilson, Angus. *The World of Charles Dickens.* New York: Viking Press, 1970.

Wilson, James D. *The Romantic Heroic Ideal.* Baton Rouge: Louisiana State University Press, 1982.

Winnicott, D. W., M.D. *Mother and Child: A Primer of First Relationships.* New York: Basic Books, 1957.

Wolf, Leonard, ed. *The Essential "Dracula,"* by Bram Stoker. New York: Plume, 1993.

Wolf, Naomi. *The Beauty Myth: How Images of Beauty Are Used Against Women.* New York: William Morrow, 1991.

———. *Promiscuities: The Secret Struggle for Womanhood.* New York: Random House, 1997.

Wolff, Robert Lee. *Sensational Victorian: The Life and Fiction of Mary Elizabeth Braddon.* New York: Garland, 1979.

Wolfit, Margaret. "Dearly Beloved Scott." *George Eliot Review* 23 (1992): 49–52.

Wollstonecraft, Mary. *A Vindication of the Rights of Woman.* Edited by Charles W. Hagelman Jr. New York: W. W. Norton, 1967.

Womanhood: The Magazine of Women's Progress and Interests: Literary, Scientific and Artistic, and of Health and Beauty Culture. Edited by Ada S. Ballin. 3 (December 1899-May 1900).

Woolf, Virginia. *Between the Acts.* New York: Harcourt Brace Jovanovich, 1969.

———. *The Common Reader: First Series.* Edited by Andrew McNeillie. San Diego and New York: Harcourt Brace Jovanovich, 1984.

———. *Jacob's Room.* In *"Jacob's Room" and "The Waves": Two Complete Novels.* New York: Harcourt, Brace, and World, 1959.

————. *The Letters of Virginia Woolf.* Edited by Nigel Nicolson and Joanne Traut-
mann. Vol. 5, *1932–1935.* New York: Harcourt Brace Jovanovich, 1979.

————. *A Room of One's Own.* San Diego and New York: Harcourt Brace Jovanovich,
1957.

————. *The Second Common Reader: Annotated Edition.* Edited by Andrew McNeillie.
San Diego and New York: Harcourt Brace Jovanovich, 1986.

Wunsch, Emma. "Split Ends: Constructions of Women's Hair from O. Henry to
hooks." Bachelor's honors thesis, Binghamton University, 1998.

Young, Douglas M. *The Feminist Voices in Restoration Comedy: The Virtuous Women
in the Play-Worlds of Etheredge, Wycherly and Congreve.* Lanham, Md.: University
Press of America, 1997.

Filmography

Tillie's Punctured Romance. 1914. Dir. Mack Sennett. Perf. Charlie Chaplin, Marie Dressler. Keystone Film Company.

Birth of a Nation. 1915. Dir. D. W. Griffith. Perf. Lillian Gish, Mae Marsh. Biograph Company.

A Fool There Was. 1915. Dir. Frank Powell. Perf. Theda Bara, Edward José, Mabel Frenyear. William Fox Vaudeville Company.

Intolerance. 1916. Dirs. D. W. Griffith. Perf. Mae Marsh, Lillian Gish. Biograph Company.

Way Down East. 1920; 1930. Dir. D. W. Griffith. Perf. Lillian Gish, Lowell Sherman. D. W. Griffith Production.

The Balloonatic. 1923. Dir. Buster Keaton, Eddie Cline. Perf. Buster Keaton, Phyllis Haver. Buster Keaton Productions.

It. 1927. Dir. Clarence G. Badger, Josef von Sternberg (uncredited). Perf. Clara Bow. Paramount Pictures.

The Battle of the Sexes. 1928. Dir. D. W. Griffith. Perf. Jean Hersholt, Phyllis Haver. Art Cinema Corporation.

Run, Girl, Run. 1928. Dir. Mack Sennett. Perf. Carole Lombard. Pathé.

The Double Whoopee. 1929. Dir. Lewis R. Foster. Perf. Stan Laurel, Oliver Hardy, Jean Harlow. Hal Roach, 1929.

Platinum Blonde. 1931. Dir. Frank Capra. Perf. Jean Harlow, Loretta Young, Robert Williams. Columbia Pictures.

Night after Night. 1932. Dir. Archie Mayo. Perf. George Raft, Constance Cummings, Mae West. Paramount.

Red Dust. 1932. Dir. Victor Fleming. Perf. Clark Gable, Jean Harlow, Mary Astor. Metro Goldwyn Mayer.

Bombshell. 1933. Dir. Victor Fleming. Perf. Jean Harlow, Lee Tracy. Metro Goldwyn Mayer.

Design for Living. 1933. Dir. Ernst Lubitsch. Perf. Miriam Hopkins, Gary Cooper, Fredric March. Paramount.

Dinner at Eight. 1933. Dir. Howard Hawks. Perf. Jean Harlow, Lionel Barrymore, Marie Dressler. Metro Goldwyn Mayer.

Gold Diggers of 1933. 1933. Dir. Mervyn LeRoy/Busby Berkeley. Perf. Dick Powell, Ruby Kheeler, Ginger Rogers. Warner Brothers.

I'm No Angel. 1933. Dir. Wesley Ruggles. Perf. Mae West, Cary Grant. Paramount Pictures.

She Done Him Wrong. 1933. Dir. Lionel Sherman. Perf. Mae West, Cary Grant. Paramount Pictures.

It Happened One Night. 1934. Dir. Frank Capra. Perf. Claudette Colbert, Clark Gable. Columbia Pictures.

Stage Door. 1934. Dir. Gregory LaCava. Perf. Katharine Hepburn, Ginger Rogers, Adolphe Menjou. RKO.

Twentieth Century. 1934. Dir. Howard Hawks. Perf. John Barrymore, Carole Lombard. Columbia Pictures.

China Seas. 1935. Dir. Tay Garrett. Perf. Jean Harlow, Clark Gable. Metro Goldwyn Mayer.

Hands across the Table. 1935. Dir. Mitchell Leisen. Perf. Carole Lombard, Fred MacMurray. Paramount Pictures.

Libeled Lady. 1936. Dir. Jack Conway. Perf. Spencer Tracy, Jean Harlow, William Powell, Myrna Loy. Warner Studios.

Mr. Deeds Goes to Town. 1936. Dir. Frank Capra. Perf. James Stewart, Jean Arthur. Columbia Pictures.

My Man Godfrey. 1936. Dir. Gregory LaCava. Perf. William Powell, Carole Lombard. Criterion.

The Princess Comes Across. 1936. Dir. William K. Howard. Perf. Carole Lombard, Fred MacMurray. Paramount Pictures.

Satan Met a Lady. 1936. Dir. William Dieterle. Perf. Bette Davis, Warren William, Marie Wilson. Warner Studios.

Swing Time. 1936. Dir. George Stevens. Perf. Fred Astaire, Ginger Rogers. RKO.

Wife vs. Secretary. 1936. Dir. Clarence Brown. Perf. Jean Harlow, Clark Gable, Myrna Loy. Metro Goldwyn Mayer.

The Awful Truth. 1937. Dir. Leo McCarey. Perf. Irene Dunne, Cary Grant, Ralph Bellamy. Columbia Pictures.

Nothing Sacred. 1937. Dir. William A. Wellman. Perf. Carole Lombard, Fredric March. United Artists.

Bringing Up Baby. 1938. Dir. Howard Hawks. Perf. Katharine Hepburn, Cary Grant. RKO Pictures.

Boy Meets Girl. 1938. Dir. Lloyd Bacon. Perf. James Cagney, Pat O'Brien, Marie Wilson. Warner Studios.

My Favorite Wife. 1938. Dir. Garson Kanin. Perf. Irene Dunne, Cary Grant. RKO Pictures.

The Philadelphia Story. 1938. Dir. George Cukor. Perf. Katharine Hepburn, Cary Grant. Metro Goldwyn Mayer.

Ninotchka. 1939. Dir. Ernst Lubitsch. Perf. Greta Garbo, Melvyn Douglas. Metro Goldwyn Mayer.

His Girl Friday. 1940. Dir. Howard Hawks. Perf. Rosalind Russell, Cary Grant. Columbia Pictures.

The Lady Eve. 1940. Dir. Preston Sturges. Perf. Barbara Stanwyck, Henry Fonda. Paramount Pictures.

The Shop Around the Corner. 1940. Dir. Ernst Lubitsch. Perf. James Stewart, Margaret Sullavan. Metro Goldwyn Mayer.

Mr. and Mrs. Smith. 1941. Dir. Alfred Hitchcock. Perf. Carole Lombard, Robert Montgomery. RKO Pictures.

Mr. Smith Goes to Washington. 1941. Dir. Frank Capra. Perf. Jean Arthur, James Stewart. Columbia Pictures.

The Palm Beach Story. 1941. Dir. Preston Sturges. Perf. Claudette Colbert, Joel McCrea, Rudy Vallee, Mary Astor. Paramount Pictures.

Sullivan's Travels. 1941. Dir. Preston Sturges. Perf. Joel McCrea, Veronica Lake. Paramount Pictures.

Roxie Hart. 1942. Dir. William A. Wellman. Perf. Ginger Rogers, George Montgomery, Adolphe Menjou. 20th Century Fox.

To Be or Not to Be. 1942. Dir. Ernst Lubitsch. Perf. Carole Lombard, Jack Benny. Romaine Films Productions.

Double Indemnity. 1944. Dir. Billy Wilder. Perf. Fred MacMurray, Barbara Stanwyck, Edward G. Robinson. Paramount Pictures.

Ladies of the Chorus. 1949. Dir. Phil Carlson. Perf. Marilyn Monroe. 20th Century Fox.

All About Eve. 1950. Dir. Joseph L. Mankiewicz. Perf. Bette Davis, Ann Baxter, Marilyn Monroe. 20th Century Fox.

The Asphalt Jungle. 1950. Dir. John Huston. Perf. Sterling Hayden, Louis Calhern, Marilyn Monroe. Metro Goldwyn Mayer.

Home Town Story. 1951. Dir. John Sturges. Perf. Jeffrey Lynn, Marilyn Monroe. Metro Goldwyn Mayer.

Let's Make It Legal. 1951. Dir. Richard Sale. Perf. Claudette Colbert, Macdonald Carey, Marilyn Monroe. 20th Century Fox.

Love Nest. 1951. Dir. Joseph Newman. Perf. June Haver, William Lundigen, Marilyn Monroe. 20th Century Fox.

As Young as You Feel. 1951. Dir. Harmon Jones. Perf. Monty Woolley, Thelma Ritter, Marilyn Monroe. 20th Century Fox.

Clash by Night. 1952. Dir. Fritz Lang. Perf. Robert Ryan, Barbara Stanwyck, Paul Douglas, Marilyn Monroe. RKO Pictures.

Don't Bother to Knock. 1952. Dir. Roy Ward Baker. Perf. Marilyn Monroe, Richard Widmark, Anne Bancroft. 20th Century Fox.

Monkey Business. 1952. Dir. Howard Hawks. Perf. Marilyn Monroe, Cary Grant, Ginger Rogers. 20th Century Fox.

We're Not Married. 1952. Dir. Edmund Goulding. Perf. Ginger Rogers, Fred Allen, Marilyn Monroe. 20th Century Fox.

Gentlemen Prefer Blondes. 1953. Dir. Howard Hawks. Perf. Marilyn Monroe, Jane Russell. 20th Century Fox.

How to Marry a Millionaire. 1953. Dir. Jean Negulesco. Perf. Lauren Bacall, Marilyn Monroe. 20th Century Fox.

Niagara. 1953. Dir. Henry Hathaway. Perf. Marilyn Monroe, Joseph Cotten, Jean Peters. 20th Century Fox.

No Business Like Show Business. Dir. Walter Lang. Perf. Ethel Merman, Marilyn Monroe. 20th Century Fox, 1954.

Rear Window. 1954. Dir. Alfred Hitchcock. Perf. James Stewart, Grace Kelly. Universal Studios.

River of No Return. 1954. Dir. Otto Preminger. Perf. Robert Mitchum, Marilyn Monroe, Rory Calhoun. 20th Century Fox.

The Seven Year Itch. 1955. Dir. Billy Wilder. Perf. Marilyn Monroe, Tom Ewell. 20th Century Fox.

Bus Stop. 1956. Dir. Joshua Logan. Perf. Marilyn Monroe, Don Murray. 20th Century Fox.

The Prince and the Showgirl. 1957. Dir. Laurence Olivier. Perf. Lawrence Olivier, Marilyn Monroe. Warner Studios.

Teacher's Pet. 1958. Dir. George Seaton. Perf. Doris Day, Clark Gable. Paramount Pictures.

Gidget. 1959. Dir. Paul Wendkos. Perf. Sandra Dee, Cliff Robertson, James Darren. Columbia Pictures.

Pillow Talk. 1959. Dir. Michael Gordon. Perf. Rock Hudson, Doris Day, Tony Randall. Metro Goldwyn Mayer.

Some Like It Hot. 1959. Dir. Billy Wilder. Perf. Jack Lemon, Tony Curtis, Marilyn Monroe. United Artists.

A Summer Place. 1959. Dir. Delmar Daves. Perf. Richard Egan, Dorothy McGuire, Sandra Dee, Troy Donoghue. Warner Studios.

Let's Make Love. 1960. Dir. George Cukor. Perf. Yves Montand, Marilyn Monroe, Tony Randall. 20th Century Fox.

The Misfits. 1961. Dir. John Huston. Perf. Marilyn Monroe, Clark Gable, Montgomery Clift, Thelma Ritter. Metro Goldwyn Mayer.

Something's Got to Give. 1962 (unfinished). Dir. Otto Preminger. Perf. Marilyn Monroe, Dean Martin. 20th Century Fox.

Darling. 1965. Dir. John Schlesinger Perf. Julie Christie, Dirk Bogarde, Laurence Harvey. Metro Goldwyn Mayer.

Blowup. 1966. Dir. Michelangelo Antonioni. Perf. David Hemmings, Vanessa Redgrave. Warner Brothers.

Belle de Jour. 1967. Dir. Luis Buñuel. Perf. Catherine Deneuve. Vista.

Where Were You When the Lights Went Out? 1968. Dir. Hy Averback. Perf. Doris Day, Robert Morse. Metro Goldwyn Mayer.

My Night at Maud's. 1970. Dir. Eric Rohmer. Perf. Jean-Louis Trintignant, Françoise Fabian. Fox Lorber.

Peau d'âne. 1970. Dir. Jacques Demy. Perf. Catherine Deneuve, Jean Marais, Delphine Seyrig. Parc Films.

Last Tango in Paris. 1972. Dir. Bernardo Bertolucci. Perf. Marlon Brando, Maria Schneider. Metro Goldwyn Mayer.

If Don Juan Were a Woman. 1973. Dir. Roger Vadim. Perf. Brigitte Bardot. Filmsonor S.A.

Index

Cook, Peter, 24

Cooper, James Fenimore, 111

coquettes: in Braddon's *Lady Audley's Secret*, 88, 90; Brontë's blonde in *Villette* as, 58; gender boundaries transgressed by, 30–32; Thackeray's Becky as, xi, 31–32, 36, *37*, 38, 40–41

Correl, Charles, 244n2

Cortez, Ricardo, 178

cosmetics: in Alcott's "Behind a Mask," 98, 99, 101; Braddon's *Lady Audley's Secret*, 89–91, 93; 1960s generation's rejection of, 224; sexuality and adultery linked to, 108; shops for, described, 239n6

cosmetic surgery, 230

Cotten, Joseph, 187

courage, 59–60

Covarrubias, Miguel, 141, 242n19

Coward, Noel, 119–21

Crawford, Joan, 146

cross-dressing: Reade's story about, 237n11; in *Some Like It Hot*, 204–9, *205*; in Thackeray's *Vanity Fair*, 31, 38–39; in *Tootsie*, 206. *See also* female impersonators

crucifixion iconography, 127

Cukor, George, 153

Cummings, Constance, 138

Curtis, Tony, roles: *The Defiant Ones*, 244n3; *Some Like It Hot*, 204–8, *205*, *207*

Dandridge, Dorothy, 223, 244n3

Dangerous Female (film), 178

Daniels, Bebe, 178

daring and adventurousness, 48, 59–60. *See also* comedy and comic spirit

dark/blond distinction: identities mistaken in, 57–58; in Romance, 9–11, 79–84. *See also* black/white symbolism; sisterhood, dark/blond

darkening: in antifeminist cartoon, 80–81, *82–83*; as evidence of sexual experience, 158; means of, 7; of yellow in orthochromatic film stock, 127

dark-haired women: attributes of, 5–10; blond cliché juxtaposed to, 227; blonde as opening door for, 60–61; blond roots of, 231; competence of, 55; as double exposure, 167; in early silent films, 122; in Eliot's *Middlemarch*, 69–77; in Eliot's *The Mill on the Floss*, 64–68; intellectuality linked to, 80–81, *82–83*; as murderers, 179–80; as Other, 23–24; reversal of representations of, 47; in Stoker's *Dracula*, 107–8

dark powers of women: in Alcott's "Behind a Mask," 100–101; beliefs in, 77; in early silent films, 122; in Stoker's *Dracula*, 102–10

Darling (film), 227, *228*; described, 225–26; Oscar for, 224

Daves, Delmar, 221

Davies, Emily, 67

Davis, Bette, 178, 245n8

Day, Doris: domesticated blond version of, 13, 221–22; popularity of, 185; sexual tease roles of, 182. Roles: *Pillow Talk*, 222, 246n1; *Where Were You When the Lights Went Out?*, 221

death: poet's fear of, 29–30; as punishment for sexuality, 109

deceitfulness, 90–91, 239n7

Dee, Sandra, 13, 185, 221

Defiant Ones, The (film), 244n3

Demy, Jacques, 14–16

Deneuve, Catherine, 14–16, 224

Design for Living (film), 119–21, 136, 170

Diamond, I. A. L., 204

Diamond Lil (play), 139, 143, 158, 242n18

"Diamonds Are a Girl's Best Friend" (song), 187, 196

DiBattista, Maria, 38, 136, 236n10, 237n13, 244n39

Dickens, Charles: *Bleak House*, 4, 226; *David Copperfield*, 86, 243n32; domesticity of, 20; satire of, 226; on "straying" curls, 243n32

Dietrich, Marlene, 10, 12–13

Dijkstra, Bram, 131

DiMaggio, Joe, 206, 209
Dinner at Eight (film), 153
Divorce Act (1857), 18
Dixon, Thomas, 122
Doctor Faustus (Marlowe), 27
domesticity and domestic: in *The Battle of the Sexes,* 135; blondness linked to, 80; in Chopin's stories, 110–14; Dickens and, 20; in *Eliza Cook's Journal,* 18–19; embodiment of, 13–14; language of, 18–19; Nazi promotion of, 161; in *Red Dust,* 152–53; sexy innocence linked to, 188–89; tyrannical treatment in, 28–29
domestic novel: as affective, 24–25; dark/ blond assumptions in, 80–84; as feminized genre, 235n7; murder by women in, 92–93; Thackeray's view of, 22, 24. *See also* sensation novel
Don Juan, 35
Donne, John, 238n2
Donoghue, Troy, 221
Don't Bother to Knock (film), 187, 193
Double Indemnity (film), 178, *179,* 180
Double Whoopee (film), 119, 148
Dracula (Stoker): Chopin's story compared with, 111; fascination with women of, 102–3; Lucy's vampirism in, 103–8; Mina's motherhood in, 108–9
drag queens, 31
Dressler, Marie, 119, 153
du Maurier, George, 159
dumb-blond jokes, 1–2, 230
Dunne, Irene, 136, 177
Dyer, Richard: on Monroe, 194–95, 203, 218; on southern white woman as angel, 126, 128, 137

economics of morality (concept), 165–66
economy: beauty's value in, 56–57; blond vamp's participation in, 131–36; language of marketplace and, 18–19, 56; men's imagination linked to advantages in, 210–13; money, power, and sex in, 32–44; prostitution and, 238n9

ecstasy, 52, 53. *See also* sexuality and desire
education: expanding opportunities for, 223; for women, 46, 50–51, 67, 78
Egan, Richard, 221
Einstein, Albert, 142
Ekberg, Anita, 217
Eliot, George: *Adam Bede,* 69; aspirations and context of, 77; on beauty/motherhood relationship, 63–64; C. Brontë compared with, 62; college support from, 67; *Daniel Deronda,* 69; darkheaded heroines of, 8; on female identity, 238n3; fictive focus of, 68–69; on marriage, 74, 129; sisterhood created by, 47. *See also Middlemarch; Mill on the Floss, The*
Eliza Cook's Journal (periodical): editorial policy of, 18–19; editor of, 235n6; founding of, 17; goals of, 7–8; on infantilization of woman, 19–20
elopements, 60–61
Elsner, Edward, 143–44
Englishwoman's Domestic Magazine, 4–5, 20, 94
English Woman's Journal, The (periodical): editors of, 18, 235n6; Eliot's view of, 64; goals of, 7–8; on Indian Mutiny, 107; on skin color, 20–21
Englishwoman's Review, The (periodical), 7–8
Ensler, Eve, 51–52, 77–78, 238n8
equality: in comic spirit, 119–*21;* Hollywood's turn from, 177–78; as prerequisite for comedy, 2, 118, 170–71, 177; in revised fairy tale, 14–16; in sexuality, 135, 136; in verbal play, 117–18, 155, 157; women's claims to, 159–62; WWII's impact on, 180
erotic/exotic nexus, 84
eroticism: in Chopin's stories, 111–15; in Eliot's *Middlemarch,* 72–73
Esquire (periodical), 180
Evangelista, Linda, *229*
Ewell, Tom, 209–16, *213*

227–28; popularity of, 146, 148; process and chemistry of, 10–11, 117, 236n9; rejection of, 223–24; sales of, 246n4; streaking and highlighting, 227. *See also* bleached hair; Clairol; platinum hair

hairpieces, 81, 97, 100

Hammett, Dashiell, 178

Hands across the Table (film), *163;* Lombard's blond hair in, 166; Lombard's sincerity in, 165; meaning of work in, 163–64; representation of city in, 162–63

Harlem Renaissance, 140–41, 242n19

Harlow, Jean: audacity of, 119; conscience and sincerity of, 165; femininity redefined by, 13; hair color of, 116–17, 148; Haver compared with, 242n23; provocatively ambiguous behavior of, 10; social class of characters of, 153–54; speech of, 136. Roles: *Bombshell*, 153–54, *156,* 165; *China Seas*, 149, 153; *Dinner at Eight*, 153; *Double Whoopee*, 148; *Hell's Angels*, 148; *Platinum Blonde*, 148, 153; *Red Dust*, 3–4, 149, 150–53, *151; Wife vs. Secretary,* 153

Harvey, Laurence, 226

Haskell, Molly, 26, 178, 195, 218, 225

Haver, Phyllis: Harlow compared with, 242n23; role in *The Battle of the Sexes*, 131–32, *133,* 134–35, 149

Hawks, Howard, 243n28. See also *Gentlemen Prefer Blondes; Twentieth Century*

Hawthorne, Nathaniel, 39–40

Hays, Matilda ("Max") Mary, 18, 235n6. See also *English Woman's Journal, The* (periodical)

Hays Office, 145, 153, 154. *See also* Production Code Administration

Hayuk, Selma, 232

H.B., 81

Heart of Show Business, The (short subject), 244n3

Hecht, Ben, 143

Hedren, Tippi, 185

Hell's Angels (film), 148

Hemmings, David, 224

Hendrix, Jimi, 224

Hennelly, Mark M., Jr., 239n11

Henry VIII (king of England), 52

Hepburn, Audrey, 189

Hepburn, Katharine, 136, 146

heroes, marital choices of, 23–24, 227, 246n5

heroines: beauty severed from attributes of, 45–47; blond and brainy, 30–32; dark-haired and intelligent, 5–7, 8; undermining conventions of, 86–87

heroinism vs. heroism, x–xi

His Girl Friday (film), 136, 162

Hitchcock, Alfred, 22, 180, 182

Hitler, Adolf, 170–71, 172

Hobson, Laura, 206

Hoffman, Dustin, 206

Holocaust, 170

Homer, *Iliad,* 35

Home Town Story (film), 191

homoeroticism, 50

homosexual impersonation, 208

Hopkins, Miriam, 13, 119–21, 136

Horne, Lena, 223, 244n3

horror stories, 102–3. *See also* ghost stories; vampires

How to Marry a Millionaire (film), *201;* comedic gold digger in, 182; cultural context of, 188–89; dizzy blonde in, 13; eyeglass scene in, 201–2; female friendships in, 200–201; music of, 186; satiric element of, 190

Hrdy, Sara Blaffer, 63

Hudson, Rock, 222, 246n1

Hughes, Howard, 148

Hunter, Evan, 180

Huston, John, 178, 192. See also *Asphalt Jungle, The*

ice-blonde. *See* cold-blooded blondes

identities: of actresses/actors, 243n30; formation of, x; mistaken, of blonde and brunette, 57–58; nature/nurture and, 48; questions about, 60; in star system, 12; Thackeray on, 243n30 imagination: female tutor of male's, 214–16; male economic advantage linked to, 210–13

I'm No Angel (film), *141, 144, 146;* body language in, 142–43; Brontë's blonde as precursor to, 145–46; love scenes in, 143; title of, 26; trial scene in, 145

imperialist impulse: coding of skin color in, 20–21; persistence of, 226; romantic fiction as expression of, 8–9; violence against women linked to, 21–25, 34–44

India: racist treatment in, 236n2; skin color and colonialism in, 20–21

Indian Mutiny (1857), 21, 107

innocence: in *Birth of a Nation,* 126–27; *Gidget*-style, 221; human beings as not, 39–40, 42; Monroe's characters as mainly, 186, 187, 188–89; in noir detective fiction, 180; pastoral setting of, 130–31; in *Roxie Hart,* 168–69; sexualized, 185, 188–89, 203

insurgency of blondes, 7–10

intellectuality/intelligence: of Austen's Elizabeth, 46; of blondes, 98–102; culture of beauty juxtaposed to, 89; dark hair linked to, 5–7, 8, 80–81, *82–83;* desirability of, 47

Ivanhoe (Scott): female body as landscape in, 52; marital choice in, 23; mentioned, 5; otherness affirmed in, 33; racial markers in, 101; Thackeray's send-up of, 17, 21–25

"I Wanna Be Loved by You" (song), 208

James, Henry, 62, 70, 75, 93

Jameson, Frederic, 23

Jane Eyre (C. Brontë): blond rebellion in, 7; context of publishing, 2–3; Jane's plainness in, 46–47; Jane's self-exploration in, 49–50; *Lady Audley's Secret* compared with, 92; *Red Dust* compared with, 152–53; reviews of, 42; selfish blonde in, 48–49; sexuality in, 52, 113

Jazz Age, 132

Jazz Singer, The (film), 115

jealousy, 59, 86–87

Johnson, Nunnally, 167, 202

Jolson, Al, 115

joy, 58–59

Joyce, James, 149

Judith (biblical), 100–101

Karns, Roscoe, 157–58, 159

Keaton, Buster, 131

Keeler, Ruby, 161–62

Kelly, Grace, 185, 222

Kennedy, John F., 189

Kinsey, Alfred, 188, 218, 245n11

Koseff, Elise, 232

Ku Klux Klan, 122–28, 184

Kundera, Milan, 220

Ladies' Association for the Repeal of the Contagious Diseases Acts, 78, 238n9

Ladies' Cabinet of Fashion, The (periodical), 4

Ladies of the Chorus (film), 191

Lady Audley's Secret (Braddon): adultery anagram and, 90; Alcott's "Behind a Mask" compared with, 98, 100, 101; angry woman in, xi, 92–93; blond vixen type established by, 77–78; commercial aggressiveness in, 84–85; confession in, 91–92; disordered curls in, 86–87; domestic violence in, 81, 84, 85–86; fraudulent handwriting in, 90–91; husband's abandonment in, 88–89; multiple readings of, 89; Pope's *Rape of the Lock* compared with, 91; Pre-Raphaelite portrait in, 87–88, 108; response to, 94; subversive energies of blondes in, 72–73

Lady Eve, The (film), 186–87

lady/maid relationship, 140–*41,* 185, 242n20

Laferla, Ruth, 232, 246n8

Lake, Veronica, 177

landscapes: as affirmation in self-development, 50; feminization of, 51–52, 57; figuration of joy and, 58–59

Last of the Mohicans, The (Cooper), 111

12–13; of *Gentlemen Prefer Blondes,* 187, 195–96, 200; of *How to Marry a Millionaire,* 186; of *Roxie Hart,* 167–68, *169,* 243n31; of *The Seven Year Itch,* 209, 212; of *She Done Him Wrong,* 140–41, 142; of *Some Like It Hot,* 208; in Thackeray's *Vanity Fair,* 35, 38–39

My Favorite Wife (film), 169, 177

My Man Godfrey (film), 163, 164, 165

My Night at Maud's (film), 225

myths and myth-making: cannibalism in, 38; nationalism and, 4–5, 65; persistence of, 112; somnambules in, 244n36; in Thackeray's charades, 34–44. *See also* dark powers of women; fairy tales and folktales

NAACP (National Association for the Advancement of Colored People), 244n2

Napoleonic Wars, 4, 6

narcissism: in Austen's *Emma,* 117–18; in *The Battle of the Sexes,* 134–35; in *To Be or Not to Be,* 173; in Brontë's *Villette,* 54–56; in *Darling,* 225–26; in Eliot's *Middlemarch,* 70–71; in Eliot's *The Mill on the Floss,* 64; in Thackeray's *Vanity Fair,* 30–31

Nathan, George Jean, 145

National Association for the Promotion of Social Sciences, 6–7

nationalism, myth-making in, 4–5, 65

National Socialist Party (Nazis, Germany), 161, 241n12. See also *To Be or Not to Be* (film)

National Union of Women's Suffrage Societies (NUWSS), 110

Newman, Alfred, 186, 209–10

Newman, John, 42

New Republic (periodical), 244n35

New Woman: male novelists' response to, 102, 106, 109; prototypes for, 8; suffragists' views of, 110

New York City: elite (blond) wives in, 230; film's representation of, 162–63; post-war hopefulness in, 186; summer heat and exodus from, 209–10

New Yorker (periodical), 185

New York Times, 230, 232

Niagara (film), *194;* antifeminism of, 182; close-up shots in, 193–94; cultural context of, 188–89; feminine evil in, 187

Night after Night (film), 137–38

nightingale, in Thackeray's charades, 38–39

nightmares, in Stoker's *Dracula,* 102–10

Nineteenth Amendment, 118, 128

Nine to Five (film), 10

Ninotchka (film), 148, 170

noir detective fiction, 180

Norbelie, Barbro Almqvist, 238n7

Nothing Sacred (film), 163, 164, 165, 175

Novak, Kim, 10, 185, 193, 222

novel. *See* domestic novel; realist fiction; sensation novel

O'Brien, Pat, 242n22

"Old, Black Joe" (song), 140

Orient and Oriental, 33–35, 101, 239n9

Orwell, George, 231

Other and Otherness, 11, 23–24, 33–35

Ott, Frederick W., 243n28

Our Bodies, Ourselves, 238n8

Pall Mall Gazette (periodical), 20, 46, 53

Pankhurst, Emmeline, 110

Paramount Pictures, 245n10

Parilla, John, 246n8

Parkes, Bessie Rayner, 18, 64, 235n6. See also *English Woman's Journal, The*

Parton, Dolly, 10

passing (and reverse passing) stories, 206–7

pastoral, 130–31, 186–87

Patmore, Coventry, 26

patriarchy and patriarchal power: Eliot on, 238n3; prerogative of, 93; woman's victory over, 100; women's community destroyed by, 52; women's refusals as challenge to, 107–8. *See also* miscegenation fears; misogyny; violence against women and children

Reade, Charles, 237n11

readers and reading: demands of, 98; reading aloud, ix–x; reality of sentiment in, 24–25, 33, 35–36, 41–42; Thackeray's address to, 39–40; truth in, 25–26

realist fiction: Collins's and Braddon's, compared, 93; fairy-tale blonde as part of, 77; paradigm shift in, 84–85, 93; Thackeray's use of, 22–27, 41–44

reality of sentiment: concept of, 24–25; reader's experience of, 33, 35–36, 41–42; truth in, 25–26, 32

Rebecca and Rowena (Thackeray): context of publishing, 17; as indictment of Romance, 30–32; women and imperialism/colonialism in, 21–25, 34

Red Dust (film), *151;* bathing scene in, 150, *151,* 154; comedic sexuality in, 3–4, 149; equality in, 177; love triangles in, 150–53; names used in, 242n24; racist stereotypes in, 243n26

red-haired women, in *Roxie Hart,* 167–69, *168, 169*

Reform Bill (1832), 69

Reid, Elizabeth Jesser, 50

Renaissance travel narratives, 8–9, 11

representations of blondes: as always heroines, always beautiful, x; blond rebellion and, 7–10; changes in, as "punctuated equilibrium," 2–4, 77–78; chaos and violence linked to, 27–29; conscience and sincerity in, 165–66, 175–77; cultural eclipse of, in 1960s, 221–25; in early silent films, 121–22; film's transformation of, 10–14; in foreign films, 223, 224, 225; hopeful and prosperous cityscape linked to 1950s, 186; main influences on, 15–16; power linked to (recent), 230–32; racial purity objectified in, 122–28, 241n12; as rapacious and aggressive, 84–85, 131–35; remembered, as double exposure, 167; reversal of, 2–4, 47; split of, in Victorian culture, 236–37n8; stereotypes in 1950s, 185–89; subjectivity restored to, 209–17;

true grit of, 27, 236n6. *See also* blondes; blondness; cold-blooded blondes; comedy and comic spirit; fairy-tale blondes; vamps

Repulsion (film), 225

Riskin, Robert, 148

River of No Return, The (film), 244n4

Roach, Hal, 119

Robertson, Cliff, 221

Robin, Leo, 195

Robinson, Jackie, 183

Rodman, Dennis, 231

Rogers, Ginger: voice of, 136. Roles: *Gold Diggers of 1933,* 161–62; *Roxie Hart,* 167–69, *168, 169; Swing Time,* 166

Rohmer, Eric, 225

Romance: blond rebellion in, 8–9; Brontë's ambiguities and, 55–56; dark/blond divide of, 9–11, 79–84; differences in, 235n7; domestic reinterpretation of, 20–21; Fatal Woman in, 29–30; persistent appeal of, 77–78; Thackeray's satire of, 21–25, 30–32

Roosevelt, Franklin D., 189

Rosen, Marjorie, 214, 217, 224, 245n11

Rossetti, Dante Gabriel, 29, 81

Roth, Phyllis A., 107

Rowe, Kathleen, 202, 208, 245n12

Roxie Hart (film), 167–69, *168, 169,* 228

"Rule Britannia" (music), 38

Run, Girl, Run (film), 119

RuPaul, 231

Ruskin, John, 32, 98, 237n12

Russell, Jane, 195–99, 200

Russell, Rosalind, 136

Saint, Eva-Marie, 185, 222

Sanger, Margaret, 240n2

Sargent, Alice, 246n6

Sarris, Andrew, 155

Satan Met a Lady (film), 178

Savi, E. W., 236n2

Schatz, Thomas, 137

school integration, 183, 184

World War II: gender impacts of, 180; racial integration after, 183; sexualized innocence in movies of, 188–89; women's roles in, 177–78

Wray, Fay, 12

Wright, J. Fielding, 183

writers. *See* female writers; male writers

Wyatt, Thomas, 222, 246n1

Young, Loretta, 148

Zellweger, Renée, 228, 229

Ziegfeld, Flo, 12

9 78